Perpetrators and Perpetration of Mass Violence

As the most comprehensive edited volume to be published on perpetrators and perpetration of mass violence, the volume sets a new agenda for perpetrator research by bringing together contributions from such diverse disciplines as political science, sociology, social psychology, history, anthropology and gender studies, allowing for a truly interdisciplinary discussion of the phenomenon of perpetration. The cross-case nature of the volume allows the reader to see patterns across case studies, bringing findings from *inter alia* the Holocaust, the genocides in Rwanda and the former Yugoslavia, and the civil wars in Cambodia and Côte d'Ivoire into conversation with each other.

The chapters of this volume are united by a common research interest in understanding what constitutes perpetrators as actors, what motivates them, and how dynamics behind perpetration unfold. Their attention to the interactions between disciplines and cases allows for the insights to be transported into more abstract ideas on perpetration in general. Amongst other aspects, they indicate that instead of being an extraordinary act, perpetration is often ordinary, that it is crucial to studying perpetrators and perpetration not from looking at the perpetrators as actors but by focusing on their deeds, and that there is a utility of ideologies in explaining perpetration, when we differentiate them more carefully and view them in a more nuanced light.

This volume will be vital reading for students and scholars of genocide studies, human rights, conflict studies and international relations.

Timothy Williams is a post-doctoral research fellow at the Center for Conflict Studies at Marburg University, Germany.

Susanne Buckley-Zistel is Professor of Peace and Conflict Studies and Director of the Center for Conflict Studies, Marburg University, Germany.

Routledge Studies in Genocide and Crimes against Humanity
Edited by Adam Jones
University of British Columbia in Kelowna, Canada

The Routledge Series in Genocide and Crimes against Humanity publishes cutting-edge research and reflections on these urgently contemporary topics. While focusing on political-historical approaches to genocide and other mass crimes, the series is open to diverse contributions from the social sciences, humanities, law, and beyond. Proposals for both sole-authored and edited volumes are welcome.

The Structural Prevention of Mass Atrocities
Understanding Risks and Resilience
Stephen McLoughlin

Constructing Genocide and Mass Violence
Society, Crisis, Identity
Maureen Hiebert

Last Lectures on the Prevention and Intervention of Genocide
Edited by Samuel Totten

Perpetrating Genocide
A Criminological Account
Kjell Anderson

The United States and Genocide
(Re)Defining the Relationship
Jeffrey S. Bachman

Perpetrators and Perpetration of Mass Violence
Action, Motivations and Dynamics
Edited by Timothy Williams and Susanne Buckley-Zistel

For more information about this series, please visit: www.routledge.com/Routledge-Studies-in-Genocide-and-Crimes-against-Humanity/book-series/RSGCH

Perpetrators and Perpetration of Mass Violence

Action, Motivations and Dynamics

**Edited by Timothy Williams
and Susanne Buckley-Zistel**

LONDON AND NEW YORK

First published 2018 by Routledge

2 Park Square, Milton Park, Abingdon, Oxfordshire OX14 4RN

52 Vanderbilt Avenue, New York, NY 10017

Routledge is an imprint of the Taylor & Francis Group, an informa business

First issued in paperback 2020

Copyright © 2018 selection and editorial matter, Timothy Williams & Susanne Buckley-Zistel; individual chapters, the contributors

The right of Timothy Williams & Susanne Buckley-Zistel to be identified as the authors of the editorial material, and of the authors for their individual chapters, has been asserted in accordance with sections 77 and 78 of the Copyright, Designs and Patents Act 1988.

All rights reserved. No part of this book may be reprinted or reproduced or utilised in any form or by any electronic, mechanical, or other means, now known or hereafter invented, including photocopying and recording, or in any information storage or retrieval system, without permission in writing from the publishers.

Notice:
Product or corporate names may be trademarks or registered trademarks, and are used only for identification and explanation without intent to infringe.

British Library Cataloguing-in-Publication Data
A catalogue record for this book is available from the British Library

Library of Congress Cataloging-in-Publication Data
A catalog record has been requested for this book

ISBN: 978-0-8153-8617-9 (hbk)
ISBN: 978-0-367-59148-9 (pbk)

Typeset in Times New Roman
by Apex CoVantage, LLC

Contents

List of figures	vii
List of tables	viii
About the authors	ix

***Perpetrators and Perpetration of Mass Violence*:**
an introduction   1
TIMOTHY WILLIAMS AND SUSANNE BUCKLEY-ZISTEL

SECTION I
Theorizing perpetrators   15

1 Thinking beyond perpetrators, bystanders, heroes:
a typology of action in genocide   17
TIMOTHY WILLIAMS

2 Violence as action   36
CHRISTIAN GUDEHUS

3 Theorizing ideological diversity in mass violence   58
JONATHAN LEADER MAYNARD

SECTION II
Motivations and dynamics   81

4 Perpetrators? Political civil servants in the Third Reich   83
DARREN O'BYRNE

5 The normality of going to war: aspects of symbolic violence
in participation and perpetration in civil war   99
DANIEL BULTMANN

vi *Contents*

6 **"We no longer pay heed to humanitarian considerations":
narratives of perpetration in the Wehrmacht, 1941–44**   117
DAVID HARRISVILLE

7 **Gender and genocide: assessing differential opportunity
structures of perpetration in Rwanda**   133
EVELYN A. GERTZ, HOLLIE NYSETH BREHM AND SARA E. BROWN

8 **Perpetrators of sexual violence in armed conflict**   151
INGER SKJELSBÆK

9 **Cross-border perpetrator recruitment in the Ivorian civil
war: the motivations and experiences of young Burkinabe
men in the *Forces Nouvelles* rebel movement**   169
JESPER BJARNESEN

10 ***Judenjagd*: reassessing the role of ordinary Poles as
perpetrators in the Holocaust**   187
TOMASZ FRYDEL

11 **Is a comparative theory of perpetrators possible?**   204
SCOTT STRAUS

Index   211

Figures

1.1	Continuum of individual impact – the impact a person has on the genocidal outcome	25
1.2	Continuum of proximity to the genocide	26
1.3	Continuous spatial classification of action in genocide	27
1.4	Typology of action in genocide	29
3.1	Typology of ideological internalization states	65
3.2	A hypothetical pre-radicalization ideological distribution	71
3.3	A hypothetical post-radicalization ideological distribution	71
7.1	Gacaca court trials in which women were found guilty	138
7.2	Percentage of Gacaca trials with a guilty verdict for women, by category	139

Table

7.1   Interviewee characteristics   141

About the authors

Jesper Bjarnesen holds a PhD in cultural anthropology from Uppsala University and has conducted research primarily on the involuntary returns of Burkinabe labour migrants from Côte d'Ivoire in the context of the Ivorian crisis. Thematically, his work centres on intergenerational dynamics, youth culture and regional mobility. Since 2013, he has worked as a senior researcher at the Nordic Africa Institute.

Hollie Nyseth Brehm is an Assistant Professor of Sociology and Criminology at The Ohio State University. She studies the risk factors of genocide, meso-level variation in genocide, gender-based violence during genocide and transitional justice. She has conducted fieldwork in Rwanda and Bosnia, and she serves on an atrocity prevention task force.

Sara E. Brown is a Fellow at USC Shoah Foundation – The Institute for Visual History and Education. She holds the first PhD in comparative genocide from the Strassler Center for Holocaust and Genocide Studies at Clark University and has worked and conducted research in Rwanda since 2004. She is the author of *Gender and the Genocide in Rwanda: Women as Rescuers and Perpetrators*.

Susanne Buckley-Zistel is Professor of Peace and Conflict Studies and Director of the Center for Conflict Studies, Marburg University, Germany. She has held positions at King's College, London, the Peace Research Institute Frankfurt and the Free University, Berlin, and fellowships at the Research Center *Governance in Areas of Limited Statehood* and the Käte Hamburger Kolleg *Global Cooperation Research*. Her research focuses on issues pertaining to peace and conflict, violence, gender and transitional justice.

Daniel Bultmann is a sociologist at the Department of Asian and African Studies, Humboldt University of Berlin. His research focuses on the sociology of armed groups and the military, peace and conflict studies, and post-conflict societies as well as disarmament, demobilisation and reintegration programs. He currently works on strategies of conversion used by former Cambodian belligerents during the process of reintegration to society, and how they convert their former social status and their acquired resources to match with conditions in a society at peace.

x *About the authors*

Tomasz Frydel is a PhD candidate in the Department of History and the Anne Tanenbaum Centre for Jewish Studies at the University of Toronto. His dissertation examines village society and the Holocaust in occupied Poland. In 2013, he was a fellow at the Institut für Zeitgeschichte in Munich and is currently a Claims Conference Saul Kagan Fellow in Advanced Shoah Studies.

Evelyn A. Gertz is a PhD candidate in the Department of Sociology at The Ohio State University and a National Science Foundation Graduate Research Fellow. Her primary research interests include political violence and conflict, the formation and maintenance of ethnic group boundaries and the processes of integration for refugees. She has conducted research in Israel and Rwanda and is currently studying identity construction among Middle Eastern Christian minorities.

Christian Gudehus is Senior Researcher at the Institute for International Law of Peace and Armed Conflict and Permanent Fellow at the Kilian-Köhler Centre for Social & Cultural Psychology and Historical Anthropology, both at the Ruhr-Universität Bochum. He is Editor in Chief of *Genocide Studies and Prevention* and Advisory Board Member of the International Association of Genocide Scholars. He is interested in the connection of memory and violence studies, on the one hand, with social theoretical approaches and qualitative social research on the other.

David Harrisville received his PhD from the University of Wisconsin–Madison in 2017, where he is currently a postdoctoral fellow sponsored by the Defense POW/MIA Accounting Agency (DPAA). He has also held fellowships at the Hebrew University and the Freie Universität Berlin. His research interests centre on the Third Reich, the Second World War and the history of morality.

Jonathan Leader Maynard is a Departmental Lecturer in International Relations at New College and the Department of Politics and International Relations at the University of Oxford, as well as a Research Associate of the Oxford Institute for Ethics, Law and Armed Conflict. His research focuses on the role of ideology in political violence and armed conflict. He is working on a book on this topic for Oxford University Press, and has published in scholarly journals including the *British Journal of Political Science* and *Terrorism and Political Violence*, as well as for news media including *The Independent* and *The New Statesman*.

Darren O'Byrne is a PhD student at Cambridge University. His research examines the role of the German state administration under Nazism by looking at the personal biographies and professional experiences of leading political civil servants. He holds a BA and an MA from University College Dublin and has held research posts at the Humboldt and Technical Universities in Berlin.

Inger Skjelsbæk is Research Professor and former Deputy Director (2009–2015) at the Peace Research Institute Oslo (PRIO). Her research interests include gender studies, political psychology, peace and conflict research, transitional justice, political extremism and research methodology. Skjelsbæk has been a visiting researcher and Fulbright Scholar at the University of California–Berkeley and at the London School of Economics. She is also Associate Professor in Cultural and Societal Psychology at the Department of Psychology and the Center for Research on Extremism at the University of Oslo.

Scott Straus is Professor of Political Science and International Studies at the University of Wisconsin–Madison. His most recent book is *Making and Unmaking Nations: War, Leadership and Genocide in Modern Africa* (Cornell, 2015), which won the 2016 best book in conflict studies from the American Political Science Association. He has previously conducted research on perpetrators in Rwanda, represented in his book *The Order of Genocide: Race, Power, and War in Rwanda* (Cornell, 2006).

Timothy Williams is a research fellow at the Center for Conflict Studies at Marburg University where he completed his PhD in 2017. His previous research has dealt with the question of why people participate in genocide, developing a conceptual model that draws on literature on the Holocaust and Rwanda as well as his own field research in Cambodia. He was awarded the International Association of Genocide Scholars' Emerging Scholars Prize in 2017 and the Raphael Lemkin Fellowship of the Armenian Genocide Memorial-Institute in 2015. He studied at Mannheim University (BA Political Science) and at the London School of Economics (MSc Comparative Politics).

Perpetrators and Perpetration of Mass Violence: an introduction

Timothy Williams and Susanne Buckley-Zistel[1]

Introduction

Why do people perpetrate violence? What does perpetration as an action signify? What motivates these actions, and how are they affected by prevailing political, social or economic dynamics? Even though the 20th century has often been labelled the century of genocides and mass violence, at the dawn of the new millennium hopes were high that the major conflicts had come to an end. Only 18 years into the 21st century, though, it is apparent that violence prevails for the foreseeable future. Despite its ever-evolving forms and expressions, its scope remains constant so that questions regarding the perpetration of violence continue to be pertinent. In this volume, we address some of them.

We do so by focusing on the individual. When Christopher Browning (1994) published his seminal monograph *Ordinary Men*, he laid the cornerstone for a micro-turn in the study of mass violence and genocide. Prior to this, much of the academic scholarship had focused on macro or meso levels, so that his introduction of the individual did not remain without controversy. The 1990s were dominated by the debate between Browning and Daniel Jonah Goldhagen (1996) and Goldhagen's many critics regarding the role of anti-Semitism in motivating individual perpetrators to participate in the Holocaust. Much other work began to emerge, primarily on the Holocaust, but soon also on Rwanda, as well as on Armenia, Bosnia and Cambodia.

This new agenda in the micro-study of genocide and mass violence has put perpetrators on centre stage. It is an important development, as it allows us to open up the phenomena of genocide and mass violence and analyse the individual cogs that together allow the machine to work. Without this understanding, these forms of violence appear merely as something that comes over a society due to macro-level political or other conditions. This neglects the agency of the individuals who are involved in the planning and implementation of genocide and mass violence, and overlooks that they all have reasons for their actions and understandings of what they are doing. By studying individual perpetrators, we can gain a deeper understanding not only of *why* genocides and mass violence occur, but also *how* they do, without exotifying perpetrators and their actions and styling them as 'others' who are fundamentally different to us 'normal' people.

2 Timothy Williams and Susanne Buckley-Zistel

By exploring motivations and dynamics of perpetration, the contributions to this volume problematise monocausal explanations and point to the situatedness of agency and the 'complexity of evil' (Williams 2017, 2014). Moreover, they raise normative questions regarding what constitutes an act of perpetration as opposed to less morally ostracised behaviour. In this sense, in Chapter 9 Jesper Bjarnesen argues that the "perception of a combatant career as fundamentally different from that of a plantation worker or a migrant working in Abidjan's informal sector may relate more to normative preconceptions about morally appropriate forms of labour than to the motivations for engaging in war, and the material and social effects of this engagement." In line with this, the study of perpetrators serves to root the actions of perpetration within the broad repertoire of human behaviour. Only by also comparing the perpetration of such atrocities with other forms of action, does it become possible to understand the dynamics in which people kill their former friends and neighbours and to comprehend the normality of participation for the people in that particular moment.

Perpetrators and Perpetration of Mass Violence brings together various insights in perpetrator research from different disciplines and from different cases. It is the first truly interdisciplinary edited volume that draws on research from political science, sociology, history, gender studies and anthropology. At the same time, it is the first book that brings together such a wealth of different cases, with research on the Holocaust but also on the genocides in Rwanda and former Yugoslavia, as well as the brutal civil wars in Cambodia and Côte d'Ivoire. As such, the volume demonstrates how similar dynamics and similar conceptual ideas can be helpful for understanding violence across these different cases.

Diversifying research agendas

Various avenues have been pursued in the micro-level study of perpetrators. The first work in this field was conducted in the many, mostly historical biographies of individual perpetrators such as Adolf Eichmann (Arendt 1963; Stangneth 2011), Albert Speer (Sereny 1995), Franz Stangl (Sereny 1983), Werner Best (Ulrich 1996), Udo Klausa (Fulbrook 2012), and Pol Pot (Short 2005a, 2005b), and of the many low-level perpetrators of genocidal violence (Abmayr 2009; Mann 2000; Schwartz 2006). However, more comparative and social scientific research has followed which is interested in looking beyond certain historical individuals and understanding broader patterns. The emerging research agenda was dominated by the Holocaust (Black 2011; Grabowski 2013; Lifton 2000 [1986]; Mann 2000), including work on Poland (Gross 2003) and Romania (Dumitru 2014; Solonari 2014). From the turn of the century onwards the radius of interest expanded to beyond the Nazi regime to include a large and growing body of research on Rwanda (e.g. Fletcher 2007; Fujii 2009; Jessee 2015; McDoom 2013a, 2013b; Smeulers and Hoex 2010; Smeulers 2015; Straus 2006), as well as on Armenia (e.g. Grigoryan 2015; Üngör and Polatel 2011; Williams 2016), Bosnia (e.g. Clark 2009; Mueller 2000) and Cambodia (e.g. Clegg et al. 2013; Hinton 2005; Williams and Neilsen 2016).

Introduction 3

First and foremost, there has been much research on the question of why people participate in mass violence, suggesting that there are many different motivations (for a systematic overview, see Williams 2017, 2014). The debate on what motivates individuals to become perpetrators was initiated by Browning (1994) and Goldhagen (1996), with their radically different interpretation of the same Reserve Police Battalion 101 setting the stage for later controversies. Goldhagen's essentialist emphasis on eliminationist anti-Semitism in the Holocaust, or Hagan and Kaiser's (2011) proposition of racism as a key motivation in the Sudan genocide, have received little support, even though such representations of perpetrators as ideologically driven or ethnic hating remain prevalent in non-academic, public perceptions. Even though explanations that draw on ideology or ethnic hatred as key explanatory factors have been widely rejected (see among many others Browning 1994; Fujii 2009; Mann 2011: 45; Moshman 2005: 185; Mueller 2000: 50; Solonari 2014; Valentino 2004: 31), more nuanced differentiations are beginning to challenge this wholesale rejection of ideology (Leader Maynard in this volume, 2014; Leader Maynard and Mildenberger 2016).

Two other strings of literature on perpetrator motivations have emerged recently. The first emphasises the importance of situations and their social dynamics (among many others Bašić 2006; Clegg et al. 2013; Dumitru 2014; Fletcher 2007; Fujii 2009; Gross 2003; McDoom 2013a, 2013b; Straus 2006, see also the contribution of Gudehus to this volume), as well as broader social-psychological explanations (e.g. Staub 2014; Waller 2002; Welzer 2006). The second string also rejects the ideological approach yet places the onus not on social dynamics but on more opportunistic explanations, such as being able to loot, the prospect of career progression, the ability to settle personal scores, the chance to pursue political interests, the possibility of raping and so on (Browning 1994; Fletcher 2007: 33; Fujii 2009: 97; Mamdani 2001: 218; Mann 2005: 32; Mueller 2000: 49, 61; Semelin 2005: 242; Straus 2006: 79; Valentino 2004). In this volume, this is reflected in the chapter by Bjarnesen as well as by Tomasz Frydel. These lines of thinking are complemented by studies that focus on emotions (Petersen 2002), as well as by contributions from the disciplines of criminology (Brannigan 2013) and organisational sociology (Kühl 2014). Significant efforts have also gone into studying perpetrators after the end of violence (see e.g. Hedlund 2015; Jessee 2015; Rauschenbach et al. 2016), for instance in the context of criminal proceedings (see Skjelsbæk's chapter). This includes, *inter alia*, the concept of complex political perpetrators (Baines 2009; for the original idea of complex political victims see Bouris 2007; see also Bernath 2015) that addresses the ambivalence that can emerge after conflict when perpetrators claim to be victims, too. It points to an emerging debate about the challenges of categorising perpetrators and non-perpetrators in a dichotomous way, for there are many people who are not just perpetrators but also victims, bystanders, rescuers and so on. In some cases, people who participate in a genocide might – if and when they have the opportunity – save others, as illustrated by Frydel in Chapter 10. Moreover, this inconsistency is the starting point for the chapter by Timothy Williams, which develops a typology of genocidal action in order to help bridge these ambivalences in individuals' behaviour.

From a methodological perspective, the field has been broadened, too. For instance, gendered analysis, as central to the chapters of Inger Skjelsbæk and Evelyn A. Gertz et al., have recently gained much traction (see also Issinger 2016; Smeulers 2015; Werner 2008). In addition, the depiction and self-depiction of perpetrators through narratives provides new insights into how societies view perpetrators and their deeds (see Skjelsbæk in this volume). Even though interviews and anthropologic studies of perpetrators are still the exception they are slowly gaining prominence (Anderson 2017; Eriksson Baaz and Stern 2013; Fujii 2009; Hinton 2005; Jessee 2015; McDoom 2013a, 2013b; Straus 2006; Williams and Neilsen 2016).

Within these various debates, *Perpetrators and Perpetration of Mass Violence* makes a contribution to forwarding the field in two ways: first, it is truly interdisciplinary, as it brings together authors from the disciplines of political science, sociology, history, gender studies and anthropology. Second, it provides an inter-contextual perspective to several different violent contexts in which perpetrators act, both in past and present. The volume has several chapters that deal with very different facets of the Holocaust, but it also ventures beyond the Holocaust, bringing it into conversation with the genocides in Rwanda and the former Yugoslavia, as well as the civil violence in Cambodia and Côte d'Ivoire. Amongst all this disciplinary and contextual diversity, the object of study remains constant, however, as all chapters deal with perpetrators and their perpetration. The precise acts in which they engage vary from direct killing of victims via participation in groups that committed crimes against humanity, to supporting acts of denunciation, to exercising bureaucratic leadership over the genocidal process. Nonetheless, despite their diversity, these acts of perpetration bear many similarities and can be explained together regarding the perpetrators' motivations and the dynamics of the perpetration itself.

It is this interdisciplinary and inter-contextual perspective that sets this volume apart from previous edited volumes on perpetrators. Most of them have focused exclusively on the Holocaust, without broadening their scope to other cases (Brunner et al. 2011; David-Fox et al. 2014; Feldman and Seibel 2005; Jensen and Szejnmann 2008; Kramer 2006; Newman and Erber 2002; Pohl and Perels 2011; Welzer et al. 2011), albeit with very different foci, geographically or thematically. Most of these volumes have a historical bent, which is not surprising given the focus on the Holocaust, although some also approach the topic from a different disciplinary perspective, most notably social psychology (Miller 2004; Newman and Erber 2002) and psychoanalytic social psychology (Brunner et al. 2011). None of these volumes go beyond just the perspective on the Holocaust, though, nor do they try to compile an explicitly interdisciplinary volume.

This volume fills this desideratum in the literature by broadening the scope to include a range of 20th-century cases, studying them from a range of disciplines. This broadening relates to the forms of violence to include genocide, civil war, mass killings and state terror, and the forms of perpetration to include killing by gun, personal attacks and sexual violence. A mere historical approach is extended by philosophical investigations and the narrative analysis of court proceedings,

Introduction 5

which moves away from analysing perpetration itself to exploring how perpetration is analysed in courtrooms, and with what effect.

Action, motivations and dynamics

Despite coming from a variety of different disciplines, studying different cases and focusing on different forms of perpetration, many of the chapters offer a conceptual as well as empirical contribution, and highlight similar aspects. Each chapter is valuable in and of itself, but taken together there are arguments that transcend the chapters.

On a conceptual level, the first main argument that runs through many of the chapters is that perpetration should be understood as action. According to Gudehus, as well as other contributors, the identification of an individual as a perpetrator is only possible through his or her action in the context of violence. In order to respond to the question 'who does what in which way,' Gudehus suggests a matrix of analytical considerations including elements such as the identification of routines or scripts, reconstructions of figuration or habitus, the detection of dynamic forces and the tracing of processes. In a similar vein, Gertz et al. locate the act of perpetration in what they call 'situated agency,' which enables and constrains participation in violence. They demonstrate how Rwandan women engaged in the genocide out of their own volition while at the same time obeying societal gender norms according to which women act in a more restrained manner, thus holding them back in contrast to male community members.

This argument also resonates in the chapters of Williams and O'Byrne, albeit in very different ways. They both argue for an approach that allows for a more complex understanding of perpetration in which individuals can engage in various types of action at different times – even if they are contradictory – and emphasise that we can describe and understand this under the analytical framework of perpetration, but not of perpetrators. For ambivalent actors whom we would not necessarily know whether to characterise as perpetrators, it allows us to sharpen our view of their actions and the consequences of these as a foundation for analysing whether they are perpetrators. This idea of perpetration as action also runs implicitly through many of the other chapters, demonstrating that a deep understanding of perpetrators is only possible through focusing the analysis explicitly on actual deeds (see the chapters of Bjarnesen, Frydel, Gertz et al., Harrisville and Skjelsbæk).

The volume's second argument suggests that ideologies may still be important when it comes to motivations for perpetration, but without them being the monolithic, all-encompassing constructions reminiscent of Goldhagen's (1996) work on eliminationist anti-Semitism. Instead, as discussed in Leader Maynard's contribution on ideological diversity, perpetrators can have varying degrees of ideological commitment, which – taken together at the societal level – need only shift a little for each person to change the ideological climate. This ties in well with other work in the volume that discusses ideology as motivation, but without assigning it core explanatory value, such as by Frydel, Bultmann or Bjarnesen.

6 *Timothy Williams and Susanne Buckley-Zistel*

Moreover, third, the ordinariness argument runs through most of the chapters, defying recent attempts to pathologise or exotify perpetrators. It is picked up in most detail by Skjelsbæk in her discussion of how perpetrators are variously narrated at the International Criminal Tribunal for the former Yugoslavia as normal or abnormal. Gertz and her colleagues point out that in public discourse male perpetration is often considered to be normal whilst women are portrayed as abnormal. Their study on Rwandan female perpetrators shows, however, that no gender distinction can be drawn in terms of perpetration.

The chapters to this volume thus illustrate that perpetrators come from ordinary surroundings and do not diverge from the mainstream population, evidenced explicitly or implicitly in Bjarnesen's discussion of Ivorian recruits, Harrisville on Wehrmacht soldiers, Frydel on Polish Gentile participants, Bultmann on Cambodian rebel recruits. All of these perpetrators came from the middle of society, with most being removed from this setting in order to perpetrate, some perpetrating from this position. The constricting power of societal roles (Bultmann, Gertz et al.), as well as the overwhelming power of German occupation (Frydel), all lead to constricted forms of agency in perpetration. Further, structural causes and economic motivations (Bjarnesen), as well as discussions of complex motivations (Frydel, Gertz et al., Skjelsbæk), emphasise maybe not the 'banality' of perpetration, but the ordinariness of it within the broad repertoire of human action.

About the volume

This volume is divided into two interlinked sections. The first is conceptual and the second more empirical, although many of the empirical chapters also have conceptual elements. In the first chapter, Timothy Williams seeks to understand violence as action and perpetrators as actors who perpetrate by developing a typology of action in genocide. Williams' typology can be used as an analytical tool for categorising any action within genocide, and is founded on two dimensions: the impact this action has on the genocide and its proximity to the killing. These two dimensions create a 14-field typology that encompasses, but differentiates in more detail, the traditional categories of perpetrators, rescuers and bystanders. Drawing on anecdotal examples from various cases, Williams shows how such a typological approach to genocidal action can allow us to better understand complex actors who act in different ways at different times, as well as to better differentiate between various actions in the grey zones between the traditional categories.

The second chapter, by Christian Gudehus, also shifts our focus towards perpetration as action. He develops a theory of action to underlie the study of perpetrators and argues that violence can best be understood as action. Gudehus draws on a rich tradition in social theory, including the concepts of frame, mentality, figuration, social norms and practices, to argue that it is a more productive analytical perspective to comprehend perpetrators and bystanders as "acting subjects" whose actions should be the starting point for analysis. This chapter's central

Introduction 7

thesis is thus that acts of perpetration, not perpetrators, are the analytically most promising avenue of inquiry; this resonates in the analysis of the empirical chapters on motivations and dynamics.

In Chapter 3, Jonathan Leader Maynard argues that there is a marked diversity regarding the degree to which ideologies are internalised by perpetrators and thus influence their actions. This requires moving beyond a black-and-white debate of whether perpetrators are ideological or not. For him, any explanation that embraces or rejects ideology falls short of its analytical potential if it does not differentiate between the diverse types of ideological internalisation states. Leader Maynard develops a typology of six categories of perpetrators reflecting their ideological stance, and shows how subtle shifts between these can lead to macro-level changes in the ideological climate.

These purely conceptual chapters are followed by empirical chapters that mix conceptual with empirical insights. In a study of high-level Nazi civil servants and their role as perpetrators of the Holocaust in Chapter 4, Darren O'Byrne analyses the nuances of what perpetration can mean in the context of a bureaucracy and how diverging acts of persecution and rescue can converge on the status of a perpetrator, or not. In detailed studies of four top-level bureaucrats he discusses how the definition of perpetration must be allowed to vary by context and cannot be reduced to merely the act of killing. Also, he argues that by moving the focus from the perpetrators to their actions, it becomes possible to view individuals as perpetrators in one situation but not in others.

Daniel Bultmann's study of symbolic violence in civil war perpetration (Chapter 5) argues against a purely economic perspective in trying to understand low-level perpetrators' participation. He argues that individuals join rebel groups in Cambodia and perceive the fulfilment of their fighting roles as normal due to their position within society so that pre-conflict social roles are reproduced in armed conflict. The concept of symbolic violence directed towards people from lower-status groups helps us understand how individual perpetrators come to see themselves as "ordinary men doing ordinary things during extraordinary times," as Bultmann writes it in his chapter.

In Chapter 6, David Harrisville studies 2,000 letters and several diaries written by members of the Wehrmacht to analyse how they understood their own perpetration, their self-perception and the atrocities that were happening around them. Harrisville draws on social-psychological theories of moral rationalisation to demonstrate how the authors of these epistles were able to exonerate themselves from guilt and uphold their own self-representations as 'decent men.' The legitimisation strategies Harrisville presents also focus on the individual acts of perpetration; however, these are then used to exculpate the individual in his own moral identity.

In the seventh chapter, Evelyn A. Gertz, Hollie Nyseth Brehm and Sara E. Brown approach women's perpetration in the 1994 genocide in Rwanda from a situated action perspective, emphasising how the structural inequality of women in Rwandan society influenced their participation in the violence. Even though many women committed acts of perpetration during the genocide, these were often related to property crimes rather than the more serious violent crimes in which

8 *Timothy Williams and Susanne Buckley-Zistel*

many men engaged. In the traditionally patriarchal society, the authors argue, fewer opportunities to perpetrate emerged for women than for men. Despite these structural constraints, however, women were able to exercise varying degrees of agency in their decisions whether to perpetrate or not, as well as in which ways they wanted to participate. The perspective forwarded in the chapter hence puts an onus on understanding the social context of an individual as a premise for understanding her or his agency and ultimately perpetration.

Inger Skjelsbæk approaches the topic of perpetrators of sexual violence in Chapter 8 by analysing how they are narrated in the proceedings of the International Criminal Tribunal for the Former Yugoslavia (ICTY). She explores the sentencing judgements of the nine principal perpetrators sentenced by the ICTY from a narrative perspective, demonstrating a broad variation in how the perpetration of sexual violence in armed conflict is explained, ranging from "chivalrous militarized individual," who could have done worse but refrained from doing so, to "opportunistic military perpetrators" who use their authority to sadistically humiliate women. The sentences also constitute a shift in international criminal justice from a laissez-faire attitude regarding sexual violence towards moral condemnation of these acts.

In Chapter 9 on cross-border recruitment of young Burkinabe men into the ranks of the *Forces Nouvelles* rebels in neighbouring Côte d'Ivoire, Jesper Bjarnesen suggests studying perpetration as a form of labour, and recruitment into rebel groups as a form of labour migration. From an anthropological perspective, he argues that normalising the study of perpetration helps to understand it as one form of economically motivated labour migration. Nonetheless, this form of perpetration only becomes possible when a socio-cultural framework legitimises it, in his context because perpetration is also seen as part of the fight against the Gbagbo regime and its persecution of Burkinabe labour migrants in Côte d'Ivoire. Bjarnesen's chapter thus argues that it is more fruitful to distance ourselves from a normative approach to perpetrators and to see perpetration as one act among many others, which – within the individual perception of the perpetrator and their socio-cultural context – can be seen as legitimate.

Tomasz Frydel's Chapter 10 focuses on the role that ordinary Polish people played during the so-called *Judenjagd*, the hunt for the Jews, in the context of the Holocaust. This chapter again engages with the ambivalences between the black-and-white categorisations of perpetrators and bystanders, underlining the necessity of a more action-centric approach to studying perpetrators and perpetration. Frydel's exploration of the agency of Polish people under German rule highlights the motivational diversity of low-level participants among the Polish Gentile population. The chapter argues that the violence can only be understood by recognising the top-down, oppressive structures of German rule, but at the same time heeding the dynamics of village society and individual motivations from the bottom up.

Finally, Scott Straus's postlogue wraps up this volume with a succinct review of the chapters, asking whether a comparative theory of perpetrators is possible. Straus argues that the chapters contribute to a systematic analysis on perpetrators

Introduction 9

in their attempt to harness the complexity of this field of research. He questions, however, whether a more general theory of perpetrators and perpetration will be possible given the broad variety of acts that perpetrator studies seeks to explain, as well as the many different contexts within which these occur. Also, Straus raises questions of methodology and research design, particularly regarding the value of comparing perpetrators to non-perpetrators, which will help improve future research on perpetrators.

Conclusion

We have compiled this book as the first interdisciplinary edited volume that brings together the insights from a range of cases beyond just the Holocaust but also contrasts them with studies of the Holocaust. It stimulates conceptual development regarding the role of perpetrators and their actions, as well as their motivations for and the dynamics of perpetration. This study of perpetrators should be seen as a beginning of contrasting cases, not as the last word on the subject.

While allowing perpetrators to be seen as ordinary human beings and taking on the perpetrator perspective are necessary to gain full understanding of why they act the way they do, it is important to emphasise for this entire volume that this approach should not be understood as exculpatory. It serves neither to diminish the significance of victim suffering, nor to argue for the legitimacy of such violence, but instead provides one stone in the mosaic of a broader understanding of the dynamics before, during and after mass violence and genocide. At the same time, the chapters of this book cannot be read as a judgement of the individual perpetrators themselves. Naturally, there are normative assumptions underlying this volume that perpetration of genocide is wrong, but this is not the topic here, for the volume seeks to describe, analyse and understand, not to judge.

While we draw this conclusion to an end, news about violence abounds. It points to gaps in research that this edited volume cannot address. They include the use of terror as a form of perpetration, the choice of young people to join violent struggles in faraway countries, the use of suicide bombing and self-immolation and many more. We very much hope that perpetrator research will dedicate itself to these forms of violence in the future and that this volume serves as a stimulation to look at the broader picture of action, motivations and dynamics.

Note

1 We are grateful to Alexandra Engelsdorfer, Alice Williams and Nadine Dammaschk for their assistance in compiling this manuscript.

References

Abmayr, Hermann G. *Stuttgarter NS-Täter. Vom Mitläufer bis zum Massenmörder.* Vol. 2. Stuttgart: Verlag Hermann G. Abmayr, 2009.
Anderson, Kjell. *Perpetrating Genocide: A Criminological Account.* London: Routledge, 2017.

10 *Timothy Williams and Susanne Buckley-Zistel*

Arendt, Hannah. *Eichmann in Jerusalem: A Report on the Banality of Evil.* New York: The Viking Press, 1963.

Baines, Erin K. "Complex Political Perpetrators: Reflections on Dominic Ongwen." *The Journal of Modern African Studies* 47, no. 2 (2009): 163–91.

Bašić, Natalija. "Die Akteursperspektive. Soldaten und 'ethnische Säuberungen' in Kroatien und Bosnien-Herzegowina (1991–1995)." In *Definitionsmacht, Utopie, Vergeltung. 'Ethnische Säuberungen' im östlichen Europa des 20. Jahrhunderts,* edited by Ulf Brunnbauer, Michael G. Esch and Holm Sundhaussen, 144–68. Berlin: LIT Verlag, 2006.

Bernath, Julie. "'Complex Political Victims' in the Aftermath of Mass Atrocity: Reflections on the Khmer Rouge Tribunal in Cambodia." *International Journal of Transitional Justice* 10, no. 1 (2015): 46–66.

Black, Peter. "Foot Soldiers of the Final Solution: The Trawniki Training Camp and Operation Reinhard." *Holocaust and Genocide Studies* 25, no. 1 (2011): 1–99.

Bouris, Erica. *Complex Political Victims.* Bloomfield: Kumarian, 2007.

Brannigan, Augustine. *Beyond the Banality of Evil: Criminology and Genocide.* Oxford: Oxford University Press, 2013.

Browning, Christopher. *Ordinary Men: Reserve Police Battalion 101 and the Final Solution in Poland.* New York: HarperCollins, 1994.

Brunner, Markus, Jan Lohl, Rolf Pohl, and Sebastian Winter (eds.). *Volksgemeinschaft, Täterschaft und Antisemitismus. Beiträge zur psychoanalytischen Sozialpsychologie des Nationalsozialismus und seiner Nachwirkungen.* Gießen: Psychosozial-Verlag, 2011.

Clark, Janine Natalya. "Genocide, War Crimes and the Conflict in Bosnia: Understanding the Perpetrators." *Journal of Genocide Research* 11, no. 4 (2009): 421–45.

Clegg, Stewart R., Miguel Pina e Cunha, Arménio Rego, and Joana Dias. "Mundane Objects and the Banality of Evil: The Sociomateriality of a Death Camp." *Journal of Management Inquiry* 22, no. 3 (2013): 325–40.

David-Fox, Michael, Peter Holquist, and Alexander M. Martin (eds.). *The Holocaust in the East: Local Perpetrators and Soviet Responses.* Pittsburgh: University of Pittsburgh Press, 2014.

Dumitru, Diana. "An Analysis of Soviet Postwar Investigation and Trial Documents and Their Relevance for Holocaust Studies." In *The Holocaust in the East: Local Perpetrators and Soviet Responses,* edited by Michael David-Fox, Peter Holquist and Alexander M. Martin, 142–57. Pittsburgh: University of Pittsburgh Press, 2014.

Eriksson Baaz, Maria, and Maria Stern. *Sexual Violence as a Weapon of War?: Perceptions, Prescriptions, Problems in the Congo and Beyond.* London and New York: Zed Books, 2013.

Feldman, Gerald D., and Wolfgang Seibel (eds.). *Networks of Persecution: Bureaucracy, Business, and the Organization of the Holocaust.* New York: Berghahn Books, 2005.

Fletcher, Luke. "Turning Interahamwe: Individual and Community Choices in the Rwandan Genocide." *Journal of Genocide Research* 9, no. 1 (2007): 25–48.

Fujii, Lee Ann. *Killing Neighbors: Webs of Violence in Rwanda.* Ithaca, NY: Cornell University Press, 2009.

Fulbrook, Mary. *A Small Town Near Auschwitz: Ordinary Nazis and the Holocaust.* Oxford: Oxford University Press, 2012.

Goldhagen, Daniel. *Hitler's Willing Executioners: Ordinary Germans and the Holocaust.* London: Abacus, 1996.

Grabowski, Jan. *Hunt for the Jews: Betrayal and Murder in German-Occupied Poland.* Bloomington: Indiana University Press, 2013.

Grigoryan, Hasmik. "Behavioral Expressions of Perpetrators in the Ottoman Empire during the Massacres and Genocide against the Armenians: Sexual Violence." Unpublished Manuscript, 2015.

Gross, Jan T. *Neighbors: The Destruction of the Jewish Community in Jedwabne, Poland.* London: Arrow, 2003.

Hagan, John, and Joshua Kaiser. "The Displaced and Dispossessed of Darfur: Explaining the Sources of a Continuing State-Led Genocide." *The British Journal of Sociology* 62, no. 1 (2011): 1–25.

Hedlund, Anna. " 'There Was No Genocide in Rwanda': History, Politics, and Exile Identity Among Rwandan Rebels in the Eastern Congo Conflict." *Conflict and Society: Advances in Research* 1 (2015): 23–40.

Hinton, Alexander Laban. *Why Did They Kill? Cambodia in the Shadow of Genocide.* Berkeley: University of California Press, 2005.

Issinger, Jan H. "Männlichkeit, Vertrauen und Gewalt. Deutsche Ordnungspolizisten als Besatzungsmacht im Zweiten Weltkrieg." In *Zwischen Geschlecht und Nation. Interdependenzen und Interaktionen in der multiethnischen Gesellschaft Polens im 19. und 20. Jahrhundert*, edited by Matthias Barelkowski, Claudia Kraft and Isabel Röskau-Rydel, 223–36. Osnabrück: Polono-Germanica, 2016.

Jensen, Olaf, and Claus-Christian Szejnmann (eds.). *Ordinary People as Mass Murderers: Perpetrators in Comparative Perspective.* Basingstoke: Palgrave Macmillan, 2008.

Jessee, Erin. "Rwandan Women No More. Female Génocidaires in the Aftermath of the 1994 Rwandan Genocide." *Conflict and Society: Advances in Research* 1, no. 1 (2015): 60–80.

Kramer, Helgard (ed.). *NS-Täter aus interdisziplinärer Perspektive.* München: Martin Meidenbauer, 2006.

Kühl, Stefan. *Ganz normale Organisationen. Zur Soziologie des Holocaust.* Berlin: Suhrkamp, 2014.

Leader Maynard, Jonathan. "Rethinking the Role of Ideology in Mass Atrocities." *Terrorism and Political Violence* 26, no. 5 (2014): 821–41.

Leader Maynard, Jonathan, and Matto Mildenberger. "Convergence and Divergence in the Study of Ideology: A Critical Review." *British Journal of Political Science* (2016): 1–27.

Lifton, Robert Jay. *The Nazi Doctors: Medical Killing and the Psychology of Genocide.* New York: Basic Books, 2000 [1986].

Mamdani, M. *When Victims Become Killers: Colonialism, Nativism and the Genocide in Rwanda.* Princeton: Princeton University Press, 2001.

Mann, Michael. "Were the Perpetrators of Genocide 'Ordinary Men' or 'Real Nazis'? Results from Fifteen Hundred Biographies." *Holocaust and Genocide Studies* 14, no. 3 (2000): 331–66.

Mann, Michael. *The Dark Side of Democracy: Explaining Ethnic Cleansing.* Cambridge: Cambridge University Press, 2005.

Mann, Michael. "Processes of Murderous Cleansing/Genocide: Comment on Hagan and Kaiser." *The British Journal of Sociology* 62, no. 1 (2011): 42–8.

McDoom, Omar. "Who Killed in Rwanda's Genocide? Micro-Space, Social Influence and Individual Participation in Intergroup Violence." *Journal of Peace Research* 50, no. 4 (2013a): 453–67.

McDoom, Omar. "Antisocial Capital: A Profile of Rwandan Genocide Perpetrators' Social Networks." *Journal of Conflict Resolution* 58, no. 5 (2013b): 865–93.

Miller, Arthur G. (ed.). *The Social Psychology of Good and Evil.* New York: Guildford Press, 2004.

12 *Timothy Williams and Susanne Buckley-Zistel*

Moshman, David. "Genocidal Hatred: Now You See It, Now You Don't." In *The Psychology of Hate*, edited by Robert J. Sternberg, 185–209. Washington, DC: American Psychological Association, 2005.

Mueller, John. "The Banality of Ethnic War." *International Security* 25, no. 2 (2000): 42–70.

Newman, Leonard S., and Ralph Erber (eds.). *Understanding Genocide: The Social Psychology of the Holocaust*. Oxford: Oxford University Press, 2002: 241–58.

Petersen, Roger Dale. *Understanding Ethnic Violence: Fear, Hatred, and Resentment in Twentieth-Century Eastern Europe*. Cambridge: Cambridge University Press, 2002.

Pohl, Rolf, and Joachim Perels (eds.). *Normalität der NS-Täter? Eine kritische Auseinandersetzung*. Hannover: Offizin, 2011.

Rauschenbach, Mina, Christian Staerklé, and Damien Scalia. "Accused for Involvement in Collective Violence: The Discursive Reconstruction of Agency and Identity by Perpetrators of International Crimes." *Political Psychology* 37, no. 2 (2016): 219–35.

Schwartz, Johannes. "Handlungsoptionen von KZ-Aufseherinnen. Drei alltags- und geschlechtergeschichtliche biografische Fallstudien." In *NS-Täter aus interdisziplinärer Perspektive*, edited by Helgard Kramer, 349–74. München: Martin Meidenbauer, 2006.

Semelin, Jacques. *Purify and Destroy: The Political Uses of Massacre and Genocide*, translated by Cynthia Schoch. New York: Columbia University Press, 2005.

Sereny, Gitta. *Into that Darkness: An Examination of Conscience*. New York: First Vintage Books, 1983.

Sereny, Gitta. *Albert Speer: His Battle with Truth*. New York: Albert A. Knopf, 1995.

Short, Philipp. *Pol Pot: A History of a Nightmare*. London: John Murray, 2005a.

Short, Philipp. *Pol Pot: Anatomy of a Nightmare*. New York: Holt, 2005b.

Smeulers, Alette. "Female Perpetrators: Ordinary or Extra-Ordinary Women?" *International Criminal Law Review* 15 (2015): 207–53.

Smeulers, Alette, and Lotte Hoex. "Studying the Microdynamics of the Rwandan Genocide." *British Journal of Criminology* 50 (2010): 435–54.

Solonari, Vladimir. "Patterns of Violence: The Local Population and the Mass Murder of Jews in Bessarabia and Northern Bukovina, July–August 1941." In *The Holocaust in the East: Local Perpetrators and Soviet Responses*, edited by Michael David-Fox, Peter Holquist and Alexander M. Martin, 51–82. Pittsburgh: University of Pittsburgh Press, 2014.

Stangneth, Bettina. *Eichmann vor Jerusalem. Das unbehelligte Leben eines Massenmörders*. Zürich: Arche, 2011.

Staub, Ervin. "Obeying, Joining, Following, Resisting, and Other Processes in the Milgram Studies, and in the Holocaust and Other Genocides: Situations, Personality, and Bystanders." *Journal of Social Issues* 70, no. 3 (2014): 501–14.

Straus, Scott. *The Order of Genocide: Race, Power, and War in Rwanda*. Ithaca, NY: Cornell University Press, 2006.

Ulrich, Herbert. *Best: Biographische Studien über Radikalismus, Weltanschauung und Vernunft, 1903–1989*. Bonn: Dietz, 1996.

Üngör, Ugur Ümit, and Mehmet Polatel. *Confiscation and Destruction: The Young Turk Seizure of Armenian Property*. London: Continuum, 2011.

Valentino, Benjamin. *Final Solutions: Mass Killing and Genocide in the Twentieth Century*. Ithaca, NY: Cornell University Press, 2004.

Waller, James. *Becoming Evil: How Ordinary People Commit Genocide and Mass Killing*. Oxford: Oxford University Press, 2002.

Welzer, Harald. *Täter. Wie aus ganz normalen Menschen Massenmörder werden*. Frankfurt: S. Fischer, 2006.

Welzer, Harald, Sönke Neitzel, and Christian Gudehus (eds.). *'Der Führer war wieder viel zu human, viel zu gefühlvoll': Der Zweite Weltkrieg aus der Sicht deutscher und italienischer Soldaten*. Frankfurt: S. Fischer, 2011.

Werner, Frank. "'Hart müssen wir hier draußen sein.' Soldatische Männlichkeit im Vernichtungskrieg 1941–1944." *Geschichte und Gesellschaft* 34 (2008): 5–40.

Williams, Timothy. "The Complexity of Evil: A Multi-Faceted Approach to Genocide Perpetration." *Zeitschrift für Friedens- und Konfliktforschung* 3, no. 1 (2014): 71–98.

Williams, Timothy. "Opportunism, Authority and Ideology: On the Motivations of Turkish Perpetrators as Portrayed in the 1919 War Crimes Trials." *International Journal of Armenian Genocide Studies* 3 (2016).

Williams, Timothy. *The Complexity of Evil: Modelling Perpetration in Genocide*. PhD Thesis, Marburg University, Marburg, 2017.

Williams, Timothy, and Rhiannon Neilsen. "'They Will Rot the Society, Rot the Party, and Rot the Army.' Toxification as an Ideology and Motivation for Perpetrating Violence in the Khmer Rouge Genocide?" *Terrorism and Political Violence* (2016): 1–22.

Section I
Theorizing perpetrators

1 Thinking beyond perpetrators, bystanders, heroes

A typology of action in genocide

Timothy Williams

Introduction[1]

When speaking to former Khmer Rouge cadres in Cambodia about their role in the genocide[2] it is quite striking that most of them present themselves not as perpetrators but instead as victims, heroes or as bystanders, all affected by but not part of the totalitarian system of mass violence instituted in Cambodia in the late 1970s. Although their self-characterisation as victims of this extremely oppressive system is certainly legitimate and possibly not unexpected, their distancing from the word perpetrator rests on the diversity of roles that they took on during this time. According to their testimonies, the perpetrators were those who had killed, not they themselves who had only been involved in arresting the victims, guarding them at security centres, interrogating them for confessions, transporting them to the location of killing or ordering their execution. In interviews I conducted with these former cadres, they were happy to speak about the actions they had been involved in, as they did not see these as acts of perpetration of genocide or mass killing.[3] This resonates with some social scientific definitions of perpetration, such as Scott Straus's (2006: 102) definition of "a genocide perpetrator (*génocidaire*) as any person who participated in an attack against a civilian in order to kill or inflict serious injury on that civilian. Perpetrators thus would be those who directly killed or assaulted civilians and those who participated in groups that killed or assaulted civilians."

In this definition, as in the diversity of actions of the former Khmer Rouge cadres, there is no recognition that these actors are part of a larger system, a cog in the machinery of killing, and that their actions are part of a process that in the end leads to the mass destruction of the victim group. Temporally, however, these actions are preconditions for the killing to occur and are thus also part and parcel of the genocide. Also, several former Khmer Rouge cadres speak of acts of resistance and rescue that they had performed in the context of their other participation. What are these individuals to be labelled as? Heroes, perpetrators, bystanders? This chapter argues that such a classification of these people is a valid starting point, but that for a fuller understanding of the process of genocide these categories can be interrogated in a more nuanced way and differentiated in greater detail. Actions of killing have a very tangible effect on the implementation

18   Timothy Williams

of genocidal policies, but so also do these other acts of arresting, guarding and so forth. They all have an impact, albeit to varying degrees, on the genocide and thus need to be analysed within the same context of the acts of killing. Equally, acts of resistance impact the occurrence of genocide, and bystanders also wield influence over the process. This chapter introduces a typology of action in genocide that pays homage to the various parts that individuals can play in the genocidal process and the influence they have on it.

Typologies are helpful for academic discourse because they allow us to reduce the complexity of reality in a *systematic* manner and thus facilitate comparison. In this way we become able to systematically compare perpetrators, bystanders and rescuers across very different contexts such as the Holocaust and the genocide of the Armenians, the 1994 genocide in Rwanda and genocide by the Khmer Rouge in Cambodia. Even though the contexts are very different, a typology can help gauge commonalities in the types of actions people are engaged in and the effects that these ultimately have. The aim of this chapter is to provide an *empirically useful* typology of genocidal action that can help researchers to position individuals' actions in relation to genocide according to what impact their actions have and how proximate they are to its implementation. This analysis is not designed to be helpful for scholars looking to discuss or develop our legal understanding of genocide perpetration, nor does it provide a framework for normative discussions of genocidal action. Instead, it assists in conceptualising the empirical complexity of action and will bring a degree of systematisation to the grey zones of traditional definitions. It does not merely 'put actors in boxes,' but allows scholars to systematically and comparatively think about perpetration, bystanding and rescuing. For research on perpetrators, this typology provides a degree of systematisation that so far has been lacking, and provides a conceptual foundation for comparative perpetrator studies to build on.

This new approach to categorising genocide actors and their actions is grounded in structural individualism, a methodological approach within analytical sociology that posits that "all social facts, their structure and change, are in principle explicable in terms of individuals, their properties, actions, and relations to one another" (Hedström and Bearman 2009: 8).[4] For genocide, this means that its genesis and manifestation can only be understood when boiled down to the individuals who constitute it, their actions and the relations they have to each other. Thus, to comprehensively approach the concept of genocidal action, all members of society who could potentially have some form of impact on the genocide and its realisation will be included in this analysis. Here I choose to focus on members of the perpetrator group, as defined by the perpetrators. In Germany, this would be all Aryan Germans, in Rwanda all Hutu, in Cambodia all Khmer not defined as enemies of the revolution[5] or in the Armenian genocide all Muslim Ottoman citizens. The argument is not that these are all perpetrators but that they are all potential perpetrators, bystanders or heroes and that they thus can all theoretically impact the genocide. Equally this does not mean that members of the victim group cannot have influence on the genocide, and it would undoubtedly also be interesting to look at various types of victims and survivors, but this would go beyond the scope

Thinking beyond perpetrators 19

of this chapter. Nonetheless, by broadening the scope of which actors to include in the analysis beyond just clear-cut cases of perpetrators, this chapter will go beyond previous work, allowing perpetration and other forms of action not to be reduced just to certain individuals but rather concentrating on the action that these people engage in and how they impact the genocide. In this way, individuals' action in the grey zones alluded to earlier can be analysed in a more nuanced way, allowing also a more refined understanding of the dynamics of genocide.

In particular, the chapter draws on examples from the historical and social scientific literature on the Holocaust, the Rwandan, Cambodian and Armenian genocides,[6] four of the most prominent genocides of the 20th century, which have received by far the most attention in the literature, thus making the difficult conceptualisation of actions in these cases particularly salient. The typology that I develop here draws on the stories of hundreds of perpetrators, bystanders and heroes as they have been told in a broad range of academic literature, testimonies of perpetrators in various archival documents, as well as on interviews conducted in Cambodia with 58 former cadres of the Khmer Rouge. While the dynamics of and action constellations in these genocides were very different, my aim for this chapter is also to find a conceptual way of describing the commonalities among types of actions across these different genocides. It is the systematic approach to looking at the varying types of genocide actions that is the contribution this chapter makes to the broader literature on perpetrators, bystanders and victims.

This chapter first briefly introduces various examples of genocidal action to highlight the complexity of the phenomenon in question and to argue the necessity for a new approach. After a short overview of previous approaches to categorising genocidal action, the typology of action in genocide is introduced, spanning two axes: 'individual impact,' which describes the consequences of an individual's actions on the occurrence of genocide, and 'proximity' to the genocide. These conceptual ideas are presented first as a continuous spatial classification of genocide action, before being reduced to a typology.

Actors in genocide who do not fit the box – a new conceptual approach

There are myriad actors intermingling in a society committing genocide, all of whom can take on numerous roles and undertake various forms of action. This section briefly presents a few of these actors as anchor points to keep in mind when proceeding with the more abstract conceptualisation. This list makes no claim to be complete, and aims only to be illustrative of the diversity of genocidal actions. The empirical examples have been chosen quite arbitrarily as illustrative examples to display the diversity of genocidal actions that these actors can engage in and to act as a starting point for conceptualisation. They are sorted roughly by hierarchy, starting with actions committed by individuals at the top and proceeding onwards to low-level actors.

When thinking of genocide actors, the first person who will probably come to mind for most is the charismatic genocidal leader, the head ideologue, the person

20 *Timothy Williams*

whose brainchild the genocide is. In Nazi Germany this person was Adolf Hitler, in the Cambodian genocide it was Khmer Rouge Brother Number One, Pol Pot. These are people who themselves probably never laid hands on a weapon to kill a member of the victim group, but who created the ideological framework justifying and demanding the genocide, and who laid the political groundwork for its implementation.

Adolf Eichmann became almost synonymous with the idea of a Holocaust *Schreibtischtäter* (literally desk perpetrators) through Hannah Arendt's (1994 [1963]) covering of his trial in Jerusalem. In his position in the Reichssicherheitshauptamt, he was administratively responsible for the organisation of the deportation of the Jews towards the East. He himself did not kill anyone, but his logistical coordination facilitated or even enabled the smooth implementation of the genocide of six million Jews in Europe. At the other end of the scale, and more positively for the victims, there are people like Oskar Schindler who at great personal risk and expense managed to save hundreds of Jews from being deported to extermination camps. He managed this by giving them jobs in his factory, jobs that were essential to the war effort, providing the legitimation for saving them (Crowe 2004).

The actions of some actors in the Ottoman Empire's genocide of the Armenians are slightly less clear, such as Mehmet Alî Efendi, Director of Customs in the Trabzon area, who coordinated some parts of the deportation and massacre of Armenians but also saved several Armenian women from the deportations (Dadrian and Akçam 2011; Yeghiayan 1990). However, he subsequently then also forced many of them to convert to Islam, and gave them to loyal followers to marry or take as household slaves. Thus, depending on the perspective, he could be considered a hero who saved their lives or a perpetrator who contributed to the genocide by enslaving these women.

When Major Trapp from Reserve Police Battalion 101 delivered the orders to eliminate the Jewish population of around 1,800 people in the Polish town of Jósefów, he gave the gathered members of his battalion the option of not participating (Browning 2001 [1994]). Although very few chose this option, some did, and thus they did not participate in the killing action. They witnessed what was happening anyway, though, and their refusal to participate was seen by their comrades and would have impacted their perceptions of what they were about to do. Thus it is all the more telling that these people did not frame their choice to be bystanders rather than killers in moral terms, but instead by stating that they were "too weak" (Browning 2001 [1994]: 64).

A further type of actor is the person who actually commits the killings, exemplified here by Pancrace, a Hutu man who killed several Tutsi during the Rwandan genocide (Hatzfeld 2003). He had joined a group of several friends, and together they had participated in several massacres, killing dozens of Tutsi victims. Pancrace can be seen as a typical low-level perpetrator who participates in killings. By contrast, Olivier was also a low-level joiner in Rwanda who, like Pancrace, participated in many killings but was also responsible for helping a young boy escape the killing, showing him which way he could run to safety (Fujii 2009).

Thinking beyond perpetrators 21

Finally, Keo Rithy[7] was a young cadre of the Khmer Rouge during its regime in the late 1970s. After the victory of the Khmer Rouge he became a soldier, but was very soon transferred to be a guard at a 'security centre'; first he guarded the perimeter of this prison before being promoted to actually guarding the prisoners themselves. In this role, he had to make sure that no prisoners killed themselves or died between interrogations. Later he was promoted again to be the personal bodyguard and messenger for the prison chief. In this capacity, he also delivered letters containing the lists of people to be executed.

This list could be expanded almost indefinitely, introducing different individuals with various life stories, all with varying nuances of participation and varying impact on the genocide in question. For example, there were Khmer Rouge cadres who crossed some people off their killing lists, but sent out the list with many other names still on it; or Rwandan women who stood by the massacres and egged on their husbands, brothers and sons, encouraging them through singing and chanting, even questioning the masculinity of men not wanting to participate. These are all people who are members of the genocidal society, and who in some way or another play a part in the way the genocide becomes realised, be it through their active support, resistance or passive attempts to disengage. The rest of this chapter takes up the challenge of trying to relate these various individuals' actions to each other and find a way to classify them as a tool for further analysis.

Categorising genocidal actors

Reflecting on the various actors presented in the previous section, some would appear to be quite clear-cut and obvious in their classifications. For example, Pancrace or other individuals who repeatedly participated in mass killings of members of the victim group can quite unambiguously be labelled perpetrators, whereas individuals such as Oskar Schindler or Olivier can be characterised as heroes. But the vast majority of individuals fall into a grey zone somewhere between these ideal types. What makes the 'obvious' cases so distinct, and how can one differentiate the other cases? Several authors have attempted to think about what kind of actors exist in genocide and how these can be related to each other, and this section will review the most important approaches. These authors have created typologies of genocide actors, although they predominantly focus on perpetrators. While the focus of this chapter is on the actions an individual is engaged in, most previous categorisations have focused on the actors themselves, and so these are presented here, before taking these insights and applying them to genocidal *actions*.

The first type of classifications put the *positions* of the individuals at the centre of their analysis. A prominent example of this approach is Raul Hilberg (1992) who suggests various types of perpetrators[8] and bystanders,[9] predominantly based on their position in the system, although also including many organisations as actors rather than just individuals. Very differently Kai Ambos (2010) creates a two-dimensional typology of perpetrators, differentiating low-, middle- and high-level individuals and state and non-state actors. Hilberg's categorisation remains

22   *Timothy Williams*

quite elite-centric and cannot claim comprehensiveness in covering all types of empirical actors who are involved in genocide, e.g. leaving out actors like Keo Rithy who played an important part in the process leading to several people's deaths but without actually being involved with the killing itself. Furthermore, both approaches suffer from the problem that individuals in these various positions can actually act in very different ways from within these positions. For example, as a low-level state actor, it is possible for an individual to engage in killing, to evade any participation or to even attempt rescuing members of the victim groups. This substantial variation in the actions in which the individuals actually engage and the diverging meanings they have for the genocide renders the classifications less meaningful for the explanation of genocide.

A further approach to classifying individuals is to examine their *motivations*. Michael Mann (2005) and Alette Smeulers (2008; see also Smeulers and Hoex 2010) both provide relatively comprehensive motivational typologies, though with differing specifications. Mann's typology is purely motivational and differentiates nine motivations for being a killer: ideological, bigoted, violent, fearful, careerist, materialist, disciplined, comradely and bureaucratic (Mann 2005: 27–9), while Smeulers concentrates on motivations but also intersperses this with certain elements of how the individuals were recruited and the positions they are in.[10] Gerhard Paul (2002) offers a less extensive and detailed compilation of Nazi perpetrators, determining perpetrators of conviction, utilitarian perpetrators, criminal extreme perpetrator (who goes above and beyond the required killing) and the traditional perpetrator following orders. Even less nuanced is the criminological typology by Herbert Jäger (1982 [1967]) who differentiates between perpetrators engaging in extreme action beyond the ordered, taking the initiative and individuals just obeying orders; these appear very similar to Lee Ann Fujii's (2009: 155) perpetrator types who went along willingly or unwittingly, or were forced.

The fundamental problem with this type of classification for forwarding the understanding of genocide is that motivations do not tell us anything about the type, intensity or effect of the *action* itself. Though motivations are undeniably pivotal to the study of perpetrators and to a full understanding of genocide, it is important to differentiate between action and motivation (for a broader discussion of violence as action see Christian Gudehus in this volume). For instance, Smeuler's profiteers speak to the motivation of opportunism. However, it is plausible that other types of actors are also opportunistic and hope to profit from the situation, such as those loyal to Mehmet Alî Efendi, the opportunistic heroes in the Armenian genocide who married women to 'save' them from deportation and killing but who took advantage of them sexually and gained free household labour; or factory owners in the Third Reich similar to Oskar Schindler who 'rescued' Jews from the gas chambers but who did this for opportunistic reasons so as to profit from their free labour. Hence, motivations alone cannot suffice to clearly categorise various genocide actors and differentiate them. Rather, it is necessary to identify the specific actions or tasks they are performing and the impact of these actions in a first step. Only then does it make sense (and is it a vital part of research) to look at motivations in order to understand why these individuals are engaging in these specific actions. Motivations alone make the classifications tenuous.

A third type of classification focuses on the degree of *complicity* of the individuals. Here, Eric Markusen (2002) classifies bystanders, assisting and perpetrators, but does not go beyond this in trying to establish the complexity of these ideal types. The idea of assisting as a culpable individual who does not "get their hands dirty" (Markusen 2002: 86), such as Keo Rithy in the preceding examples, is useful in its attempt to point out that there are influential individuals who are not involved in the killing. But a typology that rests on only these three categories is too simple and cannot grasp the pivotal nuances in various grey zones.

The fourth and final type of classification focuses on the *role* which the individual has in the genocidal action and was put forward by Lee Ann Fujii (2009: 16, 130) in her study of Rwandan perpetrators. She demarcates differences between leaders, collaborators, joiners, survivors, rescuers, evaders, witnesses and resisters. This approach appears to be extremely helpful, as it identifies various roles that individuals can have and thus shifts the emphasis from the person to their actions, demonstrating how people can engage in different actions at different times. However, though a very helpful categorisation indeed, Fujii just identifies several disparate types without stating how they are related to each other and whether the list is exhaustive. Void of defining criteria, it is unclear whether there are further types of actions that could also be included in the list. For example, it is unclear how people like Eichmann who help logistically should be categorised.

Altogether, the approaches put forth in the literature on identifying genocidal actors have contributed greatly to a more nuanced understanding of the dynamics of genocide and all have their place for various types of research endeavours. However, a systematic treatment of these actors with regard to their actions will contribute to a fuller understanding.

A typology of action in genocide

Individual impact and proximity as defining indicators of action in genocide

A new typology, as I will develop it here, needs to go beyond thinking of perpetrators, bystanders or heroes as independent, stand-alone categories. These categories are intimately interlinked and individuals can often be seen to move from one category to another and back through time and space. This is demonstrated by Mehmet Alî Efendi, who not only locally coordinated the deportation of the Armenians but also saved some of the women, albeit for dubious purposes; equally there are manifold examples of Hutu saving and hiding Tutsi friends, while still going out every day and joining in the massacres of other Tutsi. Instead, this chapter tries to include all actions within the genocidal context.

24 *Timothy Williams*

The approach chosen in this chapter is to focus on action in genocide. This emphasis on the *action* in which an individual is engaged allows us to approach the topic from a behavioural perspective. Referring back to the ideas of structural individualism and analytical sociology, action is absolutely central to explanation of social phenomena "because all the things that interest us as sociologists are the intended and unintended outcomes of individuals' actions" (Hedström and Bearman 2009: 9) and are thus also the key element to mechanisms that can explain causal processes. With this approach, the typology is consciously attempting to disentangle the many facets that can be taken at the micro-level, such as motivations, attitudes, ideologies, behaviours and many more. Thus, the conception underlying this typology rejects any idea that intentionality and action must be logically interwoven, as phenomenological approaches would posit, and while action and intentionality can be interlinked, motivations for action can broadly vary and are not constituent parts of any definition of the action themselves. A further differentiation is necessary concerning identity: a person's identity may strongly influence the action choices the individual makes, for instance with women and men choosing actions that fit certain gendered scripts or cultural expectations. However, this is of no concern here, as what we are considering is the resultant action itself. Thus, the typology developed here tries to categorise the actors along externally defined criteria rather than through their own perception. By focusing on individuals' actions as a starting point, we can create types of actions that can subsequently then be used for further analysis at the micro-level. Only then can one investigate, for instance, the motivations people have for engaging in these actions, the meaning that they ascribe to them or types of actions that are typical for certain identity scripts.

Finally, it is important to emphasise that this typology explicitly excludes the attitudinal dimension. As I have argued elsewhere with Dominik Pfeiffer, genocidal intent is mainly relevant for framing genocidal action at the macro level, but the individual low-level perpetrators act for a large number of different motivations, of which ideologies of intent will be only one (Williams and Pfeiffer 2017; on the plurality of motivations see Williams 2014). While such a differentiation would allow a distinction, for instance, between Oskar Schindler and other more opportunistic factory owners, this goes beyond the focus on action here. Intent and attitudes could provide a helpful addition to motivational analysis of genocide actors as they can signal the strength or weakness of conviction of an action depending on whether the actor is acting in line with their attitudes.

The argument I make for this approach to categorisation is that focussing on action as the behavioural manifestations of an individual's contact to genocide, not on the person themselves, allows people to engage in multiple types of action. At different times people can act differently within the genocidal proceedings. A person in a certain position can engage in various types of action from one and the same institutional position. For instance, a member of a police battalion during the Holocaust could become an implementing agent of genocidal policies killing hundreds of Jews but could equally in this exact same position be an onlooker who encourages other people through their presence, a facilitative helper who aids the logistics of the operation but refrains from actual killing or even someone who goes out of their way to save Jews. With this different perspective, any analysis can only categorise an individual's actions for a certain moment in time, and must allow for shifts and changes in action.

To define types of action in genocide I have chosen the axes of individual impact on the genocide and proximity to the killing. *Individual impact is defined here as the consequences that an individual's actions have on the actually realised genocidal outcome.* More specifically, one can ask oneself the question of what would have happened differently if the individual had not acted the way they did, and thus what impact did he or she have on the process.[11] The idea behind this factor is to gauge the consequences of an individual action. By departing from a unidimensional focus on just killing for perpetrators or virtuous saving for heroes, this allows myriad further actions to also be situated along a continuum of genocidal action. Thus, people like Keo Rithy or Adolf Eichmann, the people who arrest members of the victim group or organise the logistics, also have an impact on the genocidal outcome and the deaths of these specific people. Equally, while it is possible for some bystanders to have no impact whatsoever on the genocide, for other types of bystanders subtle effects can occur when they psychologically affect others. All of these can be located along a continuum, illustrated with some examples of impact in Figure 1.1.

Individual impact as the first defining factor stems from the idea that the essence of perpetration, rescuing and bystanding is grounded in the consequences of an individual's actions. A perpetrator, for example, is not inherently a perpetrator, born and destined to be this type of actor, but instead a perpetrator's actions define him or her as such, and it is through the effect that the actions have that we can gauge their impact and thus their defining quality. Furthermore, it is the aggregation of these individual acts that in the end make up and contest genocide, and so for a real understanding of this phenomenon we need to look at these constitutive actions.

The second factor through which I define these actions brings a spatial component to the table. *Proximity is the distance that separates an individual from the genocide; this distance is primarily defined geographically, but can also*

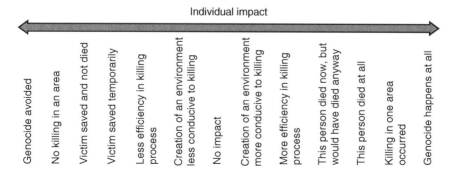

Figure 1.1 Continuum of individual impact – the impact a person has on the genocidal outcome

incorporate social or institutional measures. This means that it is not only about physical distance from the locus of killing but how intimately someone is tied to the killing procedures, e.g. someone such as Major Trapp who gives the orders to kill a certain specific group may well be seen as closer to the killing because of their close involvement with it than someone who transports the victims to the site of killing, even though the latter is closer geographically to the actual killing. This continuum of proximity is exemplified in Figure 1.2.

The rationale behind including proximity as the second factor is derived from the explanatory power that space can bring to such an endeavour. Particularly, genocide as a planned, state-driven form of political violence[12] is a joint effort combining a multitude of actions all essential for the implementation of the genocidal violence. With this organised form of violence, actions can have a strong impact from various positions within the system, and thus for a more nuanced classification it is important to weigh not just action impact, but also to gauge how close an actor is to the implementation. This measure of proximity allows various actions to be situated in relation to the machinery of death.

The following two sections relate these two dimensions to each other in typological form, first as a continuous spatial classification in which both indicators are left as continuous measures and individual actions can be placed in an endless amount of positions. Subsequently, the complexity is reduced to a more traditional typology of action in genocide.

A continuous spatial classification of action in genocide

The first type of classification presented here takes both individual impact and proximity as continuous indicators, each with infinite potential values for an individual action. Proximity varies between an action being very close to the locus of killing, for example the actor not just physically present at the site of killing, but at the other end of a weapon up close to and facing the victim. Individual impact varies between the individual's actions being the reason the genocide even occurs

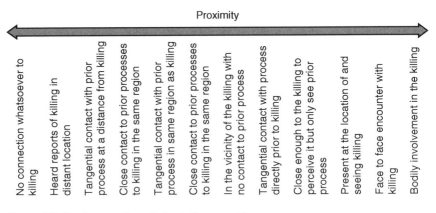

Figure 1.2 Continuum of proximity to the genocide

Thinking beyond perpetrators 27

on one extreme to the individual causing the avoidance of genocide; the threshold in the middle is that a person has absolutely no impact on the genocide, that is, that the actions performed by this person have no consequences whatsoever for the occurrence or realisation of the genocide in any way.

These two continuous scales are then related to each other in a two-dimensional model, with individual impact on the horizontal, proximity on the vertical axis (see Figure 1.3). Within this two-dimensional space, I have located the various empirical examples from the second section of this chapter as illustrative examples for ideal-typical spatial representations of various genocide actors according to their primary actions. For example, instigators of the genocide whose actions are responsible even for its genesis, but occur quite distantly from the locus of killing, such as Hitler or Pol Pot, are located on the far bottom right of the graph. Equally, Eichmann and Schindler are at the bottom of the graph: Eichmann's actions facilitated the genocide's occurrence without actually being responsible for any specific people's actual deaths but making the whole process significantly more efficient. Schindler's actions, on the other hand, were also distant from the locus of the killing, but they meant the difference between life and death for specific individuals, impacting the course of the genocide's implementation. Mehmet Alî Efendi appears twice, as his local coordination of the Armenian deportations enabled the occurrence of the killing in the area, but his actions towards some women in the victim group meant their individual safety; the latter occurred back in the city, significantly more distanced from his oversight of killings outside the city gates, thus making his actions less proximate to the genocide. Equally, Olivier appears once as a rescuer close to the killing, but also along with Pancrace, both of whose actions caused the deaths of several people. This is similar to the

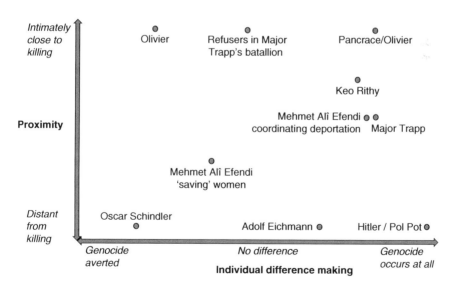

Figure 1.3 Continuous spatial classification of action in genocide

28   Timothy Williams

orders of Major Trapp; however Major Trapp was further away from the killing action, only giving the orders but not actually implementing them himself. Somewhere in between regarding proximity but with less individual impact is Keo Rithy, who facilitated the killing through his guarding and dispatching orders as a messenger, but who did not kill anyone himself. Lastly, those policemen who took up Trapp's offer to not participate had little individual impact on the genocide at all, despite being very close to the killing operations. Though their refusals could have created a moral counter-discourse that could have affected other comrades' participation, the way they framed their non-participation as weakness may have negated this impact.

A classical typology of action in genocide

Although a continual categorisation occupying a two-dimensional space enables researchers to adopt a nuanced approach to locating various actions, a certain degree of parsimony can be helpful. This parsimony allows increased comparability of individual actions across different cases, as well as a better assignment of labels to them. These categorisations of action through discrete labels allow types of actions to be clustered systematically and thus commonalities and differences between various undertaken actions can be garnered.

To create a more parsimonious typology, the indicator proximity has been dichotomised to differentiate actions that are close to and distant from the locus of killing. The indicator individual impact has been split more minutely into seven indicative categories. The number seven is to a degree arbitrary, but it allows for a symmetrical treatment of actions each side of 'no impact' on the promotion or inhibition of genocide. All categories are qualitatively different, and although any number of additional categories could have been added in between these, seven allows us to at least gauge some of the complexity of action in genocide. The median category labels the actions taken by the individual as having absolutely no impact on the genocide and its unfolding. The end points of the continuum are, as described earlier, the avoidance of genocide on the one hand and the occurrence of genocide on the other. The next strongest impact that an individual can have is whether a certain person dies or not – here we are gauging not the overall occurrence of the genocide as in the extreme cases but instead the life or death impact for certain individuals in the victim group. The final two categories then reflect whether an action has impacted the situation in general in a facilitative or inhibitive manner. This does not mean that a person specifically died because of the consequences of this action, but instead that the overall situation was influenced in a certain way, making the killing more or less likely.

This categorisation of proximity and individual impact thus creates a typology with 14 types, which is presented in Figure 1.4.[13] First we have those actions that impact the genocide so strongly that without them the genocide would not even have occurred. *Agitating* occurs when actions are distant from the killing but instigate the genocide as a whole, create the political or legal framework for it or author the ideological underpinnings, such as Hitler and Pol Pot; also, agitating

Thinking beyond perpetrators 29

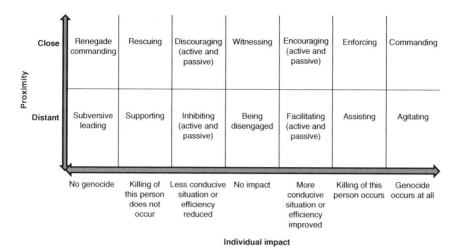

Figure 1.4 Typology of action in genocide

can fundamentally enable the genocide in other ways, such as through funding it or through inciting and enabling the genocidal ideology to even be spread in the media. *Commanding* is action without which the genocide would also not have materialised from these distant plans. Individuals engaging in commanding are up close to the killing giving the overarching orders and overseeing their implementation; here Major Trapp's or Mehmet Alî Efendi's actions could be cases in point.

Enforcing is when an individual engaging in these actions gets their hands dirty and actually executes the killing orders, such as Pancrace; these actions are intimately close to the killing and cause the death of each individual victim.[14] This action is the one most typically associated with the label of perpetrator. Slightly more distanced from the clear classification as a perpetrator but nonetheless often included in its realm is the action of assisting. *Assisting* actions are those that are also necessary for the individual to be killed but that are more distant from the killing, e.g. by being part of the arrest, guarding or transport of the victims, or in some other way enabling the killing process. Without this action there would be no victims to kill, yet the action does not occur at the actual locus of killing; Keo Rithy's actions are a good example.

Next, we have actions that create a situation that is more conducive to genocide occurring or that improve the efficiency of the situation. *Encouraging* occurs close to the nexus of killing, not actually killing, but through the presence of the actor making the environment more conducive. This is an extremely broad category in which one can differentiate between *active and passive encouraging*. Active encouraging, for instance, could be when onlookers support and cheer on the killings and are thus actively influencing the happenings towards genocide occurring. By contrast, passive encouraging occurs much more subtly when

30 *Timothy Williams*

people – conventionally classed as bystanders – make the situation more conducive to killing by simply being present at the killing and not doing anything at all, thus also not showing resistance or raising moral concerns. This inaction, thus, implicitly legitimises the killing through lack of resistance and is thus passively encouraging. *Facilitating* occurs when actors are not physically present at the killing sites, but their actions make the killing procedures easier, again being able to differentiate *active and passive facilitating*. Active facilitating, for instance, could be working in offices optimising the efficiency of killing procedures as Eichmann did in the Holocaust, developing better weaponry, or creating a more facilitative climate through propaganda in the media. More passive facilitating would be the (non-)action of the many silent members of society who implicitly legitimise an ongoing genocide and create an environment in which it can thrive purely by looking away and allowing genocidal propaganda to sediment itself in societal discourse.

The threshold between actions that promote the genocide as such and those that restrain it lies in those actions that make no difference at all. *Being disengaged* are those actions that have no bearing on the genocide and are not close to the killing, whereas *witnessing* describes those actions that have no impact on the outcome but occur at the locus of killing. Some of the policemen in Major Trapp's battalion 101 engaged in acts of witnessing, as long as their non-participation had no tangible outcomes on the killing or their comrades' psychological dispositions towards the killing. Empirically, it is questionable whether any form of action that has absolutely no impact on the materialisation of violence actually ever occurs, as all actions that are perceived by others will have some (albeit often very subtle) influence, at least on their perception of the situation due to how they interpret the inactivity.

Next, *inhibiting* is the counterpart to facilitating, in that it creates a less conducive environment from a distance and undermines the efficiency of the system, again with *active or passive inhibiting*. This can actively be through raising moral questions and creating a counter-discourse to genocidal narratives, prioritising non-genocidal actions over genocidal ones, and so on. Alternatively, passive inhibiting can be constituted by the subtle refusal to participate in practices that create a facilitative environment, e.g. still serving Jews or still going to Jewish shops in the run-up to the Holocaust, thus subtly reducing the social consensus regarding the legitimacy of the genocide. *Discouraging* actions are actions performed close to the killing itself, for instance demonstratively refusing to go along on a killing mission, thus raising a moral question mark for comrades and establishing an exit route for others. If any of Trapp's men had not framed themselves as weak, they would have been engaging in discouraging, creating a situation that makes it psychologically harder for the others to kill. A more passive form of this discouraging would be not showing up to a killing mission, rather than actively refusing it.

Rescuing is a type of action by which individual members of the victim group are saved from their fatal destinies, impacting concretely on the life of an individual, irrespective of whether this person is then killed at a later point. Such

Thinking beyond perpetrators 31

an example of this action is Mehmet Alî Efendi's saving of Armenian women, albeit with sinister intentions. *Supporting* occurs when the actions manage to save certain people, even though the actor does not hold the power of life and death at the tip of their fingers but is acting from a distance, for instance by crossing individuals off death lists or by giving Jews jobs in factories pivotal to the war effort, such as Schindler.

Lastly, we have those actions that prevent the occurrence of genocide at all. *Subversive leading* is a type of action engaged in by actors who are opposed to the genocide and through political, propaganda or violent means manage to undermine the genocidal plans from a distance. *Renegade commanding* occurs when those tasked with the implementation of genocidal plans refuse the orders given to them, and mobilise their personnel against the genocide effort, preventing the implementation of the genocide in certain areas or even at all.

It is important to reiterate that this is a typology of *action*, not of actors themselves. This is pivotal because it means that one and the same person can engage in multiple actions independently of each other without this even appearing contradictory. For example, Mehmet Alî Efendi was both *supporting* several Armenian women, while at the same time *assisting* in the coordination of the deportations.

The typology deliberately did not include the labels commonly used in the literature so as to avoid confusion between these more nuanced categories and the more overarching concepts. Nonetheless, it is instructive to relate this typology back to conventional conceptions of perpetrators, heroes and bystanders. *Perpetrators* in the narrowest sense would engage only in enforcing actions, doing the actual killing, but in a broader understanding of perpetrators as adopted implicitly by most scholars, this group would also include the actions of assisting, commanding and agitating. To a certain degree some forms of facilitating and encouraging would also be seen as the actions of perpetrators. Other types of facilitating and encouraging would be more adequately associated with the actions of *bystanders*, as would witnessing and being disengaged, as well as some types of inhibiting and discouraging. Other types of inhibiting and discouraging, as well as rescuing, supporting, renegade commanding and subversive leading would conventionally be portrayed as the actions of *heroes*. Thus, we see that these three labels are legitimately applied independently of each other, but that their borders are blurred. Furthermore, given the possibility of actors undertaking parallel actions, it renders the static attribution as perpetrator, bystander or hero more problematic still.

Conclusion

This chapter has challenged previous conceptualisations of perpetrators, bystanders and heroes by questioning the categories on which these were built and has instead introduced a more continuous typology of action that individuals can adhere to within the genocide setting. This typology followed the axes of proximity to the killing and individual impact on the genocide, defined as the

32 *Timothy Williams*

individual's impact on the occurrence and implementation of genocide. First, a spatial categorisation was developed along continuous axes in which various types of actions could be positioned in relation to each other. Subsequently this was reduced to a more consolidated typology with two categories of proximity and seven of individual impact. This then creates 14 types: commanding, agitating, enforcing, assisting, encouraging, facilitating, witnessing, being disengaged, discouraging, inhibiting, rescuing, supporting, renegade commanding and subversive leading.

In essence I have argued that categorisations relevant to genocide participation should be tied less to the person than to the action this person engages in. Thus, it is most important to look at the acts of perpetration and their consequences to define a perpetrator, and that acts of rescuing and bystanding should also take precedence as actions rather than labels ascribed to individuals. In the end, individuals are labelled according to their actions, but the actions suggested here are more nuanced than any previous categorisations. This approach allows for multi-dimensionality with one and the same individual engaging in seemingly contradictory behaviour across time and space.

Future research could attempt to broaden this typology to include not just actions by members of the perpetrator group, but all actors in society, also including the victims and survivors; this is particularly important as the actions in the typology presented here can also at the same time be located in the victim and survivor categories. Even within the group of victims, people can engage in multiple forms of action, for instance, as a victim of the regime under which they are serving but also as a facilitating or enforcing, as was the case for Jewish capos in concentration camps or for many Khmer Rouge cadres who made minor mistakes and were then re-branded enemies of the Khmer people.

The typology can furthermore be readily applied to revisit several topics salient to research into the micro-level of genocide. For instance, it would be interesting to see whether the motivations that propel the various individuals towards their actions differ systematically across the various categories. Further avenues for research using the typology would include whether engaging in various actions leads to differing responses to post-genocide societal dealing with the past or whether various types of action appeal to different demographic or psychological types of people. Also, it could prove promising to look into strategies actors find for combining multiple actions and what consequences shifts between them have for the individuals. This more nuanced approach should allow future research to pick up more strongly on differences within the group responsible for the genocide and thus forward a better understanding of the dynamics of genocide and its impact on pathways into and out of violence.

Notes

1 Acknowledgments: I would like to thank Judith von Heusinger, Mariam Salehi, Mareike Stolley and Christian Braun for their feedback on my initial ideas.
2 Although the mass killing of political enemies in Cambodia would not fall under the scope of the legal definition in the UN Convention on Genocide (Convention on the

Thinking beyond perpetrators 33

Prevention and Punishment of the Crime of Genocide 1948), it does fall under the definition of most academic definitions and commonly used lists (for an often cited list see, for example, Harff 2003).

3 I conducted interviews with 58 former cadres of the Khmer Rouge in 10 provinces of Cambodia between July 2014 and January 2015.

4 Structural individualism is not to be confused with methodological individualism, which in the tradition of economists such as Carl Menger (1963 [1883]) emphasises how any social phenomena are the result of individual actions that are based on the individuals themselves and their preferences. Structural individualism goes further than this and emphasises in its explanations the individual *in social relations* to other individuals (Hedström and Bearman 2009: 8).

5 Under the Khmer Rouge regime, it was not uncommon for cadres to also be suspected of being traitors and then subsequently redefined as enemies and killed as such. This fear of being redefined as an enemy was prevalent in most of my interviews with Khmer Rouge cadres and indeed some were imprisoned at some point while being investigated for treachery. This erodes the distinction between perpetrator and victim group yet further, but it would certainly go beyond the scope of this chapter to delve too much more deeply into this facet also.

6 The proposed typology is the endpoint of a long iterative research process that attempted to marry the concepts underlying a broad range of previous typologies in the genocide literature and my own ideas as to how genocide actors could innovatively and more appropriately be conceptualised. In a process reminiscent of grounded theory (Charmaz, 2006), at every stage these typological ideas were related to the wealth of empirical examples commonly discussed in the secondary literature, as well as the interview material and primary documents I have studied. In a prolonged iterative process, various dimensions of a typology were experimented with, and subsequently refined and honed, always relating the typology to the concepts from the literature and the empirical examples.

7 The name has been changed, but the person is based on an interview conducted by the author with a former Khmer Rouge cadre in Kandal Province, Cambodia, in August 2014.

8 Adolf Hitler, the Establishment, the old functionaries, newcomers, 'zealots, vulgarians and bearers of burdens,' physicians and lawyers, non-German governments and non-German volunteers.

9 'Nations in Adolf Hitler's Europe,' 'helpers, gainers and onlookers,' messengers, Jewish rescuers, the Allies, neutral countries, the Churches.

10 Smeulers identifies "the criminal mastermind (defined as the supreme authority), the fanatic (driven by hate and resentment), the sadist (driven by a pleasure to induce pain), the criminal (who was already involved in serious crime), the professional (who has gone through extremely coercive military training in which he was trained to become a torturer or killer), the devoted warrior (driven by a sincere belief in the ideology and the need to obey and conform to an authority), the careerist (driven by careerism), the profiteer (driven by pure self-interest or material gain), the compromised perpetrator (driven by fear) and the conformist and follower (who follow the flow)" (Smeulers and Hoex 2010: 437).

11 This is not meant to pursue a full counterfactual logic, which would also have to factor in the actions of other actors in the counterfactual situation to see how this would affect the outcome (for a broad discussion of counterfactuals and causation see Collins et al. 2004). Instead, it is a rough approximation of someone's individual impact. For instance, if an individual refuses to kill some members of the victim group, it is highly likely that they will still be killed by someone else, and in effect the victims will be dead. However, if the person does not refuse due to this duress, the effect of the action will nonetheless be that the victim is dead.

12 While the legal definition of genocide as codified in the UN Convention on the Prevention and Punishment of the Crime of Genocide (Convention on the Prevention and

34 *Timothy Williams*

Punishment of the Crime of Genocide 1948) and the many extant academic definitions (Chalk and Jonassohn 1990: 26; Jones 2006: 22; Semelin 2005: 87; Shaw 2010: 160) are all hotly contested, many do agree on the necessity of the state as an actor in the definition of genocide (Alvarez 2001: 10). As Rudolph Rummel (1994) points out, in this context labelling the state as the perpetrator is merely a "convenient personification of an abstraction" as those in control of the state are, of course, in reality people. But it is precisely these state actors who play an important role in genocide's implementation and are of core interest to the classification attempts being conducted here.

13 The titles given to each type are an attempt to most precisely describe this action in the genocide; they do not constitute the perpetrator perspective or the victim perspective, but are an attempt to present an outside view.

14 This is not to say that this victim would not have died if this individual had not killed them, as very probably someone else would have stepped in and implemented the order. Thus, in a strict sense, the counterfactual does not work, but from a simpler causal logic, it was this action that actually killed the victim.

References

Alvarez, Alex. *Governments, Citizens and Genocide: A Comparative and Interdisciplinary Approach.* Bloomington: Indiana University Press, 2001.

Ambos, Kai. "Criminologically Explained Reality of Genocide, Structure of the Offence and the 'Intent to Destroy' Requirement." In *Collective Violence and International Criminal Justice*, edited by Alette Smeulers, 153–73. Antwerpen: Intersentia, 2010.

Arendt, Hannah. *Eichmann in Jerusalem: A Report on the Banality of Evil.* New York: Penguin Books, 1994 [1963].

Browning, Christopher. *Ordinary Men: Reserve Police Battalion 101 and the Final Solution in Poland.* 1st British ed. New York: HarperCollins, 2001 [1994].

Chalk, Frank, and Kurt Jonassohn. *The History and Sociology of Genocide: Analyses and Case Studies.* New Haven: Yale University Press, 1990.

Charmaz, Kathleen C. *Grounded Theory. A Practical Guide through Qualitative Analysis.* London: SAGE, 2006.

Collins, John, Ned Hall, and Laurie A. Paul. *Causation and Counterfactuals.* Cambridge, MA and London: The MIT Press, 2004.

Crowe, David. *Oskar Schindler: The Untold Account of His Life, Wartime Activities, and the True Story Behind the List.* Cambridge, MA: Basic Books, 2004.

Dadrian, Vahakn N., and Taner Akçam. *Judgment at Istanbul: The Armenian Genocide Trials.* 1st English ed. New York: Berghahn Books, 2011 [original ed. published in Turkish, 2011].

Fujii, Lee Ann . *Killing Neighbors: Webs of Violence in Rwanda.* Ithaca, NY: Cornell University Press, 2009.

Harff, Barbara. "No Lessons Learned from the Holocaust? Assessing Risks of Genocide and Political Mass Murder Since 1955." *American Political Science Review* 97, no. 1 (2003): 57–73.

Hatzfeld, Jean. *Une saison de machettes.* Paris: Seuil, 2003.

Hedström, Peter, and Peter Bearman. "What Is Analytical Sociology All About? An Introductory Essay." In *The Oxford Handbook of Analytical Sociology*, edited by Peter Hedström and Peter Bearman, 3–24. Oxford: Oxford University Press, 2009.

Hilberg, Raul. *Perpetrators, Victims, Bystanders: The Jewish Catastrophe, 1933–1945.* New York: Harper-Collins Publishers, 1992.

Jäger, Herbert. *Verbrechen unter totalitärer Herrschaft. Studien zur nationalsozialistischen Gewaltkriminalität.* Frankfurt am Main: Suhrkamp, 1982 [1967].

Thinking beyond perpetrators 35

Jones, Adam. *Genocide: A Comprehensive Introduction*. London: Routledge, 2006.

Mann, Michael. *The Dark Side of Democracy: Explaining Ethnic Cleansing*. Cambridge: Cambridge University Press, 2005.

Markusen, Eric. "Mechanisms of Genocide." In *Will Genocide Ever End?* edited by Carol Rittner, John K. Roth and James M. Smith, 83–9. St. Paul, MN: Paragon House, 2002.

Menger, Carl. *Problems of Economics and Sociology*. Urbana: University of Illinois Press, 1963 [1883].

Paul, Gerhard. "Von Psychopaten, Technokraten des Terrors und 'ganz gewöhnlichen' Deutschen. Die Täter der Shoah im Spiegel der Forschung." In *Die Täter der Shoah. Fanatische Nationalsozialisten oder ganz normale Deutsche?* edited by Gerhard Paul, 13–92. Göttingen: Wallstein, 2002.

Rummel, Rudolph. *Death by Government*. New Brunswick, NJ: Transaction, 1994.

Semelin, Jacques. "What Is 'Genocide'?" *European Review of History: Revue europeenne d'histoire* 12, no. 1 (2005): 81–9.

Shaw, Martin. "Sociology and Genocide." In *The Oxford Handbook of Genocide Studies*, edited by Donald Bloxham and A. Dirk Moses, 142–62. Oxford: Oxford University Press, 2010.

Smeulers, Alette. "Perpetrators of International Crimes: Towards a Typology." In *Supranational Criminology: Towards a Criminology of International Crimes*, edited by Alette Smeulers and Roelof Haveman, 242–60. Antwerpen: Intersentia, 2008.

Smeulers, Alette, and Lotte Hoex. "Studying the Microdynamics of the Rwandan Genocide." *British Journal of Criminology* 50, no. 3 (2010): 435–54.

Straus, Scott. *The Order of Genocide: Race, Power, and War in Rwanda*. Ithaca, NY: Cornell University Press, 2006.

United Nations. *Convention on the Prevention and Punishment of the Crime of Genocide*. New York: United Nations, 1948.

Williams, Timothy. "The Complexity of Evil: A Multi-Faceted Approach to Genocide Perpetration." *Zeitschrift für Friedens- und Konfliktforschung* 3, no. 1 (2014): 71–98.

Williams, Timothy, and Dominik Pfeiffer. "Unpacking the Mind of Evil: A Sociological Perspective on the Role of Intent and Motivations in Genocide." *Genocide Studies and Prevention* 11, no. 2 (2017): 72–87.

Yeghiayan, Vartkes. *The Armenian Genocide and the Trials of the Young Turks*. La Verne: American Armenian International College Press, 1990.

2 Violence as action

Christian Gudehus

Introduction[1]

In the context of genocide research, perpetrators are individuals that participate in the persecution of people. They beat, shoot, betray, cordon off, rape, rob and do much more. These are actions or, to be more precise, damaging actions in the context of collective violence. The aim of this chapter is to focus on these and to present tools that help to understand and explain them. This will be done for two reasons: first, the focus on action instead of people is the consequent development of past research on violence, as will be shown in the introductory overview on the topic. Second, by doing so, violence or, more specifically, genocide research follows a trend observable in various areas of social sciences in the last decades. The aim of any research choosing a social theoretic approach to the most diverse forms of collective violence is to understand these as human activity. For this reason, in a next step selected concepts are discussed that deal with the question as to what constitutes such types of action. Heuristics that facilitate an understanding of violence are thereby unfolded. The mentioned concepts of frame, mentality, figuration or Heinrich Popitz' (2017a, 2017b [1992]) comprehension as to how social norms are established and maintained are related approaches although they are by no means identical. They have in common that they discuss the relation between individual actions and the socio-cultural worlds that are their precondition *and* result. In the following considerations on theories of action of the most diverse provenance, action moves from the status of an element of a theoretical concept to the centre of attention. This adjustment of focus further illustrates that actions or, more precisely, violent actions cannot be falsely understood to be unavoidable and quasi the mere consequence of conditions. This leaves enough room to work out the creative potential of the perception and interpretation of the world. Eventually, the view on practices – instead of actions – implies a further option to discuss violence beyond the dichotomy of individual intentionality or socio-cultural condition. The chapter closes with a short applied example and an introduction to the elements of socio-theoretical research.

There are two points to keep in mind: first, only a few approaches deal with genocides or even with violence. Most of the theories instead deal with actions in a more general manner. Second, the body of theories outlined here is complex and rooted in enduring scholarly debates so they are introduced only selectively with reference to selected authors.[2] However, their application is repeatedly outlined. Even so, the exploration of their potential and usability to answer specific research questions or to analyse material lies with those who investigate occurrences of collective violence and consider using them.

Perpetrators, victims, bystanders: from structure to person

Large parts of the research on violence and genocide have been accustomed to separate people involved in mass violence into perpetrators, victims and bystanders, at the latest since Raul Hilberg's publication with the same title (Hilberg 1992). The analytical consequences of the separation had its heuristic justification since the – also rhetorically apt – change of paradigm moved attention away from categories such as 'system' or 'structure' and towards the agents of persecution. In the publication of his comprehensive study on the destruction of the European Jews in 1961 Hilberg already used the terms 'perpetrators' and 'victims' and thereby brought to attention certain dynamics that – in ways identical with or similar to his approach – have gained special importance in the literature published since the 90s. For instance, in the part of his book titled "Perpetrators" he describes processes of the spreading of anti-Jewish acts that show – although he does not explicate it – that an action once tested can subsequently be used again to solve further 'problems' (Hilberg 1961: 1060–75). Christopher Browning and Harald Welzer use the same argument in their studies on Holocaust perpetrators (Browning 1993; Welzer 2005). Susanne Beer also applies it to people who helped Jews to escape from National Socialist persecution (Beer 2014). If such elements occur in Hilberg's early works, they do so rather incidentally in annotations, but not systematically. His discussion of these dynamics is not so much an analysis of action, of deed; instead his predominant interest lies with the overall process. In the above example of the spreading of anti-Jewish acts, for instance, Hilberg talks of a machinery gathering speed due to such processes (Hilberg 1961: 1065). Yet – and this is why this classic work is particularly suitable as an introduction to the topic – he already offers elements of what will be developed in the following under the heading "Theories of human action" as a parallel epistemological approach to the one focusing on groups such as perpetrators, victims and bystanders.[3]

If characterising terms for groups are the starting point of research, this entails a focus on the question as to what might distinguish the members of this group. Accordingly, the question is how it happened that somebody became a perpetrator. The verbs 'be'[4] or 'become,' if related to people, indicate features somebody owns; a feature that defines her or him, is an expression of her or his being. Since 'being a perpetrator' in the context of collective violence means that someone actively engages in the persecution, robbery and killing of people for reasons that in retrospect are hard to comprehend, the explanation of these acts of atrociousness from a psychological point of view requires a particular effort.[5] Accordingly, Holocaust research, which for many years was the focal point of any research on violence, moved away from a historiographic, politological and indeed also a philosophical approach towards the system, issues of power and organisation and

38   *Christian Gudehus*

shifted towards violence and, eventually, to perpetrator violence.[6] The research on National Socialism and/or the Holocaust increasingly developed into so-called perpetrator research that, however, for the most part was of a historiographic nature and manifested itself in innumerable publications and conference papers (Paul 2002; Jensen and Szejnmann 2008). Currently, perpetrator research is once more becoming an issue of interest. No analogical development of similar dimensions can be observed in victim research, which might also be due to the fact that the status of being a victim cannot be related back to a particular state of being to the same degree to which it is possible (but very problematic) for perpetrators. At best, the perspective of research focusing on group membership allows for the question of how those people assigned to the status of victims cope with what has happened to them.[7] Bystanders, in turn, are usually of interest as 'the population.' The knowledge that these non-perpetrators/non-victims had of the violence is investigated, along with how they profited by the persecution and in how far they were relevant for the dynamic of violence, i.e. whether, for instance, the actual act of witnessing – for example, when people forced to wear signs were driven through German towns – must already be understood as a part of the facilitation of violence (Wildt 2013; Hesse and Springer 2002).

Accordingly, two movements can be observed. First, research on National Socialism developed into Holocaust and genocide research and, subsequently, into research on violence. Second, this happened due to the shift of interest in research from the analysis of system and structure to the participating groups – perpetrators, victims, bystanders – , then towards an interest in violence itself. Though any summary of research traditions in the context of research on violence must necessarily remain incomplete, I have illustrated here the precursors as well as the innovative substance of social-theoretical research on violence further described in the following.

Another force behind this shift towards research on violence itself is the line of research assuming a sociological view on violence, which is particularly well developed in Germany and whose representatives have propagated for almost twenty years the investigation of executed and experienced violence (Schnell 2014; Christ and Gudehus 2013; Collins 2008). As a consequence, the attributions 'perpetrator' or 'victim' are not so much the starting point of studies written in this vein but rather the predominantly social – in contrast to psychological – constellations of the participating agents, regardless to which group they belong at any given point in time. Finally, occasionally studies may be found that go a step further and focus on the practices themselves (Buggeln 2009; Reichardt 2004). The explicit theoretical foundations for studies such as these are social theoretical traditions that consider the conditions of human action. This perspective also does not pay particular attention to those individuals carrying out the actions. Instead, the point of departure for the analyses are the actions themselves.

From person to action

The tendencies illustrated thus correspond to an analytical position that does not equate people with this – e.g. with perpetrators – or that – e.g. with bystanders – but with acting subjects whose actions can be explained.[8] This can be done in

Violence as action 39

many ways, for instance, when the relation between actions and norms are the subject of investigation. Another approach takes actions as the starting point of analysis. In this way, it is no longer perpetrators that are investigated but rather actions and their geneses and social as well as psychological meaning for the participants. A first benefit of this approach is that the concentration on actions solves a considerable definitional difficulty. In order to assess who is a perpetrator, at the outset actions or deeds must be defined whose execution makes someone a perpetrator. Accordingly, a criterion of a legal, ethical or analytical nature is required. Many instances in perpetrator research go without any such determination, in favour of the rarely explicated assumption that a perpetrator is one who participates in the persecution of people in the respectively discussed context. However, the perpetrators differ considerably at least in relation to (1) their real contribution to the deed, i.e. their actions, and (2), closely related, in the factors leading them to these actions. The first point immediately leads to the actions as objects of interest. The second does so indirectly, whenever the accurate description of actions themselves becomes part of its analysis and explanation – as the currently dominant approach demands. It becomes evident that perpetrator research has essentially investigated action for a long time. The change of perspective has almost been completed; almost all elements are present already. Currently, the change has to be labelled. Instead of speaking of perpetrator research, 'violence as action' is investigated. More precisely, 'individual action in the context of collective violence' is now the object of analysis.

Social theory: action and social change

> We believe that the theoretical development of the social sciences can be understood as revolving around three very specific questions. These are 'What is action?; 'What is social order?; and 'What determines social change?' All theorists – and this applies to both the *classical* authors of sociological theory as well as *modern* social theorists – have taken up these three questions. We should add that these are of course always closely linked: the *actions* of human beings are never entirely random. *Social orders* always develop, and these are subject to historical *change*.
> (Joas and Knöbl 2009: 18)

Accordingly, the subjects of social theory are, first, the permanent stabilisation and simultaneous change of social constellations. Second, it explores the role of individual actions as part of these dynamics. It is immediately apparent that the objects of investigation – society, action, sociality, etc. – are not even considered independently of temporal change for heuristic reasons, but that instead their fundamental principles are transition, change, the processual and dynamic forces.

In many respects, events of mass violence are places of massive societal – i.e. social and therewith also imminently psychological – change in many respects. (1) Their aim – not necessarily also their cause – is usually either to violently bring about or to avoid a particular state of social relations. For if an agreement existed between the actors – if only as regards the modes of a violence-free arrangement of relations – such violence would not be necessary. (2) Extreme violence as it

40 *Christian Gudehus*

occurs in the context of genocides changes societies and the individuals involved. This change does not exclusively entail apparently negative consequences like death, physical mutilation or a number of emotional damages that have the corresponding effects on social relationships. Extreme violence requires individuals to be ready and able to carry out the respective actions. People must learn to competently use violence (Collins 2008). This is an ability of a physical, cognitive, emotional and also social nature that is largely dysfunctional and thus undesirable beyond spaces and times of such character or other defined spaces and contexts of violence (e.g. sports, slaughterhouse, war).

All theories of human action have to analyse the relationship between the individual that, being a single person, seems to be empirically graspable and the social and physical world surrounding it. This question is of interest for historians as much as jurists, sociologists, brain researchers, socio-biologists or philosophers.

Frame

Unfortunately, 'frame' is a term used as much in everyday life as it is a defined concept in academic discussions. This indicates a difficulty: few neutral terms exist in this field. Either even such a seemingly unequivocal word as 'action' is closely connected to certain theoretical positions or the metaphorical character of many terms blurs their meaning.

At first it might be confusing that apart from its general usage another specific one exists. The choice of term is in particular inspired by the sociologist Erving Goffman, who defines it as follows: Each framework "allows its user to locate, perceive, identify, and label a seemingly infinite number of concrete occurrences defined in its terms. He is likely to be unaware of such organized features as the framework has and unable to describe the framework with any completeness if asked, yet these handicaps are no bar to his easily and fully applying it" (Goffman 1974: 21). Accordingly, frames are points of reference for every perception, interpretation and action. They contain notions as to *how the world functions* and *what people are like* and *what to do and what not to do*. In fact, such notions are a type of knowledge that in some cases is explicable and hence available whereas in others it is implicit and thus not available for the acting individuals. This frame knowledge, i.e. the competence to refer to frames, to understand them, to act in them and to know "what 'one' manages or does not manage to do, talk and arrange when, where with whom" (Soeffner 1989: 143, translated by Holste) fulfils a series of psychological functions: "It is a means of orientation and provides 'unproblematic, common and supposedly warranted *background convictions*'; it provides 'ontological safety' and it is the basis of the fear-absorbing processing of irritations that are translated back into known and accustomed patterns" (Willems 1997: 51, translated by Holste).

Mentality

Another concept commonly employed in everyday speech is that of mentality. It is used to ascribe a typical mode of behaviour to groups that is conditioned by

Violence as action 41

their way of feeling, thinking or viewing the world. No matter how superficial or often even wrong such ascriptions may be in individual cases, they are nonetheless fundamentally useful – and this in two ways. First, collectively shared modes of how situations are perceived and interpreted actually exist. They are the result of experiences likewise shared by the collective (hence, they are undergone by all or most individuals belonging to the collective and have subsequently been sedimented). Second, mentality as an aid to interpretation ('they have such and such a mentality') is itself proof for the usefulness of ready-made modes of perception in everyday life since these help to categorise and comprehend, albeit also wrongly, events with little effort and thus pave the way to be able to act at all times. As the term implies, it refers to mental, intellectual, in this case cognitive processes. When the term mentality is used in the academic context of the science of history, many definitions circle around this comprehension. They refer to dispositions, unconscious assumptions or structures that precede action (Burke 1989; Gilcher-Holtey 1998). Research on mentality focuses on the reconstruction of the modes of perception and interpretation of historical actors. In this way, a methodical circle is established: Mentality prefabricates options or potentialities to act, yet it is difficult to empirically prove this influence. In order to research and prove it, an analysis of collective action is required. Its recognisable patterns and common features shed light on the mentality that, in this conception, precedes action (Sellin 1985). However, the usage of the term varies. Gerhard Schreiber, who investigated German war crimes that took place in Italy during WWII, understands mentality to be a consequence and as such a cluster of a whole array of factors:

> Explanations for this killing legitimated by the government [. . .] – motivations determined by the situation notwithstanding – result, as mentioned above, from factors related to military considerations, power politics, occupational politics, ethnic considerations and race ideology that in total – especially when dealing with the resistance – lowered the inhibition threshold to destroy Italian life in a direct or indirect fashion, i.e. that brought into existence a mentality facilitating the ordering, execution or tolerance of murder on Italian soil.
>
> (Schreiber 1996: 38, translated by Jessica Holste)

Schreiber understands mentality as a constellation of social, political and cultural characteristics that suggests certain options to act. All in all, mentality might be described as a socially generated psychological space of action.

Figuration

Figuration, a concept developed by the sociologist Norbert Elias on the basis of historical but also qualitative empirical research, espouses the notion that relations of people, groups (of various sizes) or else institutions towards each other influence the individuals' repertoires of action (Elias and Scotson 2008; Elias

42   *Christian Gudehus*

2006; Elias 1978). Accordingly, humans are involved in social networks. Among other influences, their actions result from their relations as members of social groups of different types towards each other. With reference to Elias, Michaela Christ illustrated how the figurations of actors in a Ukrainian town continuously changed with the approach of the German troops, the siege of the town, the German occupation, the successive realisation of German racist politics, the ghettoisation of the Jews, their murder and, eventually, the conquest of the town by Soviet troops. As a consequence of these changes, the actors' perceptions of the situations shifted and therewith the perceived – and hence also considered – options to act (Christ 2011). An illustrative example is the time between the withdrawal of the Red Army from Berdičev and the Wehrmacht's occupation. It created a vacuum of power that was used by the town's citizens to raid the homes and businesses of those refugees, often Jews aware of their imperilment, who had fled from the Germans. Consequently, according to Christ, the power relations between Jews and non-Jews changed in favour of the latter. While the Jews were witnessing the distinct instability and fragility of their position, the others saw a prospectively expanding range of possibilities to become rich at the Jews' expense without punishment. Yet figurations define an individual's mode of thinking and acting on a much more fundamental level. Elias, for instance, discusses the French court of the eighteenth century and in this context describes how norms are not merely rules that are obeyed or not obeyed but an integral part of historical figurations

> whose commands individuals can escape only if they renounce contact with their social circle and membership of their social group. These norms cannot be explained by a secret buried in the breasts of large numbers of individual people; they are explainable only in the context of the specific figuration formed by these individuals and the specific interdependences binding them together.
>
> (Elias 2006: 73)

Similarly, he describes prejudice "as a normal aspect of the social beliefs of an established group in defense of its status and power against what is felt as attack of outsiders against them" (Elias and Scotson 2008: 185). It is in exactly such constellations that a relational concept of freedom and determination surfaces. Elias thinks "of 'the freedom' of each individual as part of a chain of interdependences linking people to one another and limiting individual possibilities of decision and action" (Chartier 1988: 78). Accordingly, every framework bears the potential to free and to limit at the same time. It is liberating to live in social constellations that provide relatively stable orientations for the execution of small elements of action (e.g. greetings) as well as complete life designs. However, exactly these may be perceived as restrictive, if not oppressive, depending especially on the respective positions of individuals in a given social network. This is aggravated by social sanctions placed on dissidents that warrant the relative stability of such formations. Those who do not adhere to shared interpretations must thus be ready

Violence as action 43

to pay the price in the corresponding social and psychological currency – the loss of recognition. In peaceful, pluralistic, affluent societies that also are not subject to rigid social controls, deviance is easy. This is especially true considering that there is always the chance of social change that might bring about the general recognition of one's own interpretation. This is undoubtedly different in contexts of collective violence where belonging and solidarity, expressed as value, emotion or action (for instance, in the form of customs), are of central importance to any social organisation – and probably also to physical survival.

Social norms

The aforementioned shared interpretations, their relevance for perceived or real options to act and the role of social sanctions already represent central elements of a theory of social norms. What is now of interest are the explanations as to how such norms develop, how they are related to individual actions, how they, on the one hand, are stabilised and what, on the other hand, causes their modification or even their removal. The German sociologist Heinrich Popitz has dedicated himself to these questions in his works, which are, for the most part, devoid of any explicit sociological formation of tradition and therefore also easy for laypeople to understand. Popitz defines norms as those expected forms of regular behaviour whose absence or violation causes social sanctions (for the following: Popitz 2017a). The repertoire ranges from disapproval over repressions, discrimination to punishment.

However, in complex societies, the extension of norms, if not their violation, occurs on a regular basis. Individuals violate others' expectations for various reasons. They might do so intentionally ('I violate a norm knowingly and deliberately'), but the violation might also be a side effect ('the violation of the norm was not the goal of my action') or completely unintended ('I simply acted'). It might be the consequence of creative processes ('this could be done differently') or simply of laziness and a lack of interest. People know of a norm when they expect sanctions in case of its violation or when they react to other people's violations with sanctions. In a simple case, a violation of a norm is followed by a negative reaction. As a consequence, the norm is kept intact and the social order in question is stabilised. Accordingly, not only the degree to which a norm is followed indicates its validity but also the readiness to protect it. Exactly this is the key to processes of change. Norms subdue and lose their influence on actions when their violation is sanctioned only hesitatingly or eventually not at all. Correspondingly, the expectation to be sanctioned is lowered and thus the authority of the norm fades. The fact that individuals in many cases do not know whether other members of a community obey norms also contributes to the stability of norms (Diekmann et al. 2011). There are many reasons for the absence of sanctions. One is that the lack of disapproval of violations entails considerably fewer sanctions than the violation of the norm itself. At the outset, however, it is, according to Popitz, of secondary importance whether people violate norms or else do not sanction a violation because they are lazy, disinterested or convinced they are doing the

44   *Christian Gudehus*

right thing. It is much more important that all of this takes place in the form of *actions*. Norms are produced by actions, they are stabilised by them, questioned, violated, etc. It is in this sense that non-acting does not exist. Not to sanction the violation of a norm might lead to its continuation. Accordingly, the focus is not on values that inform actions, but on social relations within which norms that inform actions are performatively negotiated.[9] Consequently, norms cannot be empirically recorded when people state which norms are valid in their opinion, but only when actual actions are observed.

With the aid of examples, Popitz illustrates how actions can fundamentally change power relations and social orders. He presents the example of a ship on which only a limited number of deck chairs is available whose distribution is, at first, unproblematic (for the following: Popitz 2017b [1992]). They are used as they are required and since the ways and times of using them differ, a casual arrangement develops. However, when new people arrive on board and others leave the ship, a minority – the new arrivals – changes this practice. These people reserve the unused deck chairs for each other. This action already establishes a norm: it results in a mutual confirmation of claims. What is done is right because others do it, too, and it is done for each other. There are multiple consequences. First, two groups are created: the privileged and the excluded. Whereas the action of the first group generates an organisational structure, this is missing in the second group that should organise itself, seek confrontation and that, eventually, should defend its newly acclaimed right. Even if the confrontation resulted in victory, completely new social orders and social norms would have been established qua action, i.e. performatively. This example is another case in point illustrating just how little effect specific intentions regarding a set of actions may have on actual consequences. The starting point was nothing but the wish to have a deck chair available at all times, a lack of trust in the old order or simply a lack of knowledge concerning the hitherto prevailing practice.

Theories of action

Frames, figurations and mentality conceptualise social conditions of individual actions. On the one hand, they all claim that options to act, even their mere perception, are considerably influenced by these 'sedimented experiences.'[10] Yet, at the same time, all these concepts emphasise that individuals are not determined but rather continuously position and reposition themselves in relation to their environment. In this context, frames may be as much consolidated as they might be varied or even extensively modified. The same holds true for social norms that are an essential element of such sedimented experiences themselves. This positioning and repositioning is the core of what might be understood as action. Theories of action are interested in exactly this process. As a matter of fact, a whole array of social scientific theories of action exist whose representatives at times attack each other and who, more importantly, emphasise the – from their point of view – fundamental and often allegedly insurmountable differences in their respective theories. This is, at least to some degree, certainly due to the prestige-generating

Violence as action   45

relevance of theory construction, which is especially typical for sociology. If one steps back, though, and looks at the fundamental assumptions from a distance, convergences come into view.

In research on the psychology of action 'acting,' 'doing' and 'behaviour' are differentiated. 'Acting' refers exclusively to those actions that are the result of processes of reflection, hence they are profoundly intentional. In contrast to this, 'behaviour' indicates actions carried out as a reflex, involuntarily. 'Doing' is a category for cases that will not fit in with the other two concepts, hence it is at least seemingly a somewhat hapless category, where an action might be planned, but the motives causing the action are hidden to the actor (Straub and Weidemann 2015: 29–37; Kaiser and Werbik 2012: 41–2). No matter if one complies with this differentiation or not, it already contains essential elements of the theorisation of human acting. First, we are once more confronted with the problem of labelling because all three terms are used almost synonymously in everyday speech and because an umbrella term does not exist, which is quite revealing. As a temporary aid, the term 'performance' could be used. More important are the already mentioned, essential criteria of differentiation, 'rationality' and 'availability.' 'Rationality' indicates to what degree actions can be the result of considerations and, thereby, of plans. 'Availability' refers to what individuals know or can know about their motives to act but also about the conditions of their actions – thus it alludes to 'frames.' There is hardly a conceivable theory of action belonging to the social or cognitive sciences that would not discuss these points. The principle opposing or complementing a profound rationality is, however, not so much irrationality or ignorance but rather something that is already implied in the approaches outlined earlier. The function of frames to serve as an aid to orientation does not, after all, imply that they have to be considered in much detail before an action is carried out. As a matter of fact, the relation between individual action and sedimented experience – be it 'figuration' or 'habitus' (Bourdieu 1972), to mention another prominent concept of the social sciences that is used in violence studies (Bakonyi and Bliesemann de Guevara 2012; Uehling 2015) – manifests itself in a set of so-called scripts, routines or automatisms of a considerably varying stability and range. The terms vary depending on the theoretical provenance. They illustrate that performance does not imply a constant, complete recreation, but rather a more or less varying repetition of tested modes of perception, comprehension and action. Or, as Hartmut Esser, a sociologist supporting a rational choice approach, formulates: "Frames and scripts are mental *models* of typical situations and sequences of action, which are stored in the memory, tied to specific contents, focused on certain aspects, and simplifying *reality* drastically" (Esser 2001: 262).

Theories of action are concerned with the evidently central difference between automatism and deliberation. Even what seem to be fundamentally different approaches converge on the view that automatised, routinised modes exist that are barely or even not at all subject to deliberation, carried out in order to assess situations and to appropriate them or to develop an action (according to a social theory perspective) (Joas 1996), or to choose one (according to the rational choice approach) (Kroneberg 2011: 17). In contrast, there are those that consider a high

46   *Christian Gudehus*

level of conscious, reflexive and, in the empathetic sense of the word, thoughtful confrontation with the situation of action a necessity, in order to do justice to the variously combined exigencies in every situation. Hartmut Esser (1993) has worked out the points of agreement between the rational choice theories and the social theory of Alfred Schütz. What interests both approaches most, in this context, are the common differentiations of routinised, habituation-based modes, on the one hand, and those that are preceded by a deliberate "choosing between projects of action like an accountant" (Esser 1993: 17) on the other. Clemens Kroneberg, Esser's student, undertakes a comparable differentiation and distinguishes a 'reflexive-calculative' mode from an 'automatic-spontaneous' mode of processing information in the framework of action processes (Kroneberg 2011: 145). Comparable insights can also be found in the writings of Hans Joas, another sociologist, though formulated quite differently:

> Given that the fundamental forms of our capacity for action lie in the intentional movement of our body in connection with locomotion, object-manipulation and communication, our world is initially structured according to these dimensions. We divide the world into categories such as accessible and inaccessible, familiar and unfamiliar, controllable and uncontrollable, responsive and unresponsive. If these action-related expectations inherent in our perception of the world are not met, we do indeed dissociate ourselves from a part of the world which now surprisingly transpires to be inaccessible and unfamiliar, uncontrollable or unresponsive, and accord it the status of an external object.
>
> (Joas 1996: 158–9)

"This means," Joas argues, "that even acts of the utmost creativity assume the pre-existence of a bedrock of underlying routine actions and external conditions which are simply taken as given" (Joas 1996: 197).

The sociologist Anselm Strauss also accepts this differentiation when he argues that essentially no action exists that is not in one way or the other based on routines:

> Routine aspects are encapsulated even in an act carried out for the first time, in form of bodily skills such as walking, culturally devised gestures, listening and speaking. Stretching the term 'routine', perhaps, one could claim that perception and memory, which are thoroughly social in character and which enter into and make possible most if not all nonreflexive action, have been routinized through repeated experiences with the world.
>
> (Strauss 1993: 193)

Again, the differences between the various approaches should by no means be negated, yet the convergence between different modes of decision making is striking, and ultimately articulates the relation between reflexive and automatised elements in any theory of action.

Violence as action   47

Lastly, these considerations imply that the relation between the reflexive and the routinised is not exclusively an opposition. The determination of the actual relation eventually depends on the individual cases under scrutiny. Exactly at this point a difference can be made out between theories that claim general validity – as they explain action on a fundamental level – and the empathetic reconstruction of violent actions. The theories aim to sensitise, and they indicate possibilities as to how actions might be understood. They cannot be transferred readily. It is a common mistake to assume that all actors are equally conditioned or even determined by frameworks and routines. However, theoretical as well as empirical research should, firstly, delineate spaces for creativity and, secondly, it should not withhold individual differences.

Adjustment, appropriation and creativity

People learn societies – i.e. how to orient themselves in social and physical environments – in manifold and complex ways. One dynamic decisive for many of these processes is composed of 'adjustment' and 'appropriation.' Everyone must continuously relate to the social and physical world (the quality of the latter naturally is also the result of social processes that may be analysed) surrounding them. For the most part, this ultimately happens in a process combining adjustment and appropriation.[11] 'Adjustment' means: I orient my performance towards the expectations I assume others have.[12] It is immediately obvious that this interpretive process requires a minimum of analytical skills and also, indeed, of creativity. The more ambiguous these expectations are in the shape of social norms or role requirements,[13] the more room is left to creativity. From an analytical vantage point, 'appropriation' is, strictly speaking, the following step. The foreign is internalised. I not only adjust, but I habitualise what is new to me. It becomes (for me and for others) something taken for granted. Accordingly, adjustment and appropriation are two closely related aspects of the same thing. Both require interpretation and creativity. The result of such processes, however, can only to a certain degree be predicted because these appropriations are, to use a term from the narrative of *Alltagsgeschichte* (the history of everyday life), eigensinnig. "At once stubbornness, willfulness, and an assertion of obstinacy (Eigen-Sinn), eigensinn denotes a type of unruly behavior that is potentially liberating for the individual but simultaneously continues to interact with the structures of power" (Steege et al. 2008: 373). Its most prominent representative, Alf Lüdtke, accordingly declares the reconstruction of forms of appropriation and practices of appropriation to be the essence of the historical research following this school of thought (Lüdtke 1997: 87). This also stimulates the violence research. The historian Elissa Mailänder-Koslov, for instance, has described very vividly the process of adjustment and appropriation undergone by female guards in German concentration camps (Mailänder-Koslov 2009). The often quite young women presumably take up their posts without a clear idea of modes of behaviour that will be expected of them. Accordingly, at the outset many are surprised, in some cases even shocked, when, for the first time, they

48 *Christian Gudehus*

are confronted with the violence their colleagues use against the prisoners. At first, they do not behave according to the social norms of the camp that do not correspond to those outside, and thus act wrongly. For instance, some newcomers initially greet prisoners or, in cases of encounters, do not trespass. Within a short time – some days or weeks – , though, a change also of the habitus becomes perceptible for the prisoners. The guards grow into their uniforms, their boots – they change their gait, their look, their facial expression and the corresponding behaviour.[14] Eigensinnig also implies that bureaucratic and juridical norms are deliberately shunned. Elissa Mailänder-Koslov shows exactly these idiosyncrasies of the guards who disobey orders in various contexts, who complain and refuse, who occasionally even argue vehemently with their male colleagues or superiors (Mailänder-Koslov 2009: 279–85). All these observations indicate a space in which performance is by no means determined but may be appropriated. On a side note, there were a number of women who left their work in the camps quite quickly for reasons that are now elusive. In these cases, the process of adjustment and appropriation was interrupted.

Interruptions like these as well as the aforementioned processes indicate individual differences and spaces of creativity. The latter may be due to a number of factors and takes various forms. The most common form of creativity (1) is the continuous navigation within requirements and routines. It is the daily adjustment in largely established social contexts accomplished by everybody. Furthermore, (2) creativity is necessary when there is no prefabricated script or routine or else when there are competing scripts and routines available to solve a problem. This applies especially in contexts of collective violence as genocides. Far more rarely, (3) creativity occurs as innovation, i.e. as a variation or further development of a rule, a technique, a process and so forth that exceeds the mere continuation or differentiation of what is accustomed. The first two variants of creativity occur within systems of rules that are handed down from one generation to the next, whereas the third may gradually exceed these. Another ideal-typical mode is (4) the intentional questioning of valid processes, the development of new points of view and questions. *New* is always a relational concept. The types of creativity vary by degrees. In the social world nothing is ever exactly the same. Similarly, innovations are based on preconditions as they depend on techniques, technologies, modes of thinking, social orders and the like. Consequently, from the vantage point of action theory, custom (or routine) and creativity are not opposites (Schäfer 2012: 17–43).

Practices

As was shown in the introduction to Popitz' approach, social norms and power relations are not only conditions but nothing less than consequences of individual action. Popitz thus has anticipated a development that in the social sciences is called 'performative turn' (Bachmann-Medick 2006: 104–43). This development, also discussed under the heading praxeology, signifies a shift of attention in the research on human interaction. The relevance of ideas for the accomplishment of

Violence as action 49

human actions is put into proportion by a focus on actions as processes of inter-pretation, of appropriation that, eventually, constitute reality. These tendencies are already implied by many of the theories outlined so far. The theory of practice goes one step further.

The different forms of sedimented experience – mentality, figuration, habitus, amongst others – but also some action-theoretical concepts are available to indi-viduals in different ways. They may to some degree become subject to reflec-tion. At the same time, individuals differ in their ability to do just this. However, this cognitive penetration of the social environment and its conditions that moti-vates and frames one's own performance is but one possible technique of inter-pretation. Another such mode of referring to the external world is of a distinctly different nature and points to the core of how human action is understood. What this means can be illustrated with the corresponding considerations of creativity:

> In the presented action model we ground creativity *in* action. Therewith, we do not search for the variable, indeterminate quality of social practices in anteceding tendencies or abilities of subjects, but in the sequence of practices themselves: in their success or failure, in their continuous new launches and the modifications of the already existent. Not the actor, but the practices with their sequences of and problems with action are the starting point of analysis.
>
> (Hörning 2004: 33, translated by Jessica Holste)

Practice theory even goes a step further, turning its focus away from the acting subject and toward practices. Andreas Reckwitz, a renowned representative of this approach, defines practices as follows: "A practice is thus a routinized way in which bodies are moved, objects are handled, subjects are treated, things are described and the world is understood" (Reckwitz 2002: 250). With reference to the acting subjects, he points out: "It invites us to regard agents as carriers of routinized, oversubjective complexes of bodily movements, of forms of interpreting, knowing how and wanting and of the usage of things" (Reckwitz 2002: 259). Once more, the objects of investigation are not even specific actions anymore, but, for instance, beating or torture understood as already acquired knowledge "out there" (Schatzki 1996: 106) that only needs to be individually appropriated, as Theodore Schatzki, another leading representative of this theory, has put it. Then these practices are available as a type of non-cognitive knowledge and may be

> understood as know-how dependent routines of behavior linked up by a prac-tical type of 'comprehension.' Knowledge of them is, on the one hand, 'incor-porated' in the bodies of the acting subjects and, on the other, regularly takes on the form of routinized relationships between subjects and the material artefacts 'used' by them.
>
> (Reckwitz 2003: 289, translated by Jessica Holste)

At this point, two aspects must be emphasised. First, the relevance attrib-uted to artefacts. They belong to the physical world that is not merely used and

50 *Christian Gudehus*

manipulated but that may itself have an action-guiding if not action-forcing character. Considering weapons, tools of torture, the construction of (concentration) camps, irons and chains etc., this immediately makes sense. Second, routines are also a part of practice theory. In no way are they described as immutable.

> What is much more important for what eventually becomes routine, however, is the 'process of working through' of practical problems and specific situations in which resistance is experienced, new things are learned, applied and linked up with other elements of practical knowledge.
> (Jaeger-Erben 2010: 260, translated by Jessica Holste)

Not only their individual appropriation but also the complexity of social and object relations necessitate variation (Reckwitz 2003). What is more:

> Apart from the fact that the mere 'application' of a practice might put to the test the practical abilities of the actor because it is conditioned by context and time, it is primarily the structural feature of a subject to be a heterogeneous cluster of knowledge that constitutes an element of unpredictability.
> (Reckwitz 2003: 294–5, translated by Jessica Holste)

In other words, individuals are exposed to too many different requirements and possibilities to be able cope with these that it is absolutely necessary for them to be idiosyncratic or else innovative. Whether practice theory really presents a new paradigm, or whether it is rather a new emphasis of already existing elements of theories, is still debated.[15] For the purpose of understanding collective violence, it provides further arguments in favour of the notion that 'doing,' its formation, its routine-like aspects and its creative components should be the focus of analysis.

The historian Sven Reichardt, undoubtedly one of the pioneers of a real praxeological science of history,[16] develops an epistemology that comprises all elements mentioned: "The connection between bodily routines of behavior, collective patterns and subjective attributions of meaning of historical actors as well as the historical anchoring of their identities and symbols become the central subjects of analysis and theory formation" (Reichardt 2007: 44, translated by Jessica Holste). Yet, Reichardt does not only theorise, he also applies. In his historical analyses of German and Italian fascist combat leagues he tests the usefulness of praxeological theory. And indeed it is the action, the shared, often violent acting that becomes the specific feature of these groups. "Not the ideology or a coherent, political program made fascism an independent and clearly distinguishable phenomenon, but the combination of the forms of its political practice with the political attitudes" (Reichardt 2009: 717, translated by Jessica Holste). Violence in this context is not merely understood to be a consequence of ideology or pressure, to be a side effect or even only an element of community formation. It is simultaneously its engine and the adhesive gluing everything together. The physicality of violence

Violence as action   51

is evident. Its execution becomes routine, a normal element of this sociality. "It was violence itself that created communality" (Reichardt 2004: 141, translated by Jessica Holste). A similar line of argumentation is applied to the National Socialist people's community that effectively was far more than an ideological concept and again was created performatively and especially by violent acts of varying intensity (Wildt 2007; Bajohr and Wildt 2009; Wildt 2013).

The approaches outlined here help to explain human action in general. It is important to bear in mind that they allow a grasp on the topic, offer a frame of interpretation, pursue and enable a specific form of understanding. They do not generate hard facts, they do not prove, but imply, argue, make plausible. This vagueness diminishes their appeal for some researchers who are looking for reliable, provable if-then relations.[17]

Applications and supplements

It transpires that, from a methodical point of view, the focus on actions and/or practices derived from social theoretical considerations at first entails the task of describing their specific features. 'Who does what in which way' is, therefore, the first question. It is followed by an interpretation drawing on a matrix of analytical considerations that offers possible explanations, but does not impose them on the situation. Elements of analysis are the identification of routines or scripts, reconstructions of figuration or habitus, the detection of dynamic forces, the tracing of processes. Although this approach starts with the reconstruction of situations, this does not mean that frames exceeding them are not relevant. Alan Kramer has analysed a case of German atrocities in Belgium during WWI with similar means (Kramer 2006). Close to a Belgian town German soldiers were constructing a pontoon bridge across a river. Previously, the town had been searched and civilians taken hostage. The latter indicates the context in which the people involved would perform in the following. They were afraid of (civilian) snipers who allegedly illegally killed German soldiers in a way that they perceived as sly or unfair. Kramer assigns this myth of the franc-tireurs to events that had occurred forty years earlier when such actions were really performed by the French: "German histories of the war 1870–1, historical novels, magazine articles, and military education manuals all helped to ensure there was a predisposition to expect *franc-tireurs* in 1914" (Kramer 2006: 20). The officers were ordered to react strongly to civilian resistance. Diverse narratives[18] circulated on such attacks that were (wrongly) considered illegal. As a matter of fact, German soldiers were fired at. Although in the situation it was at least for some Germans obvious that the aggression originated with regular troops, the frame of interpretation, the fear, the orders, the fact that hostages had been taken and so forth created a fatal dynamic that concluded with the shooting of more than seventy people – women, men and children. Kramer rightly emphasises that a dynamic cannot take the part of a subject. It is people who act. They do this rooted in experiences that are sedimented to various degrees and that not only create their modes of perception but also their sensibility.[19] They fall back on practices in which sequences such as the

52 *Christian Gudehus*

taking of hostages or mass shootings are already prefigured. The dynamic element does not imply inevitability. On the contrary, what happens cannot be determined until it takes place. A possibly uttered hint of a German soldier that civilians definitely could not have fired the shots might have been ignored or recorded. This is unknown. Again, it is apparent that – notwithstanding frames, social obligations, routines and so forth – options to act are not determined. This is the more so since frames, social obligations, routines and so forth exist simultaneously and allow for different actions. For this reason, for example, people helped Jews to evade National Socialist persecution (Gudehus 2016a).

Once more, the introduced approaches can help to explain and understand events of collective violence. They are by no means the only promising approaches and, more importantly, not exclusive. Research modes as different as individual psychology or statistics likewise contribute to the investigation of these and other phenomena. However, in this chapter the primary focus was on action and its formation.

Notes

1 I would like to thank Jessica Holste for translating the text with her usual aplomb.
2 The focus on English as an academic (lingua franca) unfortunately entails that publications written in a different language can hardly contribute to the discussion. In addition, with the laudable exception of a few studies (e.g. Ervin Staub 1989; Roy F. Baumeister 1997; James Waller 2002) social, socio-psychological and, indeed, psychological literature that does not explicitly deal with violence is not sufficiently incorporated into genocide research. It is the aim of this chapter to carefully change this. Accordingly, a number of references indicate works that so far have only been published in German.
3 Some related efforts have been made. To mention but one example, Stefan Friedrich recently suggested a socio-theoretically oriented analysis of genocidal violence: "The guiding thesis in this context is that a sociological analysis of genocide(s) must not limit itself to structural considerations, but must incorporate the social dimensions of culture and action in its analysis in equal shares" (Friedrich 2012: 14, translated by Jessica Holste).
4 Grammatically speaking 'be' is a linking verb.
5 A relatively detailed historical classification of the necessity to explain violence and the corresponding mystification of violence was undertaken a couple of years ago by Jan-Philipp Reemtsma (2008).
6 The reasons for this shift are manifold and justify a separate line of research. Many years ago, Nicolas Berg (2003) pointed out that historical West German research on National Socialism focusing especially on structural elements was motivated by biographical considerations.
7 The literature on trauma as a consequence of experienced and executed violence is comprehensive and, indeed, also makes mention of collective traumatisation if it belongs to the liberal arts (and sometimes also if it is of a social scientific nature). An overview provided from a therapeutic perspective can be found in Günter H. Seidler (2013); Anika Oettler (2013) does the same for groups or collectives.
8 Aliza Luft differentiates social practice (any action in the context of collective violence) from social categories (e.g. perpetrators). Consequently, she "treat(s) killing as one behavior among many that the same individual can engage in throughout the course of a genocide" (Luft 2015: 152).

Violence as action 53

9 On norm transformation in the context of genocidal violence, see Paul Morrow (2015), who, however, does not discuss the crucial role action plays in such processes.
10 A more elaborate account of sedimented experiences might be found in Gudehus (2016b).
11 Drawing on a different vocabulary, this process is discussed in various classical social theories. For instance, proponents of a reading from the vantage point of the sociology of knowledge are Peter L. Berger and Thomas Luckmann (1967).
12 This aspect is, for instance, discussed by Newman (2002: 61) in the context of a social psychological approach towards genocide.
13 Also in this case a reading of Popitz is recommended (2006: 117–57).
14 A classic theorisation of such processes may be found in Goffman (1961).
15 Criticism comes, for instance, from Schulz-Schaeffer (2010) und Bongaerts (2007).
16 In Germany, currently a historical praxeology is developing also as a consequence of Reichhardt's work that serves as a research perspective and method (Lucas Haasis and Constantin Rieska 2015).
17 In this context, Alex Alvarez and Ronet Bachman (2014) are a positive example. In their textbook, they draw on social theoretical concepts as well as on some classical experiments and contextualise both.
18 For information on the part that rumours play in processes of violence, see Tim Buchen (2012: 167–215).
19 Peter Lieb (2007), in his study on actions of German troops of various types in France, determines considerably more on the (nature of) specific war experiences and on the factors influencing contexts of actions that convincingly indicate which particular circumstances can encourage war crimes. He names ideological indoctrination, experience (e.g. which form of violence has been experienced and executed so far), social dynamics within units as well as situational constellations; for instance, time pressure can create a situation in which the prisoners limit the mobility of a group and thereby jeopardise it.

References

Alvarez, Alex, and Ronet Bachman. *Violence: The Enduring Problem*. Los Angeles: Sage, 2014.

Bachmann-Medick, Doris. *Cultural Turns: Neuorientierungen in den Kulturwissenschaften*. Reinbek bei Hamburg: Rowohlt, 2006.

Bajohr, Frank, and Michael Wildt (eds.). *Volksgemeinschaft. Neue Forschungen zur Gesellschaft des Nationalsozialismus*. Frankfurt am Main: S. Fischer, 2009.

Bakonyi, Jutta, and Berit Bliesemann de Guevara (eds.). *A Micro-Sociology of Violence: Deciphering Patterns and Dynamics of Collective Violence*. London and New York: Routledge, 2012.

Baumeister, Roy F. *Evil: Inside Human Violence and Cruelty*. New York: Henry Holt and Company, 1997.

Beer, Susanne. "Aid Offered Jews in Nazi Germany. Research Approaches, Methods, and Problems." *Mass Violence and Resistance* (2014). www.sciencespo.fr/mass-violence-war-massacre-resistance/en/document/aid-offered-jews-nazi-germany-research-approaches-methods-and-problems. Accessed 27 November 2017.

Berg, Nicolas. *Der Holocaust und die deutschen Historiker*. Göttingen: Wallstein Verlag, 2003.

Berger, Peter L., and Thomas Luckmann. *The Social Construction of Reality: A Treatise in the Sociology of Knowledge*. New York: First Anchor Books, 1967 [1st ed. New York: Doubleday, 1966].

54 Christian Gudehus

Bongaerts, Gregor. "Soziale Praxis und Verhalten – Überlegungen zum Practice Turn in Social Theory." *Zeitschrift für Soziologie* 36, no. 4 (2007): 246–60.

Bourdieu, Pierre. *Outline of a Theory of Practice*. Cambridge: Cambridge University Press, 1972.

Browning, Christopher. *Ordinary Men: Reserve Police Battalion 101 and the Final Solution in Poland*. New York: Harper Perennial, 1993.

Buchen, Tim. *Antisemitismus in Galizien: Agitation, Gewalt und Politik gegen Juden in der Habsburgermonarchie um 1900*. Berlin: Metropol, 2012.

Buggeln, Marc. *Arbeit und Gewalt. Das Außenlagersystem des KZ Neuengamme*. Göttingen: Wallstein Verlag, 2009.

Burke, Peter. "Stärken und Schwächen der Mentalitätsgeschichte." In *Mentalitäten-Geschichte: Zur historischen Rekonstruktion geistiger Prozesse*, edited by Ulrich Raulff, 127–45. Berlin: Wagenbach, 1989.

Chartier, Roger. "Social Figuration and Habitus." In *Cultural History: Between Practices and Representations*, edited by Roger Chartier, 71–94. Cambridge: Polity Press, 1988.

Christ, Michaela. *Die Dynamik des Tötens. Die Ermordung der Juden von Berditschew*. Frankfurt am Main: Fischer Taschenbuch Verlag, 2011.

Christ, Michaela, and Christian Gudehus. "Gewalt – Begriffe und Forschungsprogramme." In *Gewalt. Ein Interdisziplinäres Handbuch*, edited by Christian Gudehus and Michaela Christ, 1–15. Stuttgart: J. B. Metzler, 2013.

Collins, Randall. *Violence: A Micro-Sociological Theory*. Princeton, NJ: Princeton University Press, 2008.

Diekmann, Andreas, Wojtek Przepiorka, and Heiko Rauhut. "Die Präventivwirkung von Nichtwissen im Experiment." *Zeitschrift für Soziologie* 40, no. 1 (February 2011): 74–84.

Elias, Norbert. *What Is Sociology?* New York: Columbia University Press, 1978 [1970].

Elias, Norbert. *The Court Society*. Rev. ed. Dublin: University College Dublin Press, 2006 [1969].

Elias, Norbert, and John L. Scotson. *The Established and the Outsiders*. Rev. ed. Dublin: University College Dublin Press, 2008 [1965].

Esser, Hartmut. "The Rationality of Everyday Behavior: A Rational Choice Reconstruction of the Theory of Action by Alfred Schütz." *Rationality and Society* 5, no. 1 (1993): 7–31.

Esser, Hartmut. *Soziologie. Spezielle Grundlagen. Band 6: Sinn und Kultur*. Frankfurt am Main and New York: Campus, 2001.

Friedrich, Stefan. *Soziologie des Genozids. Grenzen und Möglichkeiten einer Forschungsperspektive*. Paderborn: Wilhelm Fink Verlag, 2012.

Gilcher-Holtey, Ingrid. "Plädoyer für eine dynamische Mentalitätsgeschichte." *Geschichte und Gesellschaft* 24, no. 3 (1998): 476–97.

Goffman, Erving. *Asylums: Essays on the Social Situation of Mental Patients and Other Inmates*. Garden City, NY: Anchor Books, 1961.

Goffman, Erving. *Frame Analysis: An Essay on the Organization of Experience*. New York et al.: Harper Colophon Books, 1974.

Gudehus, Christian. "Helping the Persecuted. Heuristics and Perspectives (Exemplified by the Holocaust)." *Mass Violence and Resistance* (2016a). www.sciencespo.fr/mass-violence-war-massacre-resistance/en/document/helping-persecuted-heuristics-and-perspectives-exemplified-holocaust. Accessed 27 November 2017.

Gudehus, Christian. "On the Significance of the Past for Present and Future Action." In *Theorizing Social Memories: Concepts and Contexts*, edited by Gerd Sebald and Jan Wagle, 84–97. London and New York: Routledge, 2016b.

Violence as action 55

Haasis, Lucas, and Constantin Rieska (eds.). *Historische Praxeologie. Dimensionen vergangenen Handelns.* Paderborn: Ferdinand Schöningh, 2015.

Hesse, Klaus, and Philipp Springer. *Vor aller Augen. Fotodokumente des nationalsozialistischen Terrors in der Provinz.* Essen: Klartext Verlag, 2002.

Hilberg, Raul. *The Destruction of the European Jews.* Chicago: Quadrangle Books, 1961.

Hilberg, Raul. *Perpetrators, Victims, Bystanders: The Jewish Catastrophe, 1933–1945.* New York: Aaron Asher Books, 1992.

Hörning, Karl H. "Soziale Praxis zwischen Beharrung und Neuschöpfung. Ein Erkenntnis- und Theorieproblem." In *Doing Culture – Neue Positionen zum Verhältnis von Kultur und sozialer Praxis,* edited by Karl H. Hörnig and Julia Reuter, 19–39. Bielefeld: Transcript, 2004.

Jaeger-Erben, Melanie. *Zwischen Routine, Reflektion und Transformation – die Veränderung von alltäglichem Konsum durch Lebensereignisse und die Rolle von Nachhaltigkeit. Eine empirische Untersuchung unter Berücksichtigung praxistheoretischer Konzepte.* Doctoral Thesis, Technische Universität Berlin, 2010.

Jensen, Olaf, and Claus-Christian W. Szejnmann (eds.). *Ordinary People as Mass Murderers: Perpetrators in Comparative Perspective.* Basingstoke: Palgrave Macmillan, 2008.

Joas, Hans. *The Creativity of Action.* Chicago: University of Chicago Press, 1996.

Joas, Hans, and Wolfgang Knöbl. *Social Theory: Twenty Introductory Lectures.* New York: Cambridge University Press, 2009.

Kaiser, Hans-Jürgen, and Hans Werbik. *Handlungspsychologie.* Göttingen: Vandenhoeck & Ruprecht, 2012.

Kramer, Allen. "The War of Atrocities: Murderous Scares and Extreme Combat." In *No Man's Land of Violence: Extreme Wars in the 20th Century,* edited by Alf Lüdtke and Bernd Weisbrod, 11–33. Göttingen: Wallstein, 2006.

Kroneberg, Clemens. *Die Erklärung sozialen Handelns. Grundlagen und Anwendung einer integrativen Theorie.* Wiesbaden: VS Verlag, 2011.

Lieb, Peter. *Konventioneller Krieg oder NS-Weltanschauungskrieg? Kriegführung und Partisanenbekämpfung in Frankreich 1943/44.* München: Oldenbourg Verlag, 2007.

Lüdtke, Alf. "Alltagsgeschichte: Aneignung und Akteure. Oder – es hat noch kaum begonnen!" *Werkstattgeschichte* 17 (1997): 83–92.

Luft, Aliza. "Toward a Dynamic Theory of Action at the Micro Level of Genocide: Killing, Desistance, and Saving in 1994 Rwanda." *Sociological Theory* 33, no. 2 (2015): 148–72.

Mailänder-Koslov, Elissa. *Gewalt im Dienstalltag. Die SS- Aufseherinnen des Konzentrations- und Vernichtungslagers Majdanek 1942–1944.* Hamburg: Hamburger Edition, 2009.

Morrow, Paul. "The Thesis of Norm Transformation in the Theory of Mass Atrocity." *Genocide Studies and Prevention* 9, no. 1 (2015): 66–82.

Newman, Leonard S. "What Is a 'Social Psychological' Account of Perpetrator Behavior? The Person Versus the Situation in Goldhagen's *Hitler's Willing Executioners.*" In *Understanding Genocide: The Social Psychology of the Holocaust,* edited by Leonard S. Newman and Ralph Erber, 43–67. Oxford: Oxford University Press, 2002.

Oettler, Anika. "Gewaltfolgen – kollektiv." In *Gewalt. Ein interdisziplinäres Handbuch,* edited by Christian Gudehus and Michaela Christ, 250–6. Stuttgart: J. B. Metzler, 2013.

Paul, Gerhard (ed.). *Die Täter der Shoah. Fanatische Nationalsozialisten oder ganz normale Deutsche?* Göttingen: Wallstein Verlag, 2002.

Popitz, Heinrich. "Social Norms." *Genocide Studies and Prevention* 11, no. 2 (2017a): 3–12.

Popitz, Heinrich. *Phenomena of Power: Authority, Domination, and Violence.* New York: Columbia University Press, 2017b [1st German ed. 1992].

56 Christian Gudehus

Popitz, Heinrich. *Soziale Normen*. Frankfurt am Main: Suhrkamp, 2006.

Reckwitz, Andreas. "Toward a Theory of Social Practices: A Development in Culturalist Theorizing." *European Journal of Social Theory* 5, no. 2 (2002): 243–62.

Reckwitz, Andreas. "Grundelemente einer Theorie sozialer Praktiken: Eine sozialtheoretische Perspektive." *Zeitschrift für Soziologie* 32, no. 4 (2003): 282–301.

Reemtsma, Jan Philipp. *Vertrauen und Gewalt. Versuch über eine besondere Konstellation der Moderne*. Hamburg: Hamburger Edition, 2008.

Reichardt, Sven. "Praxeologie und Faschismus. Gewalt und Gemeinschaft als Elemente eines praxeologischen Faschismusbegriffs." In *Doing Culture. Neue Positionen zum Verhältnis von Kultur und sozialer Praxis*, edited by Karl H. Hörnig and Julia Reuter, 129–53. Bielefeld: Transcript, 2004.

Reichardt, Sven. "Praxeologische Geschichtswissenschaft. Eine Diskussionsanregung." *Sozial.Geschichte* 22, no. 4 (2007): 43–65.

Reichardt, Sven. *Faschistische Kampfbünde. Gewalt und Gemeinschaft im italienischen Squadrismus und in der deutschen SA*. 2nd ed. Köln, Weimar, and Wien: Böhlau Verlag, 2009 [2002].

Schäfer, Hilmar. "Kreativität und Gewohnheit. Ein Vergleich zwischen Praxistheorie und Pragmatismus." In *Kreativität und Improvisation. Soziologische Positionen*, edited by Udo Göttlich and Ronald Kurt, 17–43. Wiesbaden: Springer VS, 2012.

Schatzki, Theodore. *Social Practices – A Wittgensteinian Approach to Human Activity and the Social*. Cambridge: Cambridge University Press, 1996.

Schnell, Felix. "Gewalt und Gewaltforschung." *Docupedia-Zeitgeschichte* (2014). http://docupedia.de/zg/Schnell_gewalt_gewaltforschung_v1_de_2014. Accessed 27 November 2017.

Schreiber, Gerhard. *Deutsche Kriegsverbrechen in Italien: Täter-Opfer-Strafverfolgung*. München: C. H. Beck, 1996.

Schulz-Schaeffer, Ingo. "Praxis, handlungstheoretisch betrachtet." *Zeitschrift für Soziologie* 39, no. 4 (2010): 319–36.

Seidler, Günter H. "Gewaltfolgen – Individuell." In *Gewalt. Ein interdisziplinäres Handbuch*, edited by Christian Gudehus and Michaela Christ, 243–50. Stuttgart: J. B. Metzler, 2013.

Sellin, Volker. "Mentalität und Mentalitätsgeschichte." *Historische Zeitschrift* 241, no. 3 (1985): 555–98.

Soeffner, Hans-Georg. *Auslegung des Alltags – Der Alltag der Auslegung*. Frankfurt am Main: Suhrkamp, 1989.

Staub, Ervin. *The Roots of Evil: The Origins of Genocide and Other Group Violence*. Cambridge: Cambridge University Press, 1989.

Steege, Paul, Andrew Stuart Bergerson, Maureen Healy, and Pamela E. Swett. "The History of Everyday Life: A Second Chapter." *The Journal of Modern History* 80, no. 2 (2008): 358–78.

Straub, Jürgen, and Doris Weidemann. *Handelnde Subjekte. 'Subjektive Theorien' als Gegenstand der verstehend-erklärenden Psychologie*. Gießen: Psychosozial, 2015.

Strauss, Anselm. *Continual Permutations of Action*. New York: Aldine de Gruyter, 1993.

Uehling, Greta. "Genocide's Aftermath: Neostalinism in Contemporary Crimea." *Genocide Studies and Prevention* 9, no. 1 (2015): 3–17.

Waller, James. *Becoming Evil: How Ordinary People Commit Genocide and Mass Killing*. Oxford: Oxford University Press, 2002.

Welzer, Harald. *Täter. Wie aus ganz normalen Menschen Massenmörder werden*. Frankfurt am Main: S. Fischer, 2005.

Wildt, Michael. *Volksgemeinschaft als Selbstermächtigung. Gewalt gegen Juden in der deutschen Provinz 1919 bis 1939*. Hamburg: Hamburger Edition, 2007.

Wildt, Michael. "Picturing Exclusion: Race, Honor, and Anti-Semitic Violence in Nazi Germany Before the Second World War." In *Violence and Visibility in Modern History*, edited by Jürgen Martschukat and Silvan Niedermeier, 137–55. New York: Palgrave Macmillan, 2013.

Willems, Herbert. *Rahmen und Habitus. Zum theoretischen und methodischen Ansatz Erving Goffmans: Vergleiche, Anschlüsse und Anwendungen*. Frankfurt am Main: Suhrkamp, 1997.

3 Theorizing ideological diversity in mass violence

Jonathan Leader Maynard

Introduction

A paradox holds back understanding of perpetrators of mass violence. On the one hand, close empirical research has consistently emphasized perpetrators' heterogeneity – the mix of motives and mindsets found amongst members of the organizations and societies that engage in violence (e.g. Bartov 1994; Browning 2001; Browder 2003; Straus 2006; Gerlach 2010: 1–5). At the same time, both overarching theories of mass violence and summative characterizations of particular cases tend to homogenize perpetrator groups through causal stories that efface diversity (see also Bloxham 2008: 204). Accounts of perpetrators have been orientated around, for example, bureaucratic compartmentalization (Bauman 1989), conformity to authority and peer pressure (Roth 2005; Zimbardo 2007), willing ideological endorsement of violence (Goldhagen 1997; Weitz 2003; Semelin 2005), petty material self-interest and hooliganism (Mueller 2000), rational conflict decision making (Kalyvas 2006; Wood 2014), or intense inter-group hate (Kaufman 2001; Suny 2004; Kaplan 2005). Frequently, these accounts are presented as opposing dichotomies: 'willing executioners' vs. 'ordinary men,' 'ideology' vs. 'self-interest,' or 'greed' vs. 'grievance' (see also Matthäus 2007: 233; Bloxham 2008; Szejnmann 2008: 47). Simultaneously, typologies sort cases into neat but essentialist categories: 'ideological' violence, 'ethnic' violence, 'developmental' violence, and so forth (du Preez 1994: 66–78).

Few actually claim that these portrayals are apt for all perpetrators, and most scholars recognize that perpetrators act from varied and fluid motives (Kalyvas 2006: 24–5; Henriksen and Vinci 2008: 88; Smeulers 2008; Karstedt 2012: 500). Indeed, such variation explains how all homogenizing accounts find empirical research to support them (Bloxham 2008: 204). For every study like Christopher Browning's *Ordinary Men* (2001), often invoked to demonstrate the ideologically uncommitted nature of perpetrators,[1] there are equally influential ones like Omar Bartov's *Hitler's Army* (1994), which highlight ideological belief amongst perpetrators. Rather than being ignorant of diversity, theorists generally resort to homogenizing explanations, I suggest, because of underlying weaknesses in our analytical tools for grappling with heterogeneity. This chapter seeks to address those weaknesses.

Theorizing ideological diversity 59

It is not the first attempt to do so (Smeulers 2008; Bloxham 2008). But here I focus on one particular form of perpetrator diversity, namely *ideological* diversity, where conceptualization and theory remains especially lacking (Leader Maynard 2014). Scholars of mass violence frequently talk of ideology – whether to affirm or downplay its importance. But there is little effort to distinguish the different ways in which ideology might matter for different sorts of perpetrator. Instead, it is often assumed that an emphasis of 'ideology' involves portraying perpetrators as 'fanatics' driven to violence by intense ethnic animosity or transformative revolutionary projects. This assumption leads several leading scholars to strike a sceptical tone regarding ideology's relevance, since empirical research often shows that relatively few perpetrators conform to such a portrayal (Valentino 2004: 24, 55; Kalyvas 2006: 4–5; Waller 2007: 40–53, 102, 124, 185; Fujii 2008: 570–1; Fujii 2009; Karstedt 2013: 394).

But such scepticism is misplaced, because ideological explanations need not take this form. The dichotomous assumption that ideology either involves devoted fanatical belief or is basically epiphenomenal fails to attend the much broader range of ways in which individuals can, *often partially and selectively*, internalize or make use of ideologies that justify violence (Browder 2003: 495; Leader Maynard 2014; Leader Maynard 2015). Ideological beliefs do not need to be held with one hundred percent conviction, with explicit and self-conscious emphasis, on the basis of many years of prior commitment, or to the exclusion of other motives. On the contrary, most contemporary approaches to the study of ideology argue that it is ubiquitous and ordinary, though variant (van Dijk 1998; Norval 2000: 316; Jost 2006; Freeden 2013: 115–16, 118, 121; Malešević 2010: 63).[2] Consequently, a perpetrator who lacks extreme manifestations of ideology may still have internalized many beliefs derived from extant ideological frameworks.

This is not to deny that ideologies sometimes serve merely as a "pretext" (Fujii 2008: 570), post-hoc "rationalization" (Waller 2007: 49) or "afterthought" (Zimbardo 2007: 11) – though even this does not necessarily make them causally irrelevant (Leader Maynard 2014: 828). But I argue that close empirical research shows that most perpetrators do sincerely internalize justificatory ideologies *to some degree*, and that ideology plays a central but complex role in mass violence. Even beliefs internalized to a limited extent and with little advanced theoretical content may significantly reconstitute how a perpetrator thinks about the nature of their actions, and the moral status of their victims, in ways *vital* to their participation in killing (Slim 2007: 121–2). Between 'total internalization' of an ideology and 'zero internalization' is most of what matters: forms of partial internalization that bring key beliefs and justifications into an individual's thinking – potentially enabling, constraining, or guiding violent behaviour.

Consequently, labelling some perpetrators or cases 'ideological' and others 'non-ideological' is unhelpful. Research on mass violence needs to take a more nuanced approach, which requires a better theorization of ideological diversity. In this chapter I advance such theorization, in three steps. First, I explain why perpetrators' ideological diversity matters. Second, I advance a conceptual framework for better grappling with such diversity, centred around a new typology for

60 *Jonathan Leader Maynard*

different degrees of ideological internalization. Third, I offer some preliminary hypotheses on how different ideological diversities in different parts of the apparatus of mass violence matter in perpetration.

Why does ideological diversity matter?

It is not self-evident that we ought to care about perpetrators' ideological diversity. To some, the present tendency to skirt around diversity could simply reflect commitments to parsimony. For all their diversity, perpetrators all seem to perpetrate the outcome of interest: violence. As Claus-Christian Szejnmann (2008: 41) notes: "whilst individuals had different biographical patterns and showed individual forms of behaviour . . . their murderous impact was frighteningly homogenous" (see also Browder 2003: 486). There might also be psychological grounds for thinking that individual diversity is unlikely to lead to divergent behaviour. The related social-psychological phenomena of *groupthink* (Janis 1982) and *situational conformity* (Asch 1956; Zimbardo 2007; Waller 2007; Milgram 2010) seem to suggest that individuals will largely conform to the dominant views of a group, or to other pressures to perpetrate such as orders from an authority figure (Roth 2005). The complex diversity of the group might therefore seem unimportant in explaining overall participation in violence.

But this is a mistake. For a start, groupthink and situational conformity, though important, do not provide valid causal accounts of mass violence on their own (Newman 2002). Individuals do not respond to groupthink and situational pressures uniformly, and the *intensity* and *direction* of groupthink and conformity pressures reflect the ideological makeup of groups and authority figures. In SS units operating in Eastern Europe shared attitudes towards brotherhood, loyalty, and a brutal martialism underpinned intense group pressures to *engage* in violence (Kühne 2008: 59–65, 68–72). But in the French town of Le Chambon-sur-Lignon, residents were – through the efforts of the local pastors André Trocmé and Edouard Theis – pressured to *resist* the Nazi and Vichy persecution of Jews, saving over a thousand lives (Rochat and Modigliani 1995). Furthermore, the explanatory power of groupthink and conformity research – derived from studies of bureaucratic decision making and non-lethal behaviour in laboratory experiments[3] – can be overstated with respect to real world lethal mass violence. Killing is not easy, and even under the most intense situational pressures to kill, remarkable numbers of ordinary front-line soldiers in war cannot (Collins 2008; Grossman 2009). Conformity to 'situations' does not automatically produce participation in violence absent individuals' beliefs, attitudes, and training (Grossman 2009). And sophisticated theorists of obedience and conformity – including Stanley Milgram and Philip Zimbardo – recognize this, affirming the relevance of ideology as a key influence on the way individuals construct representations of the situations they find themselves in (Newman 2002: 51, 60–2; Zimbardo 2007: 9–11, 226–8, 273–4; Milgram 2010: 143–7). The authority, for example, of a religious leader, a government official, a local zealot, or a state institution is not given by 'the situation,' but constructed by ideological conceptions – and individuals'

Theorizing ideological diversity 61

responses to orders from such sources can therefore vary from unquestioning deference to haughty indignation (see also Bloxham 2008: 214–15).

Other arguments for downplaying the significance of diversity rest on a failure to examine variation in degrees and forms of mass violence and to compare occurrences of mass violence with non-occurrences (see Straus 2012b, 2015). Take James Waller's (2007: 15) claim that "political, social or religious groups wanting to commit mass murder do. Though there may be other obstacles, they are never hindered by a lack of willing executioners." There is a degree of truth here – it is never the case that *no* potential perpetrators of mass violence can be found. But this can obscure how *variation* in the availability of mass killers, and the ideological attitudes of broader societies, can shape the intensity of mass violence and, indeed, whether it happens in the first place (McDoom 2012: 121). During the invasion of Poland in 1939, senior German army officers protested against Nazi instructions to slaughter groups of Polish civilians, with Hitler eventually rescinding the orders (Fein 1979: 4; Matthäus 2007: 220). The contrast between this and their response later in the war, after more prolonged radicalization, is marked. Typically, as John Hagan and Winona Rymond-Richmond (2008: 892) note, "authorities' activation of ethnic attacks from 'above' requires locally led 'resonance from below.'" And the same is true of resistance to violence. As François Rochat and Andre Modigliani (1995: 202) explain, the rescue of Jews in Le Cambon-sur-Lignon rested on the determined attitude of the moral leaders of the village – the pastors Trocmé and Theis – but also the way "their response resonated strongly with the beliefs of many people of Le Chambon." Both perpetration of and resistance to violence are shaped by the ideological makeup of the individuals and groups involved.

Certain ideological compositions of potential perpetrator groups can block violence outright. Sometimes this is through resistance and refusal to participate, but more typically weak ideological endorsement of violence acts as a pre-emptive restraint, leading policymakers to anticipate that radical orders will carry high political costs. In the varying implementation of the Holocaust in Nazi-occupied and Nazi-allied Europe, how states acted ranged from full implementation of Nazi plans, through various forms of partial or minimal implementation, through to active obstructionism, protection, and rescue. As Semelin (1993: 137) observes: "The governments' attitudes were generally determined by the degree of anti-Semitism within local opinion – that is, the extent of social division on the 'Jewish problem' within the countries." The ideological balance of society can thus affect whether elites pursue mass violence in the first place.

But even when policymakers do decide to initiate campaigns of mass violence, the ideological composition of potential perpetrators and broader society can affect how the violence unfolds. *Potential* perpetrators do not all perpetrate, and *actual* perpetrators do not all behave the same way (Smeulers 2004: 239; Fujii 2008: 574–6). Faced with a campaign of mass violence, agents possess a broad repertoire of possible responses, ranging from strictly implementing or even going beyond their orders, through to evasion, non-implementation, or outright resistance (Browder 2003: 488). Key causal processes, shaped by ideological

62   *Jonathan Leader Maynard*

diversity, alter the scale, distribution, and form of mass violence. I focus here on two such processes:

i   *leakage* – the reduction of violence through, for example, non-implementation, desertion, diversion, rescuing, or publicization (Browning 2001: 65–7; Üngör 2013: 6–7, 14–15, 19; Oppenheim et al. 2015);
ii   *cascade* – the escalation of violence, through joining, collaboration, or the exploitation or emulation of campaigns of violence for other purposes (Weitz 2003: 131–2, 187; Gerlach 2010: 65–6, 97–9, 106–12).

Levels of leakage and cascade make the difference between a fragmented and limited paroxysm of violence and a horrifyingly efficient, disciplined campaign, as well as everything in between. The intensity of these processes is thus of considerable theoretical and moral importance.

My argument here accords with recent efforts to call attention to the complexity of mass violence, including tensions and divergences between centre and periphery, multipolar and multicausal dynamics, microvariation in patterns of violence, and the often messy mix of motives and actors who come together in coalitions to make it occur (Kalyvas 2003; Szejnmann 2008; Gerlach 2010; Klusemann 2010; Owens et al. 2013; Karstedt 2013: 393–4; Collins 2013). But I wish to argue that theorists err in sometimes suggesting that such complexity undermines an emphasis of ideology. It does challenge excessively monolithic, crude accounts of ideology's role. But it increases the need for more nuanced approaches focused on ideological diversity and the multiple causal processes that link ideology with violent behaviour.

Even in the Holocaust, for example – the archetype of a centrally directed and purposeful campaign of mass killing – processes of leakage and cascade shaped by ideology are visible. Some groups of perpetrators engaged in selective non-implementation, while others spread violence beyond the domain of official instructions on their own initiative or with the participation of locals. Thomas Kühne (2008: 55), for example, offers a vignette of the three company leaders of the 1st battalion of the German 691st infantry regiment in Operation Barbarossa. Ordered to kill the Jewish population of an occupied Russian village, the three leaders reacted in contrasting ways: "Lieutenant Kuhls, a member of the Nazi Party and the SS, carried out the order with his company without hesitation." By contrast, "Lieutenant Sibile, a teacher aged 47 . . . told his superior officer than he 'could not expect decent German soldiers to soil their hands with such things' [and] said his company would only shoot Jews if they were [established to be] partisans." Captain Friedrich Nöll, meanwhile, was gravely disquieted by the order, but "after initial evasiveness . . . reacted as ordered" though passed the duty on to his company sergeant-major. As Kühne (2012: 141) notes elsewhere:

> Not all . . . embraced mass murder unanimously. Carrying out mass murder meant integrating different individuals and social entities, varying degrees of willingness to participate, different perpetrators, collaborators

Theorizing ideological diversity   63

and accomplices, sadists, fanatics, cold-blooded killers, occasional doubters, more serious dissenters, and unwilling yet submissive collaborators.

Homogenizing explanations therefore misrepresent mass violence and cannot adequately account for variation within and across cases. Mass violence is not the product of a single intention, master cleavage, underlying motivation, or kind of perpetrator (Kalyvas 2003; Karstedt 2012: 500). Ideological diversity, and the effort to manage it, is a critical ingredient of the political and psychological dynamics that produce mass violence.

Conceptualizing ideological diversity

Some efforts to grapple with perpetrator diversity have been made, primarily by developing typologies. Michael Mann (2005: 27–9) distinguishes between ideological, bigoted, violent, fearful, careerist, materialist, disciplined, comradely, and bureaucratic killers. Alette Smeulers (2008: 244–60) identifies criminal masterminds, fanatics, criminals/sadists, profiteers, careerists, devoted warriors, followers/conformers, compromised perpetrators, and professionals. Michael MacQueen (cited in Szejnmann 2008: 42) typologizes Lithuanian perpetrators of Nazi mass killing into revenge seekers, careerists, turncoats, the greedy, anti-Semites, and accidental perpetrators.

Such typologies represent a step forward, but none of them adequately tackles ideological diversity. They tend to essentialize perpetrators' motives somewhat, and compartmentalize ideology so that it appears relevant for only one or two perpetrator categories (or case categories, see du Preez 1994: 66–78). Again, a role for ideology is implicitly presented as limited to the highly committed true believer. As I have pointed out elsewhere, this is a serious mistake, since all the categories listed previously can be vitally bound up with ideology, albeit some more so than others (Leader Maynard 2014: 823–824; Alvarez 2008: 215). Colonialist mass violence, for example, undoubtedly relied on profiteering killers, careerist killers, bigoted killers, and sadistic killers. But all these motivations were facilitated and encouraged by pervasive colonialist ideologies, which dehumanized indigenous victims, convinced perpetrators of their racial superiority, advanced particular exploitative notions of territory and property rights, and so forth. In so doing, colonialist ideologies made campaigns of violence by profiteers, careerists, bigots, and sadists possible against indigenous peoples, when such violence would have been prohibited against fellow Europeans or Christians (Smith 2011: ch. 3–4; Bellamy 2012). Ideology can thus be vital even for those whose primary motive is not the realization of some ultimate ideological project.

Since ideology's relevance cannot be limited to certain motivational categories *a priori*, existing typologies should abandon singular categories that seem to exhaustively contain 'ideological' perpetrators. Instead, we need an orthogonal typology that tracks the varying ways individuals internalize ideology and which cuts across all the motivational categories just described.

64 *Jonathan Leader Maynard*

Before I outline such an ideological typology, a few other bits of a conceptual toolkit are needed. I define ideology as *a distinctive overarching system of normative, semantic, and/or purportedly factual ideas that provides a general understanding of the political world and guides political behaviour.* This is a broad conception – in my view the best way to operationalize ideology for social science, consistent with recent trends amongst specialist theorists of ideology (Hamilton 1987; Freeden 1996; Gerring 1997; van Dijk 1998; Norval 2000; Knight 2006; Jost 2006; Jost et al. 2009; Leader Maynard and Mildenberger 2016). It does not render ideology 'too broad,' so that it loses all analytical power, but self-consciously uses it to denote a general category of phenomena (as with concepts like 'culture,' 'psychology,' 'personality,' or 'economics'). A lengthy defence of this definition is tangential to my purposes here, and I refer readers to elaborations available elsewhere (Leader Maynard 2014: 823–5; Leader Maynard 2015: 191–3; Leader Maynard and Mildenberger 2016).

When we talk about ideologies, we do so with reference to two overlapping but distinct objects of analysis. *Personal ideologies* denote the distinctive systems of ideas that shape the actual political thinking of a given individual and are, at the most fine-grained level of detail, unique. No 'socialist' or 'Nazi' or 'liberal' thinks exactly the same way, and their personal ideology is really a unique variant of these more abstract ideal-types. These abstracted ideal-type labels, by contrast, typically denote *shared ideologies.* They describe systems of ideas used with sufficient similarity amongst a number of persons to make it analytically productive to talk about their common ideological system. A productive analogy can, here, be drawn with languages. Every individual has their own unique way of speaking English, Urdu, Catalan, or Cockney. But we can usefully abstract from those differences to identify the language they speak in common. So, too, with ideologies. And we can talk about both languages and ideologies at varying levels of abstraction: identifying very precise strains of rural French or left-libertarianism, or very broad 'Latin languages' or 'the Liberal tradition.' All of this is analytically powerful if done reflectively.

I confine ideologies to denoting individuals' and collectives' *overall* systems of ideas for thinking about politics. But those systems are built from sub-systems: ideologies do not just possess random notions about healthcare, the good life, or violence but patterned *ideational clusters* that makeup the overall ideology. Clusters might be theories, doctrines, myths, narratives, or any other set of notions below the level of an overall ideology. Importantly for my typology, clusters can be transmitted without taking the whole rest of the ideology with them, embedding themselves in the minds of those who may not be wholesale converts to their source-ideology. Clusters are, however, likely to look more plausible in some ideologies than others, so as they are disseminated into a given population, they will more often 'pollinate' individuals who are ideologically similar to their propagators.

A typology of ideological internalization

In parsimoniously grappling with mass violence we are generally concerned with how far a particular perpetrator has internalized the content of dominant violence-justifying

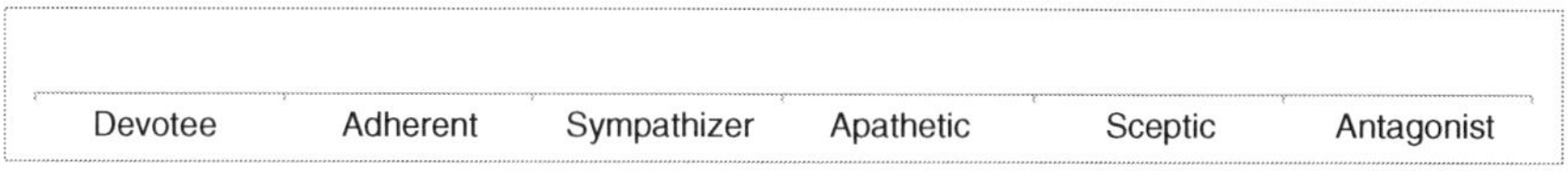

| Devotee | Adherent | Sympathizer | Apathetic | Sceptic | Antagonist |

Figure 3.1 Typology of ideological internalization states

ideologies like Nazism, Stalinism, Maoism, Hutu Power ideology, or jihadist funda-mentalism. We question, in other words, how far an individual's personal ideology matches such more general shared ideologies. I refer to this as an individual's *inter-nalization state*. In reality, there is a fine-grained continuum of internalization states ranging from total internalization, through many forms of partial internalization, to no internalization, and finally various forms of active rejection. But I suggest that we can legitimately simplify somewhat, distinguishing individuals according to six distinct internalization states: **devotees**, **adherents**, **sympathizers**, **apathetics**, **sceptics**, and **antagonists**. These describe individuals' stance with respect to *some specific ideology*, not ideologies in general (a devotee of one ideology will be an antagonist of another, for example). Throughout my discussion of the internaliza-tion states that follows, I assume that the ideology in question is an ideology whose advocates call for mass violence.

Crucially, this focus on internalization states is intended to highlight, rather than obscure, how ideology can affect agents' behaviour in ways *besides inter-nalization* – ideologies can still matter when internalization is weak or absent. Many individuals, for example, may instrumentalize or "wear" ideologies for self-interested reasons (Browder 2003: 494–5; Gutiérrez Sanín and Wood 2014: 217–20) or rather unreflectively conform to social pressure to comply with ide-ologies (Newman 2002) despite having limited underlying belief in them. But which causal mechanisms predominate in linking ideologies to perpetrator behav-iour is likely to vary according to the perpetrators' levels of internalization, as I discuss next in describing the six internalization states (see Figure 3.1).

Devotees

Matching the archetypal image of the 'true believer,' devotees are characterized by confident, committed, and comprehensive internalization of a given ideology. In other words, they internalize the ideology with immense faith in its validity, with loyalty and inflexibility, with acceptance of almost all elements of the ideol-ogy (and only this ideology), and with the perception that the ideology is central to the entirety of their political life. Even within this category, there is variance in the style of devotion. Some devotees may have sophisticated, intellectualized versions of the ideology, others more vernacular strains. Even strong belief can often be an inchoate bundle of rather vague passions rather than a set of system-atized doctrines. Devotees don't all match the crudest images of wild-eyed fanat-ics, and they could be cognitively reflective (strong commitment needn't equal blind fundamentalism). Some devotees of extreme violence-justifying ideologies may even be personable and urbane around many who disagree with them despite

66 *Jonathan Leader Maynard*

the intensity of their views. But their complete confidence and commitment to their wholesale adoption of the ideology, and the central importance they attach to it, remains. Genuine belief in the ideology drives devotees' behaviour – pressure to conform or instrumentally use the ideology, though potentially extant, hardly matters for the devotee since they would fervently work to support the ideology whether such pressure existed or not. Devotees hardly ever generate leakage; whereas their enthusiasm for the cause will often encourage them to drive forward campaigns of violence on their own initiative even in the absence of strong additional motives to do so, generating cascade.

Adherents

Adherents identify with and operate under the violence-justifying ideology, but to a weaker, more conditional, and more selective extent than devotees. Whether reflectively or unreflectively, they have real confidence in the ideas they have internalized, though this may be open to challenge. They feel committed to the ideology and are consequently hard to turn away from it, but not implacably so. They internalize almost all major elements of the ideology, and are confident in its core ideas, but may be ambivalent or sceptical about some of its more peripheral elements (on core and periphery, see Freeden 1996; Freeden 2013). Their internalization of the ideology is also less exclusive than that of devotees, and may co-exist with ideational clusters of other provenances. Importantly, for our purposes, these could include ideological restraints on violence. For example, a genuine adherent to Nazi ideology could still retain considerable attachment to non-Nazi Christian morality, which might conflict with Nazi prescriptions. If this happened to a devotee, they would unequivocally side with the Nazi prescriptions. But the adherent may be much more genuinely conflicted by such internal dissonance, with scope for a number of outcomes (and a considerable role for situational factors). Adherents attach importance to the ideology's content and prescriptions in political and social life, and are likely to be motivated to various forms of active involvement in ideological activities, including violence, as a consequence. But pressures to conform to or instrumentalize ideology may also be relevant, since adherents are more sensitive to such pressures than devotees. This all gives them some limited potential for leakage, but still considerable potential for cascade, especially when other reinforcing motives are engaged.

Sympathizers

Sympathizers have internalized significant clusters of the ideology, reflecting a positive disposition towards it. But their internalization could be with varying degrees of confidence, could be derivative of other, deeper concerns, and is selective, non-committal, and not necessarily of central importance to them. Indeed, sympathizers probably don't actively *identify* with the ideology at all, so may not be best described as, for example, 'Nazis,' 'Stalinists,' 'Hutu extremists' or 'Serbian nationalists.' Nevertheless, sympathizers are vitally characterized by a serious

Theorizing ideological diversity 67

degree of real internalization – they genuinely sympathize with the ideology. Since they are sympathetic anyway, they will easily conform to the ideology under social pressure and willingly instrumentalize the ideology if they see this as personally useful, or if they see the ideology as the legitimate framework of an organization they work for – the military or party or state bureaucracy, for example. They are likely to accept justifications of actions like voting for a party that espouses the ideology or implementing policies called for by that party. Critically, for our concerns here, the selective material they have internalized may provide the necessary motivations or legitimations for the individual to participate in mass violence. For example, many of the non-Nazi Wehrmacht soldiers who were convinced it was their sacred duty to obey the orders of the Führer, or the ordinary Hutu who were not true extremists but nevertheless accepted claims that the invading RPF was about to launch a genocide of its own against the Hutu, are sympathizers as conceptualized here. According to circumstances and other motives, sympathizers create considerable potential for cascade, but also some potential for leakage.

Apathetics

Apathetics[4] are characterized by little internalization of the ideology in question, but little internalization of the ideology's main competitors too. This is not to say that apathetics have *no* personal ideology: a range of different foundations for apathy exist, and they may not be completely apathetic about politics *in general*. But the apathetic attaches little importance to the violence-justifying ideology in question. For example, an apathetic with respect to Nazism in the early 1930s could be heavily invested in the local politics of their town in the Western Rhineland. But the grand national battles between Nazis, Liberals, Social Democrats, and Communists are a world away, as far as they are concerned. If heading to the ballot box, they might even happen to vote Nazi, but do so fairly unreflectively, and attach little significance or commitment to the decision. Apathetics may still have internalized, in a rather presumptive, latent or unconscious, fashion, some components of the ideology in question. Our hypothetical Rhenish apathetic might find Hitler's statements about betrayed war veterans somewhat convincing, for example, just as their equivalent apathetic in 1950s China or 1990s Yugoslavia might vaguely accept Maoist accounts of the revolution or Serbian myths about national origins. They may have been affected by latent ideological frames or ideologically encouraged dehumanization (see also Snow 2004; Smith 2011). And whatever beliefs or lingering discontents apathetics do have may provide a foundation for them to be subsequently converted to sympathizers (or sceptics) via persuasion. But unlike sympathizers, apathetics presently have little confidence in such internalized material and attach limited personal importance to it. Moreover, those internalized elements co-exist with many other beliefs from other sources (perhaps including some that delegitimize violence), creating competing pressures on the apathetic that they would prefer not to have to resolve. Apathetics are highly susceptible to social pressure to conform to the ideology and may well instrumentalize ideology – unlike sympathizers, though, their motives for

68   *Jonathan Leader Maynard*

doing so rest almost entirely on the extraneous instrumental benefits of wearing rather than being supported by underlying approval. The most important thing to say about apathetics is that their behaviour in mass violence is generally driven by external incentives to comply with the ideology, and they will generate leakage when these are weak, and cascade when strong. Still, their personal ideologies may exert a balance of pressure in one direction or the other that is not wholly irrelevant. And the fact that they *are* ideologically apathetic, rather than sceptical or antagonistic, matters.

Sceptics

Sceptics may still have internalized some elements of a violence-justifying ideology (often latently or unreflectively), but they are poorly disposed towards it overall. Rather than confidence in the ideology, they doubt its claims; rather than commitment to it, they consciously (but perhaps privately) reject it. Moreover – unlike the apathetic – they attach significance to their doubts, finding many elements of the ideology actively unappealing, and are highly reluctant to wear the ideology for instrumental purposes, doing so only under strong social pressure. The source of much of this scepticism is their internalization of competing ideas, which stand in opposition to the ideology and undermine its pronouncements. They probably also lack full confidence in, or commitment to, these opposing notions (otherwise they would become an antagonist). But they are more convinced by them than by the violence-justifying ideology. Sceptics could still become perpetrators, but only unwillingly and under strong social pressure to conform, and they will be reluctant to instrumentalize the ideology unless the incentives to do so are severe. They generally seek out ways to avoid participation, potentially including desertion or defection from the campaign of mass violence (though this may require considerable courage). Sceptics thus generate high potential for leakage, and almost none for cascade. As with apathetics, sceptics might have (weakly) internalized some elements of the violence-justifying ideology that could facilitate their reluctant involvement in violence and/or serve as a rationalization for it. But their overarching scepticism makes them doubt or actively reject the legitimacy of the violence, and predisposes them to escape or oppose it.

Antagonists

Antagonists confidently and consciously reject the ideology, refuse to countenance its claims, and attach considerable importance to this rejection. This still encompasses a variety of specific ideological stances. The rejection need not be completely comprehensive – there is often common ground even between fundamentally opposed ideologies. But antagonists firmly deny the validity of the ideology as a whole. Consider, for example, Clemens August Graf von Galen, the outspoken Bishop of Münster who denounced Nazi euthanasia programmes, the Gestapo, and the persecution of the Church. Von Galen was very far from a political liberal – he was a strong German nationalist and political conservative, opposed the Weimar

Theorizing ideological diversity 69

Republic and democracy, and was, like the Nazis, convinced by the *Dolchstoßleg-ende* (the stab-in-the-back myth). Nevertheless, he became an increasingly committed antagonist of Nazism, engaging in vigorous opposition to it. Most antagonists are far more distant from the violence-justifying ideology, as with the pastors of Le Chambon-sur-Lignon (Rochat and Modigliani 1995: 198–204), the members of the Danish government who saved over 95 per cent of the Jews of the country from Nazi persecution (Semelin 1993: 151–4), or the most determined individual rescuers like the Swedish diplomat Raoul Wallenberg. As all this suggests, antagonists will do everything possible to avoid participation in mass violence and, with some courage and opportunity, will actively work to resist it. They create a range of obstacles to mass violence by their mere existence, and will generate high levels of leakage if they have any capacity to do so by refusing to participate and trying to organize others to do the same. Severe coercion may be able to cudgel them into silence or even force them into limited forms of participation. But short of this they will agitate against the violence-justifying ideology, and especially courageous antagonists will ignore the strongest pressures to comply, even if this involves extreme danger or death.

These categories are obviously simplifications. Some individuals will occupy the grey zones between categories, and in the muddy real world of cognition, there are often ambiguities and complexities in an individual's ideological state. This typology also must not obscure the importance of variation in the *content* of the relevant ideologies – variation that can exist within these various categories as well as between different violence-justifying ideologies. Sometimes it may actually be ideological differences *amongst those who are devotees or adherents* which are critical in fragmenting or holding back mass violence. Ideologies are made of a rich variety of actual content that belies the typical reduction of them to just animosity towards some out-group.

Nazism, for example, was much more than just anti-Semitic hatred, but a complex morass of myths – like the *Dolchstoßlegende* or the fiction of Aryan racial history – normative principles – like the *Fuhrerprinzip* or the prohibition of *Rassenschande* (racial shame) – theories of social change – like Social Darwinism – emotionally laden concepts – the *Volksgemeinschaft*, the *Führer*, the *Untermensch* – and beliefs about matters of fact – that democracy promotes instability and disorder, that Jews really are the central driving force of Bolshevism (or rather *Jüdischer Bolschevismus*). The same is true of all other ideologies. A growing body of research charts how variation in this substantive content of different ideologies shapes variation in patterns of violence (Drake 1998; Asal and Rethemeyer 2008a, 2008b; Thaler 2012; Straus 2015; Staniland 2015). In many cases, such as mass violence against Jews across Europe during World War II, a range of overlapping but distinct violence-justifying ideologies may be in operation, that provide differing justifications for violence, different conceptions of who the proper targets of such violence are, different distributions of devotees, adherents, sympathizers, apathetics, sceptics, and antagonists, and different resulting patterns of violence. So, it is not just the varying degree of internalization that matters but the varying content of what is internalized, too.

70   *Jonathan Leader Maynard*

Still, whilst a simplification, this typology of internalization states represents perpetrators' ideological diversity better than existing frameworks. Given that individuals are not simply either devotees – totally internalizing a violence-justifying ideology – or antagonists – totally rejecting it – the varying populations of these different categories in any specific context describes a complex ideological topography that shapes mass violence.

Crucially, this topography is dynamic, with a gradual trickle of individuals between categories, and occasional floods – rapid ideological transitions – as the balance between categories is radically altered. With respect to Nazi Germany, the years of Hitler's rapid military triumphs from 1938 to 1940 were probably one such period of rapid change (preceded by an intense but slower ideological shift under Nazi rule from 1933–8), as were the years 1945–7, in the opposite direction. This flux in the ideological topography reflects the fact that individuals' internalization states are not fixed but shift in response to ideological propagation, material incentives, and their interpretations of personal experiences – including during campaigns of mass violence themselves (Fujii 2008: 569–70; McDoom 2012: 121). Most individuals shift their ideological stances only slowly and by degrees, but rather rapid transitions at the individual level are also possible. Take, for example, Oskar Schindler's gradual shift from apathy towards Nazism until c.1935, to being a clear sympathizer from around 1935–40 (but probably not an adherent, despite opportunistically joining the Nazi Party in 1939), followed by his rapid shift to scepticism from roughly 1940–42 and then to a dedicated antagonist – perhaps definitively achieved when he witnessed the brutal liquidation of the Warsaw Ghetto on March 14, 1943 (Wundheiler 1986).

One advantage of the typology of internalization states is that it permits more plausible representations of how processes of ideological radicalization towards violence take place, whether amongst society at large, broad organizations (like governing regimes, political parties, the military, terrorist organizations, or paramilitaries), or narrow groups of elite policymakers. For significant radicalization towards violence to occur, it is not necessary to 'convert' huge numbers into devotees of a violence-justifying ideology. Instead, most social radicalization involves shifts, by individuals of various ideological persuasions, in a *predominantly radicalizing direction*. Indeed, a patterned shift of relatively small individual changes, whether in response to significant events or to campaigns of ideological dissemination, can in aggregate substantively reshape the ideological landscape.

I provide an illustration of this process in Figures 3.2 and 3.3. Figure 3.2 describes a hypothetical pre-radicalization ideological distribution in which the vast bulk of a group lack any serious internalization of the violence-justifying ideology. Most are apathetics or sceptics. The arrows, however, indicate the broad trajectory of a radicalization process (perhaps the product of a shocking exogenous event or a sustained propaganda campaign). Ideological change is never one-directional, since radicalizing appeals will create some 'backlash,' repelling some (the smaller, rightwards arrows). Yet, despite individual members of the population radicalizing by only one or two steps, the resulting change in the ideological

Theorizing ideological diversity 71

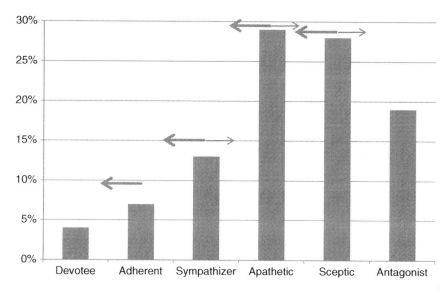

Figure 3.2 A hypothetical pre-radicalization ideological distribution

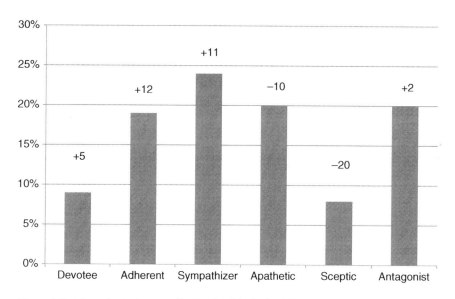

Figure 3.3 A hypothetical post-radicalization ideological distribution

topography can be dramatic, as shown by the hypothetical post-radicalization distribution depicted in Figure 3.3 (numbers indicate the change in each category).

Devotees (and even devotees plus adherents) still make up a minority of the population in the post-radicalization distribution of Figure 3.3, by some distance.

72   *Jonathan Leader Maynard*

Yet it is easy to see how that distribution creates vastly more opportunities and pressures for violence than a less radicalized one. The radicalized society contains far more people whose ideological attitudes are likely to lead them to support or even cascade mass violence, and far fewer likely to oppose it or generate leakage – and policymakers know this. This may be sufficient to cross the 'tipping point' where mass violence becomes a serious possibility, and to sustain it once underway.

Diversity and violence

Obviously, however, it is not only the overall balance that matters, but *who* is a devotee or an adherent, and where in critical power structures they are. The effect of ideological diversity varies in different parts of the *apparatus of violence* – the overarching arrangement of individuals, institutions, and practices involved (see also Bloxham 2008). In this final section I offer some hypotheses regarding this relationship derived inductively from existing research on mass violence.

I share the widespread view that ideological attitudes are generally most important amongst elite policymakers (Valentino 2004: 2–3; Straus 2012a: 549). But there is cross-case variation. A critical determinant is the *concentration of organizational power* in the context in question, related to the distance that violence is occurring from centres of power (Malešević 2010).

In what I call 'tight' campaigns of mass violence, very high organizational power grants violent centres extensive control over their 'peripheries.' *Diversity amongst policymakers at the centre is therefore most significant.* If policymakers are highly ideologically diverse, with many sceptics or antagonists to violence-justifying claims, mass violence is likely to be limited, incoherent, or avoided. In most cases where mass violence is a serious possibility, however, policymakers are likely to be of similar internalization states – being devotees or adherents to a shared ideology (Straus 2015: 66). Even here, though, ideological differences amongst these devotees/adherents could impede or fragment violence, perhaps by leading some members of the elite to feel that alternatives to mass violence are available or that there are other political priorities that violence would undermine. As Alex de Waal, Jens Meierhenrich, and Bridget Conley-Zilkic point out, varying degrees of elite dissension are frequently an important factor in the limitation, breakdown, or eventual halting of campaigns of mass violence, as, for example, in East Pakistan in 1970–71, Somalia in the late 1980s, or Sudan in the early 1990s (de Waal et al. 2012: 21–2; see also Straus 2015: 79–80). But if policymakers with high organizational power are broadly united on the desirability and permissibility of mass violence then mass violence is likely to be more purposeful and extensive.

However, even contexts with concentrated organizational power often leave room for considerable agency amongst local elites, other intermediaries between central policymakers and direct killers, or potential resisters. Their ideological dispositions can thus be important. Whilst the Holocaust involved numerous apathetic bureaucrats, the significance of large numbers of sympathizers in both state administrative structures and the military officer corps is widely recognized

Theorizing ideological diversity 73

(Bartov 1994; Lozowick 2000; Bloxham 2008: 210). Jürgen Matthäus' study of some of the earliest mass killings of Jews in the Nazi invasion of the Soviet Union, for example, has made clear the degree to which local initiatives by German officers, and the civilian population, were critical. "The beginnings of the Holocaust in Lithuania," Matthäus, writes, "suggest that the push for these extreme 'measures' came from officers in the field . . . [and the June 1941 Bialystok] massacre, which followed an order to search for Red Army soldiers and Jews, was initiated by a few determined officers who, it appears, inspired others to participate" (Matthäus 2007: 223–4). Indeed, as Matthäus (2007: 220–2) also points out, the Nazi leadership was originally relatively cautious in pushing for mass killing, and sensitive to potential resistance from the troops. But large-scale ideological endorsement of violence ensured that "none of the perceived dangers in the radicalization of anti-Jewish policy had materialized" (Matthäus 2007: 234). This early violent entrepreneurship by men who appear evident Nazi devotees, coupled with a broader abundance of sympathizers and apathetics, helped enable and escalate the more systematic genocide that followed (Matthäus 2007: 224).

The presence of adherents and sympathizers to a broader anti-Semitism amongst the local population was also critical: Matthäus (2007: 230) concludes that "the Holocaust . . . could not have evolved on Lithuanian soil if imported German violence had not harmonized with residual anti-Jewish sentiment among the local population," and frequently local pogroms preceded or occurred in absence of Nazi directives. This is obviously not to exculpate more senior officers or the central leadership – their massive ideological radicalization of ordinary Germans, sanctioning of violent entrepreneurs, and more direct pressure on others, was the key factor in facilitating cascade and engendering the Holocaust proper (Matthäus 2007: 224–7). But even the ideological attitudes of German figures of authority varied. General Joachim Lemelsen, for example, whilst endorsing many Nazi framings of the war against the USSR, issued instructions to his soldiers stating: "A Russian soldier who has been taken prisoner while wearing a uniform, and after he had put up a brave fight, has the right to decent treatment" (Bartov 1994: 85) and five days later protested that "in spite of my instruction . . . still more shootings of POWs and deserters have been observed. . . . This is murder" (Bartov 1994: 86). By contrast, the commander of the German 12th Infantry Division instructed his soldiers: "Prisoners behind the front-line . . . Shoot as a general principle! Every soldier shoots any Russian found behind the front-line who has not been taken prisoner in battle" (Bartov 1994: 84). So even in tight campaigns, the ideological attitudes of local authorities could vary – and this can affect spatial variation in violence.

But organizational power is not always so strong. The Rwandan genocide, Maoist or Khmer Rouge mass violence, and the Holocaust outside areas of direct Nazi occupation, were not 'tight' but more akin to what I term 'segmented' mass violence: where actual implementation relies on the co-operation of a number of semi-independent power centres or agents. In polycratic segmented campaigns, ideological diversity amongst *intermediaries* – such as local elites or bureaucrats – operating between the centre and the potential direct killers or resisters can significantly shape the pattern of violence. To what extent do these intermediaries

74 Jonathan Leader Maynard

internalize the violence-justifying ideology of the centre, and to what extent do other influential ideologies amongst intermediaries remain compatible with that ideology? If the balance of internalization states is more skewed to the devotee/adherent end of the scale, or other ideologies share an interest the centre's program of violence, leakage is likely to be low and cascade high. Conversely, high numbers of apathetics, sceptics, and antagonists generate leakage.

In areas of Europe outside of direct Nazi control, local ideological diversity therefore often contributed to more restrained practices of mass violence. Semelin notes how public protests by religious figures against Nazi mass killings in Europe could pose obstacles towards violence in Hungary and parts of Romania, but rarely did so in areas under the most direct German control, like Bohemia-Moravia and directly occupied Greece (Semelin 1993: 141–2).[5] The interaction of control and ideology thus shaped substantial variation in leakage and corresponding levels of violence (Semelin 1993: 129–30; Dawidowicz 1987: 480). Similarly, in Rwanda, violence was delayed, resisted, and reduced in areas of the state where support for the ruling MRND regime was weak, local resonance for justifications of violence lacking, and government control more limited (Straus 2015: 308–10).

By contrast, when the ideological topography is skewed towards the stronger internalization states, we may see more cascade than leakage in areas where the centre is not in direct control. In Indonesian killings of alleged 'communists,' for example, levels of violence were in fact *higher* in areas of weak military control where local civilian populations, who bought into the regime's justifications of violence, enacted intense mob violence on their own initiative (Gerlach 2010: ch. 2). Had the local civilian population been dominated by those sceptical or antagonistic to the regime's presentation of violence, the intensity of killing would have been considerably reduced. Similarly, in Khmer Rouge Cambodia, as Eric Weitz (2003: 187) observes:

> The violence was so extensive, the loss of life so great, both because it was decreed from the center of power *and* because the regime had given completely free rein to cadres on the ground, many of them no older than teenagers, who decided on their own who could live and who should die. [. . .] Without lists, Cambodians were subject to an even greater extent to the arbitrary determinations of individual cadres in the villages and labor camps in which they lived.

The scale of Khmer mass violence was not solely a product of state coercion but the ideological makeup of groups the state could use to carry out its will, generating cascade. Ideology is not the sole factor shaping this sort of variation within and across cases, but it is a central determinant.

Some mass violence involves even less organizational power than segmented campaigns. In 'loose' campaigns, there may be incitement and the issuing of orders (or perhaps just unofficial sanctioning) by authority figures. But the occurrence and extent of violence depends mainly on the ideological attitudes and reaction of potential direct killers themselves, and perhaps relevant intermediaries between them and the 'centre.' Decentralized terrorist campaigns take this form, as do most mass lynchings in the American south or anti-Semitic pogroms in Tsarist Russia. Devotees, adherents, or sympathizers amongst the actual direct killers are needed to get such violence off the ground. With weak application of coercive pressures, sceptics and antagonists will not get involved, and apathetics are likely to do so only with extensive other motivational pressures.

Conclusion

In this chapter, I have made the case that scholars of mass violence need to more deeply theorize perpetrator diversity, and ideological diversity in particular. Ideology is neither the only nor a determinative cause of mass violence. But alongside other important factors it significantly shapes the probability of mass violence and the scale and form it takes when it does occur. I have highlighted empirical evidence on how different distributions of violence-justifying ideologies and their constitutive clusters can encourage or block mass violence, or affect processes of leakage and cascade once mass violence is underway. And I have provided a typology of ideological internalization states that can provide a conceptual handle on diversity, as well as offering some initial hypotheses on how these internalization states impact on patterns of mass violence.

All of this is, however, an early step. Clearly, we need more research on the impacts of different ideological diversities, and the dynamics of diversity amongst policymakers, intermediaries, direct killers, and broader publics and constituencies. I have drawn some hypotheses regarding how ideological topographies might change in ways that radicalize a society towards violence, but we need more empirical research on such questions, which the typology offered here might facilitate. And future research also needs to be built on a more developed account of the specific causal mechanisms that link ideologies with the concrete decision-making processes behind mass violence (Cohrs 2012; Gutiérrez Sanín and Wood 2014). All of this will allow scholars to engage in a more sophisticated manner with the vital but complex role ideology plays, and avoid reducing it to fanatical motivation or epiphenomenal façade.

Notes

1 Though Browning (2001: 184–6, 194, 216) actually affirms the significance of ideology.
2 Not all theorists of ideology are so expansive: an important tradition in political science imposes much more demanding criteria of elaboration and consistency (Converse 1964; Luskin 1987). But this stance is not popular in the rest of the literature on ideology, and is increasingly challenged (Jost 2006; Leader Maynard and Mildenberger 2016).
3 Even participants in the famous Milgram experiments were told that they would cause no lasting harm (see also Mastroianni 2015).
4 Given no better terms, I'm nominalizing this adjective.
5 There are exceptions: Semelin (1993: 142–3) notes the success of the February–March 1943 protests by German women in Berlin against the incarceration of their Jewish husbands, which led to the release of Jews even at the height of the Holocaust.

76   Jonathan Leader Maynard

References

Alvarez, Alex. "Destructive Beliefs: Genocide and the Role of Ideology." In *Supranational Criminology: Towards a Criminology of International Crimes*, edited by Alette Smeulers and Roelof Haveman, 213–32. Antwerpen: Intersentia, 2008.

Asal, Victor, and R. Karl Rethemeyer. "Dilettantes, Ideologues, and the Weak: Terrorists Who Don't Kill." *Conflict Management and Peace Science* 25, no. 3 (2008a): 244–63.

Asal, Victor, and R. Karl Rethemeyer. "The Nature of the Beast: Organizational Structures and the Lethality of Terrorist Attacks." *The Journal of Politics* 70, no. 2 (2008b): 437–49.

Asch, Solomon E. "Studies of Independence and Conformity: I. A Minority of One Against a Unanimous Majority." *Psychological Monographs: General and Applied* 70, no. 9 (1956): 1–70.

Bartov, Omer. *Hitler's Army: Soldiers, Nazis and War in the Third Reich*. Oxford: Oxford Paperbacks, 1994.

Bauman, Zygmunt. *Modernity and the Holocaust*. Cambridge: Polity Press, 1989.

Bellamy, Alex J. "Mass Killing and the Politics of Legitimacy: Empire and the Ideology of Selective Extermination." *Australian Journal of Politics and History* 58, no. 2 (2012): 159–80.

Bloxham, Donald. "Organized Mass Murder: Structure, Participation, and Motivation in Comparative Perspective." *Holocaust and Genocide Studies* 22, no. 2 (2008): 203–45.

Browder, George C. "Perpetrator Character and Motivation: An Emerging Consensus?" *Holocaust and Genocide Studies* 17, no. 3 (2003): 480–97.

Browning, Christopher R. *Ordinary Men: Reserve Police Battalion 101 and the Final Solution in Poland*. London: Penguin Books, 2001.

Cohrs, J. Christopher. "Ideological Bases of Violent Conflict." In *Oxford Handbook of Intergroup Conflict*, edited by L. R. Tropp, 53–71. New York: Oxford University Press, 2012.

Collins, Randall. *Violence: A Microsociological Approach*. Princeton: Princeton University Press, 2008.

Collins, Randall. "Micro and Macro Sociological Causes of Violent Atrocities." *Sociologia, Problemas e Práticas* 71 (2013): 9–22.

Converse, Philip Ernest. "The Nature of Belief Systems in Mass Publics." In *Ideology and Discontent*, edited by David Apter, 206–61. London: Free Press of Glencoe, 1964.

Dawidowicz, Lucy S. *The War Against the Jews 1933–45*. London: Penguin Books, 1987.

de Waal, Alex, Jens Meierhenrich, and Bridget Conley-Zilkic. "How Mass Atrocities End: An Evidence-Based Counter-Narrative." *The Fletcher Forum of World Affairs* 36, no. 1 (2012): 15–31.

Drake, C. J. M. "The Role of Ideology in Terrorists' Target Selection." *Terrorism and Political Violence* 10, no. 2 (1998): 53–85.

du Preez, Peter. *Genocide: The Psychology of Mass Murder*. London: Bowerdean and Boyars, 1994.

Fein, Helen. *Accounting for Genocide: National Responses and Jewish Victimization during the Holocaust*. New York: Free Press, 1979.

Freeden, Michael. *Ideologies and Political Theory: A Conceptual Approach*. Oxford: Oxford University Press, 1996.

Freeden, Michael. "The Morphological Analysis of Ideology." In *The Oxford Handbook of Political Ideologies*, edited by Michael Freeden, Lyman Tower Sargent and Marc Stears, 115–37. Oxford: Oxford University Press, 2013.

Fujii, Lee Ann. "The Power of Local Ties: Popular Participation in the Rwandan Genocide." *Security Studies* 17, no. 3 (2008): 568–97.

Theorizing ideological diversity 77

Fujii, Lee Ann. *Killing Neighbors: Webs of Violence in Rwanda*. Ithaca, NY: Cornell University Press, 2009.

Gerlach, Christian. *Extremely Violent Societies: Mass Violence in the Twentieth-Century World*. Cambridge: Cambridge University Press, 2010.

Gerring, John. "Ideology: A Definitional Analysis." *Political Research Quarterly* 50, no. 4 (1997): 957–94.

Goldhagen, Daniel. *Hitler's Willing Executioners: Ordinary Germans and the Holocaust*. London: Abacus, 1997.

Grossman, Dave. *On Killing: The Psychological Cost of Learning to Kill in War and Society*. New York: Back Bay Books, 2009.

Gutiérrez Sanín, Francisco, and Elisabeth Jean Wood. "Ideology in Civil War: Instrumental Adoption and Beyond." *Journal of Peace Research* 51, no. 2 (2014): 213–26.

Hagan, John, and Wenona Rymond-Richmond. "The Collective Dynamics of Racial Dehumanization and Genocidal Victimization in Darfur." *American Sociological Review* 73, no. 6 (2008): 875–902.

Hamilton, Malcolm B. "The Elements of the Concept of Ideology." *Political Studies* 35, no. 1 (1987): 18–38.

Henriksen, Rune, and Anthony Vinci. "Combat Motivation in Non-State Armed Groups." *Terrorism and Political Violence* 20, no. 1 (2008): 87–109.

Janis, Irving. *Groupthink*. Boston: Houghton Mifflin Company, 1982.

Jost, John T. "The End of the End of Ideology." *American Psychologist* 61, no. 7 (2006): 651–70.

Jost, John T., Christopher M. Federico, and Jaime Napier. "Political Ideology: Its Structure, Functions and Elective Affinities." *Annual Review of Psychology* 60, no. 1 (2009): 307–37.

Kalyvas, Stathis N. "The Ontology of 'Political Violence': Action and Identity in Civil Wars." *Perspectives on Politics* 1, no. 3 (2003): 475–94.

Kalyvas, Stathis N. *The Logic of Violence in Civil War*. Cambridge: Cambridge University Press, 2006.

Kaplan, Robert D. *Balkan Ghosts: A Journey Through History*. New York: Picador USA, 2005.

Karstedt, Susanne. "Contextualizing Mass Atrocity Crimes: The Dynamics of 'Extremely Violent Societies.'" *European Journal of Criminology* 9, no. 5 (2012): 499–513.

Karstedt, Susanne. "Contextualizing Mass Atrocity Crimes: Moving Toward a Relational Approach." *Annual Review of Law and Social Science* 9, no. 1 (2013): 383–404.

Kaufman, Stuart J. *Modern Hatreds: The Symbolic Politics of Ethnic War*. Ithaca, NY: Cornell University Press, 2001.

Klusemann, Stefan. "Micro-Situational Antecedents of Violent Atrocity." *Sociological Forum* 25, no. 2 (2010): 272–95.

Knight, Kathleen. "Transformations in the Concept of Ideology in the Twentieth Century." *American Political Science Review* 100, no. 4 (2006): 619–26.

Kühne, Thomas. "Male Bonding and Shame Culture: Hitler's Soldiers and the Moral Basis of Genocidal Warfare." In *Ordinary People as Mass Murderers: Perpetrators in Comparative Perspective*, edited by Olaf Jensen and Claus-Christian W. Szejnmann, 55–77. Basingstoke: Palgrave Macmillan, 2008.

Kühne, Thomas. "Great Men and Large Numbers: Undertheorising a History of Mass Killing." *Contemporary European History* 21, no. 2 (2012): 133–43.

Leader Maynard, Jonathan. "Rethinking the Role of Ideology in Mass Atrocities." *Terrorism and Political Violence* 26, no. 5 (2014): 821–41.

78 *Jonathan Leader Maynard*

Leader Maynard, Jonathan. "Combating Atrocity-Justifying Ideologies." In *The Responsibility to Prevent: Overcoming the Challenges to Atrocity Prevention*, edited by Serena K. Sharma and Jennifer Welsh, 189–225. Oxford: Oxford University Press, 2015.

Leader Maynard, Jonathan, and Matto Mildenberger. "Convergence and Divergence in the Study of Ideology: A Critical Review." *British Journal of Political Science*, FirstView Online Version (2016): 1–27.

Lozowick, Yaacov. *Hitler's Bureaucrats: The Nazi Security Police and the Banality of Evil*. London: Continuum, 2000.

Luskin, R. C. "Measuring Political Sophistication." *American Journal of Political Science* 31, no. 4 (1987): 856–99.

Malešević, Siniša. *The Sociology of War and Violence*. Cambridge: Cambridge University Press, 2010.

Mann, Michael. *The Dark Side of Democracy: Explaining Ethnic Cleansing*. Cambridge: Cambridge University Press, 2005.

Mastroianni, George R. "Obedience in Perspective: Psychology and the Holocaust." *Theory & Psychology* 25, no. 5 (2015): 657–69.

Matthäus, Jürgen. "Controlled Escalation: Himmler's Men in the Summer of 1941 and the Holocaust in the Occupied Soviet Territories." *Holocaust and Genocide Studies* 21, no. 2 (2007): 218–42.

McDoom, Omar Shahabudin. "The Psychology of Threat in Intergroup Conflict: Emotions, Rationality, and Opportunity in the Rwandan Genocide." *International Security* 37, no. 2 (2012): 119–55.

Milgram, Stanley. *Obedience to Authority: An Experimental View*. London: Pinter & Martin Ltd., 2010.

Mueller, John. "The Banality of 'Ethnic War'." *International Security* 25, no. 1 (2000): 42–70.

Newman, Leonard S. "What Is a 'Social-Psychological' Account of Perpetrator Behavior? The Person Versus the Situation in Goldhagen's *Hitler's Willing Executioners*." In *Understanding Genocide: The Social Psychology of the Holocaust*, edited by Leonard S. Newman and Ralph Erber, 43–67. New York: Oxford University Press, 2002.

Norval, Aletta. "The Things We Do with Words – Contemporary Approaches to the Analysis of Ideology." *British Journal of Political Science* 30, no. 2 (2000): 313–46.

Oppenheim, Ben, Abbey Steele, Juan F. Vargas, and Michael Weintraub. "True Believers, Deserters, and Traitors: Who Leaves Insurgent Groups and Why." *Journal of Conflict Resolution* 59, no. 5 (2015): 794–823.

Owens, Peter B., Yang Su, and David A. Snow. "Social Scientific Inquiry into Genocide and Mass Killing: From Unitary Outcome to Complex Processes." *Annual Review of Sociology* 39 (2013): 69–84.

Rochat, François, and Andre Modigliani. "The Ordinary Quality of Resistance: From Milgram's Laboratory to the Village of Le Chambon." *Journal of Social Issues* 51, no. 3 (1995): 195–210.

Roth, Paul A. "Social Psychology and Genocide." In *The Oxford Handbook of Genocide Studies*, edited by Donald Bloxham and A. Dirk Moses, 142–62. Oxford: Oxford University Press, 2005.

Semelin, Jacques. *Unarmed Against Hitler: Civilian Resistance in Europe, 1939–1943*. Westport, CT: Praeger, 1993.

Semelin, Jacques. *Purify and Destroy: The Political Uses of Massacre and Genocide*. London: Hurst & Company, 2005.

Theorizing ideological diversity   79

Slim, Hugo. *Killing Civilians: Method, Madness and Morality in War*. London: Hurst & Company, 2007.

Smeulers, Alette. "What Transforms Ordinary People into Gross Human Rights Violators?" In *Understanding Human Rights Violations: New Systematic Studies*, edited by Sabine C. Carey and Steven C. Poe, 239–56. Aldershot: Ashgate Publishing, 2004.

Smeulers, Alette. "Perpetrators of International Crimes: Towards a Typology." In *Supranational Criminology: Towards a Criminology of International Crimes*, edited by Alette Smeulers and Roelof Haveman, 233–66. Antwerpen: Intersentia, 2008.

Smith, David Livingstone. *Less Than Human: Why We Demean, Enslave and Exterminate Others*. New York: St. Martin's Griffin, 2011.

Snow, David A. "Framing Processes, Ideology, and Discursive Fields." In *The Blackwell Companion to Social Movements*, edited by David A. Snow, Sarah A. Soule and Hanspeter Kriesi, 380–412. Oxford: Blackwell Publishing, 2004.

Staniland, Paul. "Militias, Ideology, and the State." *Journal of Conflict Resolution* 59, no. 5 (2015): 770–93.

Straus, Scott. *The Order of Genocide: Race, Power and War in Rwanda*. Ithaca, NY: Cornell University Press, 2006.

Straus, Scott. " 'Destroy Them to Save Us': Theories of Genocide and the Logics of Political Violence." *Terrorism and Political Violence* 24, no. 4 (2012a): 544–60.

Straus, Scott. "Retreating from the Brink: Theorizing Mass Violence and the Dynamics of Restraint." *Perspectives on Politics* 10, no. 2 (2012b): 342–62.

Straus, Scott. *Making and Unmaking Nations: War, Leadership and Genocide in Modern Africa*. Ithaca, NY: Cornell University Press, 2015.

Suny, Ronald Grigory. "Why We Hate You: The Passions of National Identity and Ethnic Violence." *Berkeley Program in Soviet and Post-Soviet Studies Working Paper Series*. Berkeley: University of California, 2004.

Szejnmann, Claus-Christian W. "Perpetrators of the Holocaust: A Historiography." In *Ordinary People as Mass Murderers: Perpetrators in Comparative Perspective*, edited by Olaf Jensen and Claus-Christian W. Szejnmann, 25–54. Basingstoke: Palgrave Macmillan, 2008.

Thaler, Kai M. "Ideology and Violence in Civil Wars: Theory and Evidence From Mozambique and Angola." *Civil Wars* 14, no. 4 (2012): 546–67.

Üngör, Uğur Ümit. "Mass Violence in Syria: A Preliminary Analysis." *New Middle Eastern Studies* 3 (2013): 1–22.

Valentino, Benjamin A. *Final Solutions: Mass Killing and Genocide in the 20th Century*. Ithaca, NY: Cornell University Press, 2004.

van Dijk, Teun. *Ideology: A Multidisciplinary Approach*. London: Sage Books, 1998.

Waller, James. *Becoming Evil: How Ordinary People Commit Genocide and Mass Killing*. Oxford: Oxford University Press, 2007.

Weitz, Eric D. *A Century of Genocide: Utopias of Race and Nation*. Princeton, NJ: Princeton University Press, 2003.

Wood, Reed M. "Opportunities to Kill or Incentives for Restraint? Rebel Capabilities, the Origin of Support, and Civilian Victimization in Civil War." *Conflict Management and Peace Science* 31, no. 5 (2014): 461–80.

Wundheiler, Luitgard N. "Oskar Schindler's Moral Development During the Holocaust." *Humboldt Journal of Social Relations* 13, no. 1/2 (1986): 333–56.

Zimbardo, Philip. *The Lucifer Effect: How Good People Turn Evil*. London: Rider Books, 2007.

Section II

Motivations and dynamics

4 Perpetrators? Political civil servants in the Third Reich

Darren O'Byrne

Introduction

Despite our ever-increasing interest in Nazi perpetrators, we still lack a precise definition of the term. Indeed, although much literature examines various persons and groups as perpetrators, few scholars have focused on what it is that makes them perpetrators. Instead, it is merely accepted that the subjects of perpetrator research – *Täterforschung* in German – are such, as scholars look to explain how and why they participate in acts of mass violence (Paul 2002). So in order to answer the question – whether state bureaucrats can be accurately described as perpetrators – we first need look at the dominant images that emerge in perpetrator research to see if they conform to what is there.

By and large, historians have taken either a broad or narrow view of perpetration (Longerich 2009). Saul Friedlander and Raul Hilberg, for example, – the latter being among the first to use the term in a historical context – have both advocated a broader understanding of the term, viewing as perpetrators anyone involved in the persecution and murder of the Jews (Friedlander 2009; Hilberg 2006). In one of its earliest manifestations, therefore, the term 'perpetrator' was Holocaust-specific. Defining perpetration solely in terms of the Nazis' 'Final Solution' to the Jewish Question, however, can be problematic for a number of reasons. For one, it is well known that the Jews were just one of a number of victim groups persecuted and even murdered during the Third Reich. Although finding a solution to the Jewish 'problem' was undoubtedly among the most pressing concerns for the Nazi leadership, and was different in terms of the underlying motivations behind it (Evans 2014: 24), the eventual fate of others such as the Sinti and Roma or the 'hereditarily ill,' to take but three examples, was largely the same (Bastian 2001; Klee 2009).

Another problem with Holocaust-specific definitions of perpetration is that they can also give rise to questions concerning the precise timeframe in which perpetration occurs. For in describing as perpetrators "all people who played a specific role in the formulation or implementation of anti-Jewish measures" (Hilberg 2006: ix), be it during or before the Second World War, one is forced to ask, at what point does perpetration begin? Or, to put it differently, when does a perpetrator become a perpetrator? This point becomes particularly acute

84 Darren O'Byrne

when considering that many of the regime's early discriminatory measures, aimed at Jews and other minorities, had been drafted long before 1933. Consider Christopher Browning's point concerning the Nazi regime's first significant piece of racial legislation, the Law for the Restoration of a Professional Civil Service (RGBl 1933: 377), as an example. "Even before Hitler's assumption of power," he argues, "schemes were being hatched in the Interior Ministry to purge the Civil Service, end the naturalization of *Ostjuden* (Eastern European Jews), and prohibit the changing of names to disguise Jewish identity" (Browning 1983: 145). In other words, the basic outline of this law was drafted during the Weimar Republic and merely implemented after Hitler became chancellor. However, if we accept that mass violence was in fact an outgrowth of these policies, and would hardly have been possible without them, then it might be argued that perpetration actually predated the Third Reich. One of the biggest problems with broader definitions of perpetration, therefore, is one of periodization.

Narrower definitions of Nazi perpetrators, on the other hand, have a far more clearly defined timeframe. Indeed, since its emergence as a field of study in its own right, *Täterforschung* has focused almost exclusively on the SS and police battalions that participated, either directly or indirectly, in the atrocities committed during the Second World War (Mallmann and Paul 2014). Thus, we are no longer talking about participation in the Holocaust *per se*, but rather mass violence in all its forms. Yet, even here the term 'perpetrator' is nowhere expressly defined. Instead, given their proximity to the killing, and the fact that they represent the regime that is driving the violence, it is merely assumed that they are perpetrators, as historians look to explore the apparatus and membership of these organizations, the relationship between center (Berlin) and periphery (the occupied territories), as well as the complex and varying motivations of the actors involved (Longerich 2010: 2–4). Just like broader understandings of the term, however, atrocity-centric understandings of perpetration can be problematic. For one, they fail to recognize that violence was just one form of persecution in Nazi Germany; a manifestation, in fact, of the broader structural conditions that facilitated and encouraged persecution in all its forms, and without which the atrocities would never have materialized. Secondly, the overwhelming focus, particularly in German language research, on the 'policing' organizations criminalized after the war underlines the extent to which legal terminology and scholarly research have almost become intertwined. Indeed, Stefan Kühl has shown how "there appears to be a broad consensus in scholarship that everyone who took part in the Holocaust – regardless of whether they were convicted by a court – are best described by using criminal categories" (Kühl 2014: 257–8).

The fact remains, however, that there were some SS and police functionaries who were not involved in planning or implementing Nazi atrocities, and many non-members – including some civil servants – who actually were. Finally, by focusing solely on wartime atrocities, we risk losing sight of the complex division of labor that characterized even the Nazi murder apparatus. The actions of perpetrators on the ground were many, and not all of them led directly to the gas chambers. The recently convicted SS-*Unterscharführer* and Auschwitz bookkeeper,

Political civil servants in the Third Reich 85

Oskar Gröning, is a case in point. In July 2015, a Lüneburg court found Gröning guilty of being an accessory to the murder of 300,000 Hungarian Jews and sentenced him to four years in prison. According to the findings of the court, his role consisted primarily of counting the money of the deportees and sending it on to SS headquarters in Berlin. Therefore, although Gröning was an important cog in the machinery of destruction, he did not, as far as we know, physically murder anybody. Instead, his and others' roles within the system were in fact a by-product of the decision to kill millions of people.

Thus, both broad and narrow definitions of Nazi perpetrators exhibit certain limitations. Whereas the former provides for an almost limitless application of the term, the latter's emphasis on atrocity can lose sight of the fact that Babi Yar and Auschwitz were but manifestations of a system that promoted and legitimized persecution in many forms. Many of these problems stem from our inability to provide a single, overarching definition of the term. And for good reason; there is no single definition of perpetration. Perpetration, rather, varies according to context and, as the scope of this present volume shows, cannot be limited to one time, place or group. That said, it is still incumbent on historians who engage in perpetrator research to provide a definition of perpetration that reflects the historical circumstances in which it occurs. For before we can determine who the perpetrators are, we first need to define what perpetration is. And to achieve this, historians should focus on the different *acts* that make perpetrators what they are (Mallmann and Paul 2014: 23).

During the Third Reich at least, it is abundantly clear that perpetration involved more than the mere act of killing, just as being a victim was about more than being killed. "Perpetration", rather, according to Mary Fulbrook, "was also possible through administration, 'Germanization', stigmatization, camps, ghettos etc" (Fulbrook 2012). Although perpetrators in the narrow sense were also engaged in acts such as these, they usually belonged to the SS and police units active in the occupied eastern territories, and it is their roles as killers, along with their motivations for killing, that interests historians the most (Wildt 2003). But if we accept that these acts also constitute perpetration, then it becomes clear that it was not limited to the SS and police battalions in the East, and was just as visible in Germany prior to and during the Second World War. In fact, all but one of the acts perpetrated in the East – that of mass murder – were replicated by senior civil servants over the course of the Third Reich. After all, with its innumerable laws and decrees, it was the bureaucracy who brought about the "civic and social death" of the German Jews, "thus delivering them into the hands of the SS" (Browning 1983: 146). Thus considered, it can be reasonably assumed that much civil service behavior back in Berlin – which basically involved legislating for the identification, disenfranchisement and sometimes even death of the regime's victims – was, indeed, tantamount to perpetration, and that broader definitions of Nazi perpetrators, despite their obvious flaws, are just as valid as those that appear in *Täterforschung*.

In what follows, then, I will further elucidate the nature of civil service perpetration by showing how the actions of senior civil servants facilitated persecution

86   Darren O'Byrne

and, in some cases, even murder in Nazi Germany. Rather than treating the bureaucracy as a whole, however, I will examine four different, high-ranking civil servants – Friedrich-Wilhelm Kritzinger, Franz Schlegelberger, Johannes Krohn and Wilhelm Stuckart. For, as Richard Overy has argued, each case needs to be treated on its own merits, because even within each historical situation there are often different forms of perpetration (Overy 2009). Taking Overy's point to its logical conclusion, however, the concluding section then examines other aspects of civil servants' behavior, showing that other acts in other situations were not, in fact, tantamount to perpetration. Indeed, sometimes civil servants actively worked against the stated aims of the regime. Focusing on the Janus-faced nature of their conduct, therefore, it will be shown that although perpetration was indeed a widespread phenomenon in the German bureaucracy under Nazism, the singular term 'perpetrator' can sometimes fail to capture the complexity of civil servants' behavior. Thus, perpetration in Nazi Germany will be examined as a context-specific phenomenon, meaning that it was possible to be a perpetrator in one context, and not in another.

Civil servants being perpetrators

Like all modern bureaucracies, the German administration under Nazism was characterized by a highly complex division of labor. Hence, it is unsurprising that some government departments were more directly concerned with persecution than others. That said, because persecution was a matter of administration, and therefore a concern for the civil service, practically everyone who chose to serve the state in Nazi Germany helped to decide the fate of its victims. The Justice Ministry's Franz Schlegelberger is a case in point. One of the few secretaries of state to serve both the Weimar and National Socialist governments, Schlegelberger oversaw the slow but deadly evolution of legal policy in Germany and the annexed eastern territories. Like many bureaucrats of his rank, Schlegelberger worked tirelessly to align the aims of the new leadership and the interests of the civil service early on. So it should come as no surprise that he, too, helped give legal expression to many of the regime's primary ideological objectives. During the first few months of Hitler's rule, in fact, he helped resuscitate the Law for the Restoration of a Professional Civil Service (BBG) – the first drafts of which had been prepared during the Weimar period – , which provided the legal basis for purging racially and politically undesirable officials from state employment (Adam 2003: 47–8). Perhaps the first significant piece of racial legislation introduced by the regime, the BBG also provided the framework for the further removal of Jews and other 'non Germans' (Majer 2003) from other spheres of public life, and by 1934, Schlegelberger issued further directives to the courts banning the appointment of Jewish lawyers in cases where legal aid was required. Of course, such efforts need to be seen as part of the regime's overall attempt to 'cleanse' German society of Jewish influence. And it is widely accepted that Schlegelberger and the Justice Ministry were responding, at least in part, to pressure from Nazi party radicals, who were already pushing policy in this direction

Political civil servants in the Third Reich 87

(Nathans 1990: 45–6). Whether he was the driving force or not, however, it has long been accepted that motivations play no part in determining who the perpetrators are (Browning 1998). All that mattered was compliance, which Schlegelberger duly provided. This willingness to cooperate was also on display when it came to removing Jews from the legal profession outright. Indeed, Schlegelberger was one of the key figures behind the implementation of the Fifth Decree to the Reich Citizenship Law, which again revoked the right of Jews to practice law in Germany and the incorporated Austrian territories (RGBl 1938: 1146). Acting on behalf of lawyers who were 'German,' he first suggested the measure in mid-1938, whereupon the law was enacted the following September (BArch B R 43-II/1535). Schlegelberger also personally dictated some of the law's more detailed provisions, particularly those relating to the legal representation of Jews themselves. Where this was required, he insisted, they should be represented by other Jews conditionally licensed by the judicial administration. Rather than calling them lawyers, however, he suggested they be referred to as 'legal advisors' (BArch B R 3001/20253).

As we can see, Schlegelberger played an active role in the identification and progressive disenfranchisement of minorities before 1939, many of whom would later be killed by the National Socialist regime. But it was during the war that he made his most radical contribution to the regime's persecutory agenda. With the invasion of Poland, persecution came to include state-sponsored occupation, ethnic cleansing, forced labor and mass murder. All these were matters of administration and therefore required the complicity of senior bureaucrats like Schlegelberger. With areas such as the Sudetenland and Western Poland now incorporated into 'Greater Germany,' German courts were instilled in areas where there lived significant numbers of Czechs, Poles and, of course, Jews. His role in the persecution of the Jews before the war proved his readiness to execute the regime's will. During the war, however, he looked to fend off SS attacks on his administrative competence by calling for even harsher treatment of 'non-Germans.' In 1941, for example, he complained "that the administration of Justice showed an incomprehensibly considerate attitude towards the Polish people, who are irreconcilably hostile to us." Presenting them as a danger to public safety, he expressed the hope that from now on "the heaviest punishments [would] be inflicted on Polish criminals" (Majer 2003: 336). Similarly, Schlegelberger ordered the courts to administer "exemplary punishments to Jews in 1942." Referring specifically to the lenient treatment of a Jew who sold a bottle of brandy, and Jews who used the Hitler salute in Moscow, he ordered that in future such cases should be treated as treason (Majer 2003: 341). At the time, convicted acts of treason carried the death penalty.

Such calls for the harsher treatment of Poles and Jews found their ultimate expression in the Decree Concerning Criminal Justice in the Incorporated Eastern Territories (RGBl 1941: 759). According to the decree, 'non-Germans' were to be subject to special law in the incorporated territories. Going forward, Jews and Poles were to be sentenced to death if they, for example, committed acts of violence against Germans or even uttered anti-German remarks. To be sure, much

88   *Darren O'Byrne*

of the law's content reflected the wishes of Hitler, Himmler and Martin Bormann, with Schlegelberger even managing to thwart the latter's attempts to introduce corporal punishment (Neliba 2005: 20). However, it was the Justice Secretary who completed the final draft, adding the caveat that neither Poles nor Jews were entitled to legal representation, and it was he who signed an appendage the following month ordering the new law to be applied even in cases heard before it was introduced (von Alten 2009: 68–9).

These are just some of Schlegelberger's acts that were tantamount to perpetration. Like him, the Reich Chancellery's Friedrich-Wilhelm Kritzinger was another high-ranking bureaucrat who perpetrated through administration; in other words, by helping to formulate and implement a range of discriminatory policies. Unlike Schlegelberger, however, whose administrative mandate was largely limited to matters of jurisprudence, practically all laws enacted during the Third Reich landed on Kritzinger's desk because of the Chancellery's role as a coordinating office between senior government agencies and as their main point of contact with Hitler (Rebentisch 1989: 69–71). Thus, whereas other ministries only became involved in the political process when it concerned them, the Chancellery coordinated discussions and perfected legislative drafts on issues ranging from the euthanasia program to the persecution of the Jews (Mommsen 1966a: 272). Kritzinger's own department within the Chancellery was directly responsible for processing and transferring the legislative initiatives of and between the Interior and Justice ministries; the Supreme Command of the Armed Forces; the Finance, Labor and Economics ministries; as well as the German railway and postal services. Following his appointment in 1938, therefore, he communicated with the Reich's most important agencies about a wide range of discriminatory policies. For example, documents concerning the persecution of the clergy and the murder of 'hereditarily ill' – the so-called euthanasia program – carry his signature. By and large, these were merely passed on to the relevant departments (Mommsen 1966a: 378–9).

As with most civil servants, however, Kritzinger played a far more active role in the promulgation of anti-Jewish legislation. Like most administrative agencies in the Third Reich, the Chancellery had an office that dealt exclusively with Jewish affairs. Aptly named "Jews and Half-Jew Matters," Kritzinger was its chief from 1940 (Mommsen 1966a: 370). This helps explain why he was invited to the now infamous Wannsee conference in 1942, a meeting convened by the leader of the Reich Security Main Office (RSHA), Reinhard Heydrich, to coordinate a 'Final Solution' to the Jewish Question. Beyond the fact that he was present, the only surviving evidence of the meeting reveals nothing of Kritzinger's reaction to what was discussed (PAAA R 100857). Nevertheless, his mere presence suggests that Heydrich expected the Chancellery's full cooperation in the endeavor. In the months preceding the conference, moreover, Kritzinger was also involved in discussions concerning contentious position of half and quarter Jews, Jews in mixed marriages, as well as those pertaining to the Eleventh Decree to the Reich Citizenship Law (RGBl 1941: 1146). With a view to legalizing the deportations that were already taking place, an Interior Ministry draft law stipulated that all Jews in Germany be made stateless and their property transferred to the Reich,

Political civil servants in the Third Reich 89

a move which Kritzinger agreed with in principle. However, in light of the massive legal difficulties such a move would entail, and because there would soon be no Jews left in Germany, he argued that Jews should only me made stateless once they crossed the German border, more often than not in trains bound for the East. With the help of his direct superior, Hans-Heinrich Lammers, Kritzinger was able to ensure that the final draft of the law reflected his wishes. Following Hitler's approval, it was passed in November 1941. And although it failed to create a semi-legal basis for the deportations themselves, it did essentially sanction the consequences of deportation, such as the loss of property and rights that were attached to citizenship (Mommsen 1966a: 388). Like the aforementioned SS Bookkeeper and Perpetrator, Oskar Gröning, therefore, Kritzinger was not complicit it mass murder *per se* but rather in acts that came about as a result of the regime's genocidal practices.

Kritzinger's stint in the Reich Chancellery spanned the years 1938 to 1945, a period that witnessed the deadly evolution of Nazi racial policy. The Labor Ministry's Johannes Krohn, conversely, was forced out of office in 1939 following a years-long turf war with the leader of the German Labor Front, Robert Ley, who set his organization up as a kind of shadow Labor Ministry that progressively usurped the administrative mandate of the actual Labor Ministry (BAK N 1430 and Rüdiger Hachtmann 2011). Having been relieved of his duties, therefore, Krohn was not in a position to assist the regime in its wartime excesses in a way similar to Schlegelberger and Kritzinger, at least not in his capacity as Labor Secretary. Indeed, it fell to his successor, Friedrich Syrup, to help oversee the regime's forced labor program during the war (NMT XIV: 827–32); a slice of luck that arguably helped save his reputation after 1945 (Rohrbeck 1954). This does not mean, however, that Krohn did not commit acts of perpetration. As we saw earlier, perpetration was also possible through administration, even before the war. And during his time in the Labor Ministry, he too played his part in identifying and disenfranchising the regime's victims. Although the Labor Ministry's involvement in the legislative process was limited to areas that concerned it, whilst in office Krohn and his Minister, Franz Seldte, were largely able to defend its position as the Reich's foremost authority on social, labor and health policies (Süß 2003: 51). Furthermore, considering Seldte's disinterest in social matters, along with Krohn's expertise in this area (Krohn 1926, 1938), it is unsurprising that the Labor Secretary would help formulate a raft of discriminatory social legislation. The Law Concerning Tenancy Arrangements for Jews (RGBl 1939: 864), for example, signed by Krohn in April 1939, provided for the eviction of Jews from their homes if their landlord was German, and insisted that the resultant homeless families be accepted by other Jews still in possession of their apartments. "Eventually, these *Judenhäuser* [Jewish Houses] were filled from floor to ceiling" (Hilberg 2003: 170).

To be sure, we know that neither Krohn nor the Labor Ministry was the original source of this initiative. It was in fact a compromise measure between Hermann Göring and Heydrich (Heim 2009: 242). However, the documents sent the Chancellery for final approval in March 1939, stated that all participants, Krohn included, agreed with the draft proposal to remove the Jews from German

90 *Darren O'Byrne*

"residential space" (BArch B R 43-II/1171a). Similarly, Krohn was also involved in the development of discriminatory healthcare policies in the Third Reich. Because there was no actual Health Ministry in Nazi Germany, the administration of healthcare was shared among different departments. The Labor Ministry, therefore, was able to exert influence in this area because statutory health provision was a matter of social insurance (Süß 2003: 51). Winfried Süß maintains that the Labor Ministry's approach to healthcare policy was "conservative in a narrow sense, and merely concerned with the maintenance of the status quo" (ibid.). However, given the speed with which things developed in the Third Reich, it could be argued that even the status quo was constantly in flux. In this area, too, Seldte was a disinterested observer, and he ceded responsibility to Krohn and his successors. This explains why it was Krohn and not his minister, who signed some of the Third Reich's most discriminatory health legislation. For example, the Third Decree Concerning the Implementation of the Law for the Prevention of Genetically Diseased Offspring, signed by Krohn in February 1935, ensured that state health insurance funds would cover the costs of sterilizing those judged to be incurably ill, whereas a Decree Concerning the Participation of Jews in State Health Insurance Funds, signed by Krohn in October 1938, severely inhibited Jews' ability to practice medicine by refusing Jewish doctors the right to claim costs from state health insurance funds (RGBl 1938: 367).

These are just some of the discriminatory laws and decrees Krohn helped formulate during his time in the Labor Ministry. As with Schlegelberger and Kritzinger, there is little in the archives to suggest he was the driving force behind these policies. Like them, in fact, there is much to suggest that he too was responding to the radical demands of the new regime, at least in part. As with perpetrators in other contexts, however, personal motivations have no bearing on their status as perpetrators. People were persecuted and even killed despite the varying motivations of the actors involved. What mattered most was compliance with the general program, which Krohn duly provided.

Another person who acted in this manner was Wilhelm Stuckart. The only member of the group without a departmental portfolio before Hitler took power, Stuckart entered the Education Ministry – first as department head, then as State Secretary – in June 1933, not because of his expertise in this field but because of his long-standing ties to the Nazi Party (BArch SSO 167B). Appointed two months after the enactment of the BBG, one of his first tasks as leader of the ministry's education department was to help purge schools and universities of their politically and racially undesirable teachers and professors, whereupon "by March 1934, German universities had lost numerous world-renowned scholars thanks to the work of Stuckart and his colleagues" (Jasch 2012: 79). Despite his obvious willingness to assist the regime in pursuit of its ideological goals, however, he was soon removed from office by his minister, Bernhard Rust, for allegedly challenging the latter's authority, and was forced to spend a short period on the margins of power before his eventual transfer to the Interior Ministry in 1935. In light of his previous fall from grace, Stuckart obviously had something to prove in his new post, not only to the Interior Minister – the long-time Nazi

Political civil servants in the Third Reich 91

Wilhelm Frick – but also to "Hitler himself, who intervened to prevent Stuckart from being consigned to provincial oblivion" (Caplan 1980: 44). And whereas the enactment of the BBG allowed Stuckart to prove his worth to the Nazi education administration, the passing of the Nuremburg Laws would provide him with ample opportunity to do so in the Interior Ministry. Indeed, as head of the Department for Constitutional and Legislative Matters (BArch R 601/1817), in autumn 1935 Stuckart was at the forefront of the regime's efforts to rob Jews of their full citizenship, make it illegal for Jews to have sex with non-Jews, and everything else that the Nuremburg Laws entailed (Kershaw 2010: 345). He even wrote the official commentary to the laws with Hans Globke the following year (Stuckart and Globke 1936).

Having remained in office after 1939, moreover, Stuckart was also involved in a variety of measures that either led to, or were the result of, the regime's murderous excesses during the war. For example, it was he who signed a secret decree in 1939 calling for the forced registration of 'deformed' babies and small children in preparation for the euphemistically labeled child 'euthanasia' program, which in fact amounted to the systematic mass murder of apparently handicapped children (Jasch 2012: 287). Like his colleagues, moreover, he too was involved in discussions concerning the Final Solution to the Jewish Question. As we have just seen, Stuckart had helped pave the way for the mass murder of the Jews before the war by promulgating laws that both identified and disenfranchised the proposed victim group, "thus delivering them into the hands of the SS" (Browning 1983: 146). But even after the regime's conception of the Final Solution shifted from a 'territorial solution' to one based on murder, the complicity of civil servants was still required, be it in providing a 'legal' safeguard for the deportations themselves or in defining who was to be murdered (Jasch 2012: 290). So it should come as no surprise that Stuckart, too, was involved in debates concerning the position of quarter and half Jews – the so-called *Mischlinge* – , as well those relating to Jews in mixed marriages (*Mischehen*); issues that dominated the aforementioned Wannsee Conference. Although it is still being debated whether the wholesale destruction of all Jews was discussed at the conference, the fact that it was even called suggests that their deportation to the East had already been decided upon. Who 'they' were, however, was not. Just as in Germany before the war, despite the best efforts of the regime it was not always clear who the Jews were, and who, consequently, was to be subjected to discriminatory measures; a particularly vexing question in light of the ongoing deportations. Like Kritzinger, who was invited to represent the Reich Chancellery, Stuckart was present as the Interior Ministry's representative. But whereas little is known about the former's reaction to what was being discussed, the only surviving document from the meeting suggests that the latter was one of its most vocal participants. Like most of his colleagues at the meeting, it appears that Stuckart had nothing against the deportations in principal; a position supported by his previous contributions to the regime's discriminatory agenda. In relation to the *Mischlinge* and *Mischehen* living in Germany, however, he argued against their deportation for largely the same reasons that Kritzinger rejected Stuckart's proposal to make them stateless; the endless administrative

92 Darren O'Byrne

difficulties. That said, so as to not hinder the regime's efforts to 'solve' the Jewish problem, Stuckart suggested – ultimately in vain – that those Jews who were not deported should be forcibly sterilized (PAAA R 100857).

These are just some of the ways political civil servants in the Third Reich perpetrated through administration. Such acts may not have led directly to, and were always far removed from, mass violence. But they were part of the broad web of persecution that either led to, or emerged from Nazi atrocities. Indeed, through their innumerable laws and decrees it was men like Schlegelberger, Kritzinger, Krohn and Stuckart who first helped define the objects of Nazi persecution – the victims – before implementing a program of political, social and economic disenfranchisement that threatened the already fragile existence of various minority groups in Hitler's Germany. Once that country was at war, moreover, at a time when persecution came to include occupation, ethnic cleansing, forced labor and mass murder, those who remained in office invariably helped facilitate these acts because they, too, were matters of administration that required the legal know-how and technical expertise these men possessed. They may not have been the driving forces behind these policies. In some instances, in fact, civil servants even spoke out against the regime's excesses. As was mentioned earlier, however, motivations carry little weight in determining who the perpetrators were. The only thing required was compliance, which each of the men surveyed here duly provided. Thus, in the sense that they legislated for the identification, disenfranchisement and, indirectly, sometimes even murder – acts which, in and of themselves, comply with Fulbrook's broader definition of perpetration through administration – , it is fair to conclude that Schlegelberger, Kritzinger, Krohn and Stuckart were perpetrators.

But if we accept the points made earlier, that perpetration was both context-specific and defined by the acts themselves, how then do we define other acts in other contexts? And how does an analysis of the broad spectrum of civil service behavior affect our understanding of these men as perpetrators? In the following section, then, I will explore the margins of the term perpetrator by examining some civil servants' acts that were not, in fact, tantamount to perpetration. Indeed, as will be shown below, Schlegelberger, Kritzinger, Krohn and Stuckart occasionally worked against the stated aims of the regime in ways that appear to contradict their singular definition as perpetrators. Taken together with the previous section, therefore, it will be shown that perpetration was a context-specific phenomenon, meaning that it was possible to be a perpetrator in one context and not in another.

Civil servants not being perpetrators

Schlegelberger and Kritzinger, for example, were part of a group of civil servants that provided assistance to the former Minister of Justice from the Weimar period, Curt Joël, under whom both men had served before Hitler took power. Defined as a full Jew according to the Nuremburg Laws of 1935 – drafts of which Schlegelberger and Kritzinger, who both worked in the Justice Ministry at the time, would have helped shape – Joël should have been subjected to the full gamut

Political civil servants in the Third Reich 93

of restrictions these laws embodied. Thanks to the intervention of his former colleagues, however, he managed to evade some of the harsher measures that came about as a result of his loss of citizenship. Indeed, thanks in no small part to Kritzinger's personal intervention, Joël's successor as Justice Minister, Franz Gürtner, promised to stick up for Joël should his existence be threatened by these measures. Such assistance took shape in a number of different ways. In the aftermath of the Night of the Broken Glass, for example, he was exempted from a special tax ordering Jews to pay for the damages, mostly to their own property, inflicted by Nazi thugs during the pogrom. And whereas other Justice Ministry officials intervened to ensure that Joël received the same food rations as a full German citizen (*Reichsbürger*), it was Schlegelberger who obtained him German's clothing card, which exempted him from the restrictions placed on Jews obtaining clothes during the war (Godau-Schüttke 1981: 221–7). When Joël became sick, moreover, Kritzinger intervened personally to ensure that his former boss was sent to one of Berlin's best hospitals instead of the vastly under-provided-for hospitals that had been set up specifically to treat Jews. And when he or his family members were threatened with deportation, Kritzinger was among those who helped ensure this never happened (FUA E7/2276).

As with most civil servants who stood trial after the war, such acts were presented to the courts as evidence of the defendants' 'resistance' to the Nazi regime. Unlike most, however, Schlegelberger's and Kritzinger's claims were actually backed up by the Joël family. The same was also true of Schlegelberger's efforts to save former colleagues from the judiciary from losing their jobs and, later on, from being deported. According to his biographer Eli Nathans, in fact, Schlegelberger worked to delay the deportation of his former colleague and childhood friend – a Jewish Supreme Court judge named Alexander Cohn – "and once this was no longer possible, he ensured that Cohn and his wife were sent to Theresienstadt, the least murderous of all the Nazi concentration camps." Similarly, he is known to have helped former colleagues classified as *Mischlinge* by the regime, with one district court judge confirming that Schlegelberger helped him transfer to a small Prussian town where it was easier to hide his identity, whilst the wife of another, Johannes Koffka, told the courts that Schlegelberger helped Koffka remain in office until 1942 (Nathans 1990: 42–4). The irony behind these acts is that Schlegelberger, as we saw earlier, was at the forefront of efforts to remove Jews from the German legal profession in their entirety. Therefore, isolated acts such as these should in no way obscure the ways these men facilitated persecution and even murder during the Third Reich. In themselves, however, they do highlight the limits of the term perpetrator as a tool of historical analysis, underlining the extent to which it can sometimes fail to capture the complexity of human behavior. For although people became perpetrators in one situation, this was not always the case in others.

Stuckart, similarly, was part of a group of intellectuals who became quite critical of Nazi occupation policies during World War Two; policies which, originally, Stuckart helped to formulate. Set up in 1939 to discuss the urgent the questions surrounding the domination, organization and administration of German-dominated

94 *Darren O'Byrne*

Europe, the group looked to posit an alternative model of 'rational' domination based on radical ethnic principles (Herbert 1996: 278–9). Arguing in favor of a European community of nations separated strictly along racial lines – and led, of course, by the continent's dominant race; the Germans – , the group wrote a number of articles lamenting the regime's excessive and indiscriminate use of force. In stark contrast to the denationalizing policies being pursued by Hitler and others, Stuckart even argued that "German hegemony should not mean denationalization and repression. National Socialism, rather, by virtue of its own explicit nationalism, respected national differences and would offer freedom from domination . . . with each 'worthy' group being allowed to develop independently and enjoy its own living space" (cited in Mazower 2008: 246–7).

Even within this critique, it should be noted that Stuckart's blatant racism is clearly on display. Indeed, the group's blueprint for the racial reordering of Europe was to follow a strict racial hierarchy. Whereas some groups were to be treated in a conciliatory manner, toughness was required with the most primitive, inferior or racially poisonous peoples. The basic point, however, made in another article, was that "the Germans had become indiscriminately and excessively violent; one could not expect to expel or annihilate all other people on the continent since that defeated the purpose of establishing German hegemony in the first place" (Mazower 2008: 232–47). So although their message was abstruse and couched in a virulent racism, the group nevertheless offered, "elliptically but unmistakably, a new direction for German rule" (Mazower 2008: 232–47). Why did Stuckart – a man who had and would continue to do so much to assist the regime in the realm of racial policy – speak out against the murderous course taken by the regime during the war? Although it cannot be proven, it is certainly possible that it offended his sense of moral decency on some level. Indeed, Kritzinger, who also assisted the regime in this area, is known to have been disgusted by the occupations policies practiced in Poland (Mommsen 1966a: 397). What is known, is that Stuckart was frustrated by the fact that his original blueprint for occupation was not being followed, and that his ministry – and therefore he himself – was dwindling in significance as a result of the proliferation of extra- or quasi-state institutions which were progressively eroding the Interior Ministry's administrative mandate (Rebentisch 1991: 477). So his attempts to influence occupation policy in this direction need to be seen, at least in part, as a response to his own loss of power, as an *attempt*, indeed, to remain significant.

The same might also be said of Krohn's efforts to ensure that Jews who fought in World War One were not removed from the legal profession. In the eyes of the law, though not always in practice, this group was originally protected against some anti-Semitic measures because of their previous sacrifices for Germany. By 1938, however, conservative elements within the regime – some of whom supported the Jewish war veterans' cause – were either on the defensive or in decline, whereas more radical elements within the regime were growing in confidence and stature. As always, this latter group favored the broadest possible definition of who the Jews were, and therefore wanted all of them – whether full, half or quarter, veteran or non-veteran – removed from the legal and other professions. As

Secretary of State in Germany's foremost social policy ministry (the Labor Ministry), and therefore responsible for considering how these Jews should survive or be provided for in light of losing their livelihoods, Krohn's office was asked to clarify its position on the matter in early summer 1938. In response, the Justice Ministry's proposal to revoke the special position of Jewish war veterans, Krohn's office issued an impassioned plea to respect those Jews who had sacrificed so much for Germany and allow them to continue serving at the bar. "I feel compelled to make these deliberations" it was argued, "so that the necessary special position of the wartime injured and war participants in the Third Reich, including the Jewish war veterans who are lawyers, does not go unnoticed in relation to important matters of state policy," by which was meant the progressive attack on the economic position of the Jews. In conclusion, however, the letter stated that "even if they cannot be exempted from economic constraints or suppression, this should not lead to a devaluing of soldierly worth in the eyes of the public" (BArch B R 3001/20253). On some level, at least, there can be little doubt that Krohn identified with the proposed victims; he too had fought and was severely injured during the First World War. But, very much like Stuckart, there was also another, more strategic element to his protests. After 1933, it had become part of the Labor Ministry's administrative mandate to treat the cases of injured Jewish war veterans who, despite their special status, were nevertheless subjected to the regime's discriminatory measures, which essentially meant trying to ensure that the 'non-Aryan' war wounded received the same benefits, pensions and employment protection as their 'Aryan' counterparts (Geheren 2016). Had Krohn simply conceded to the demands of the radicals – whose position would eventually win the day anyway – , it would have meant the further erosion of his administrative mandate, which, as we saw earlier, was being increasingly usurped by the German Labor Front around this time. Thus, it is partly against the backdrop of the internecine power struggles that defined the Third Reich that Stuckart's and Krohn's protests need to be seen.

Conclusions

By focusing on the actions of Franz Schlegelberger, Friedrich-Wilhelm Kritzinger, Wilhelm Stuckart and Johannes Krohn, the preceding analysis has shown that it was possible for a person to be a perpetrator in one situation and not in another. Perpetration in the Third Reich involved far more than the act of killing. It also included legislating for the persecution and sometimes even murder of the regime's victims; a phenomenon Mary Fulbrook has referred to as "perpetration through administration" (Fullbrook 2012). Therefore, in the situations where they acted in ways that facilitated these ends, these men can be considered as perpetrators. At the same time, however, it has also been shown that not all civil service behavior was tantamount to perpetration. In some instances, in fact, civil servants actually worked against the stated aims of the regime, either by helping, or attempting to help, individual or groups of Jews, or by trying to change the course of Nazi occupation policy during World War Two.

96 *Darren O'Byrne*

How, then, does this affect our understanding of these men as perpetrators? Most importantly, it shows that perpetration was a context-specific phenomenon. Although I have examined only the most extreme examples at opposite ends of the behavioral spectrum, so much of what people did in Nazi Germany had no bearing on the fate of the regime's victims and therefore cannot be considered as typical perpetrator behavior. Because perpetration was situational, historians need to focus how people interact with these situations, not as perpetrators *a priori* but as complex individuals acting in complex historical circumstances; an approach that will also benefit the analysis of behavior that was not tantamount to perpetration. For if historians focus on individual actors solely as perpetrators, they will only end up examining those aspects of their behavior that makes them perpetrators, failing to comprehend that the complexity of human behavior defies overtly simplistic, and essentially legal definitions like perpetrator, bystander, sometimes even victim, as recent studies of rape during the Holocaust have controversially shown (Hedgepeth and Saidel 2010). During the course of this, or any historical period, the fine margins between these categories were often in flux, meaning that it was possible for a person to be many or all of these things over time. With regards to Schlegelberger, Kritzinger, Stuckart and Krohn, these men were both critical of the regime and yet actively complicit in its crimes; something we risk losing sight of when referring to them merely as perpetrators.

References

Archival sources

Freiburg University Archive (FUA).
German Federal Archive, Berlin (BArch B).
German Federal Archive, Koblenz (BArch K).
Institute for Contemporary History, Munich (IfZ).
Political Archive of the German Foreign Office, Berlin (PAAA).

Printed primary sources

Heim, Susanne (ed). *Die Verfolgung und Ermordung der europäischen Juden durch das nationalsozialistische Deutschland. Band II: Deutsches Reich 1938 – Aug. 1939.* München: Oldenbourg Verlag, 2009.
Reich Law Gazette (RGBl). http://alex.onb.ac.at/tab_dra.htm
United States Military Tribunals (NMT). 1946–49. Vol. I – XV, 2009. https://www.loc.gov/rr/frd/Military_Law/NTs_war-criminals.html

Secondary literature

Adam, Uwe-Dietrich. *Judenpolitik im Dritten Reich.* Düsseldorf: Droste Verlag, 2003.
Bastian, Till. *Sinti und Roma im Dritten Reich: Geschichte einer Verfolgung.* München: Beck Verlag, 2001.
Browning, Christopher. "The German Bureaucracy and the Holocaust." In *Genocide: Critical Issues of the Holocaust: A Companion to the Film, Genocide,* edited by Alex Grobman, Alex Landes and Sybil Milton, 145–9. Los Angeles: Rossel Books, 1983.

Political civil servants in the Third Reich 97

Browning, Christopher. *Ordinary Men: Reserve Police Battalion 101 and the Final Solution in Poland.* New York: Harper Perennial, 1998.

Caplan, Jane. "Recreating the Civil Service: Issues and Ideas in the Nazi Regime." In *Government, Party and People in Nazi Germany*, edited by Jeremy Noakes, 34–56. Exeter: University of Exeter Press, 1980.

Evans, Richard J. *The Third in History and Memory.* Oxford: Oxford University Press, 2014.

Friedlander, Saul. *Nazi Germany and the Jews: 1933–1945.* New York: HarperCollins, 2009.

Fulbrook, Mary. "A Small Town Near Auschwitz: Ordinary Nazis and Holocaust." Presentation at the *European Summer Institute on the Holocaust and Jewish Civilization.* London, England, 18–29 June 2012.

Geheren, Michael. *Betrayed Comradeship: German-Jewish World War 1 Veterans under Hitler.* PhD Thesis, University of Chicago, 2016.

Godau-Schüttke, Klaus-Detlev. *Rechtsverwalter des Reiches: Staatssekretär Dr. Curt Joël.* Frankfurt am Main: Verlag Peter D. Lang, 1981.

Hachtmann, Rüdiger. "Elastisch, dynamisch und von katastrophaler Effizienz: Zur Struktur der Neuen Staatlichkeit des Nationalsozialismus." In *Der prekäre Staat: Herrschen und Verwalten im Nationalsozialismus*, edited by Sven Reichhardt and Wolfgang Seibel, 29–74. Frankfurt am Main: Campus Verlag, 2011.

Hedgepeth, Sonja M., and Rochelle G. Saidel. *Sexual Violence Against Jewish Women During the Holocaust.* New England: Brandeis University Press, 2010.

Herbert, Ulrich. *Best: Biographische Studien über Radikalismus, Weltanschauung und Vernunft, 1903–1989.* Berlin: Dietz Verlag, 1996.

Hilberg, Raul. *The Destruction of the Europen Jews.* Third Edition. Vol. I. New Haven and London: Yale University Press, 2003.

Hilberg, Raul. *Perpetrators Victims Bystanders: The Jewish Catastrophe 1933–1945.* New York: HarperCollins, 2006.

Jasch, Hans-Christian. *Staatssekretär Wilhelm Stuckart und die Judenpolitik: Der Mythos von der sauberen Verwaltung.* München: Oldenbourg Verlag, 2012.

Kershaw, Ian. *Hitler: A Biography.* London and New York: W. W. Norton, 2010.

Klee, Ernst. *'Euthanasie' im NS Staat: Die Vernichtung lebensunwerten Lebens.* Frankfurt am Main: Fischer Verlag, 2009.

Krohn, Johannes. *Die Ausdehnung der Unfallversicherung auf gewerbliche Berufskrankheiten.* Berlin: Verlag des Reichsarbeitsblattes, 1926.

Krohn, Johannes. *Die Reform der deutschen Sozialversicherung.* Stuttgart and Berlin: W Kohlhammer Verlag, 1938.

Kühl, Stefan. *Ganz normale Organisationen: Zur Soziologie des Holocaust.* Berlin: Suhrkamp Verlag, 2014.

Longerich, Peter. "Was kann die Biographie-Forschung zur Geschichte der NS-Täter beitragen." Paper presented at the conference *Täterforschung im globalen Kontext.* Berlin, Germany, 28–30 January 2009.

Longerich, Peter. *Holocaust: The Nazi Persecution and Murder of the Jews.* Oxford: Oxford University Press, 2010.

Majer, Diemut. *Non-Germans Under the Third Reich: The Nazi Judicial and Administrative System in Germans and Occupied Eastern Europe with Special Regard to Occupied Poland.* Baltimore and London: Johns Hopkins University, 2003.

Mallmann, Klaus Michael, and Gerhard Paul. *Karrieren der Gewalt: Nationalsozialistische Täterbiographen.* Darmstadt: Primus Verlag, 2014.

Mazower, Mark. *Hitler's Empire: Nazi Rule in Occupied Europe.* London: Allen Lane Publishing, 2008.

98 *Darren O'Byrne*

Mommsen, Hans. "Aufgabenkreis und Verantwortlichkeit des Staatssekretärs der Reichskanzlei, Dr. Wilhelm Friedrich-Wilhelm Kritzinger." *Gutachten des Instituts für Zeitgeschichte* 12 (1966a): 369–98.

Mommsen, Hans. *Beamtentum im Dritten Reich: Mit ausgewählten Quellen zur nationalsozialistischen Beamtenpolitik.* Stuttgart: Deutsche Verlagsanstalt, 1966b.

Nathans, Eli. *Der Unrechtsstaat: Franz Schlegelberger.* Baden-Baden: Nomos Verlag, 1990.

Neliba, Günter. *Staatssekretäre des NS-Regimes: Ausgewählte Aufsätze.* Berlin: Duncker & Humblot, 2005.

Overy, Richard. "Perpetrator Research in International Context." Paper presented at the conference *Täterforschung im globalen Kontext.* Berlin, Germany, 28–30 January 2009.

Paul, Gerhard. *Die Täter der Shoah. Fantastische Nationalsozialisten oder ganz normale Deutsche.* Göttingen: Wallstein Verlag, 2002.

Rebentisch, Dieter. *Führerstaat und Verwaltung im Zweiten Weltkrieg: Verfassungsentwicklung und Verwaltungspolitik, 1939–1945.* Stuttgart: Steiner Verlag, 1989.

Rebentisch, Dieter. "Wilhelm Stuckart: 1902–1953." In *Persönlichkeiten der Verwaltung,* edited by Kurt G. A. Jeserich and Helmut Neuhaus, 474–8. Stuttgart: Kohlhammer Verlag, 1991.

Rohrbeck, Walter. *Beiträge zur Sozialversicherung: Festschrift für Johannes Krohn.* Berlin: Duncker & Humblot, 1954.

Stuckart, Wilhelm, and Hans Globke. *Reichsbürgergesetz vom 15. September 1935, Gesetz zum Schutze des deutschen Blutes vom 15. September 1935, Gesetz zum Schutze der Erbgesundheit des deutschen Volkes (Ehegesundheitsgesetz) vom 18. Oktober 1935 nebst allen Ausführungsvorschriften und den einschlägigen Gesetzen und Verordnungen.* München and Berlin: C. H. Beck Verlag, 1936.

Süß, Winfried. *Der Volkskörper im Krieg: Gesundheitspolitik, Gesundheitsverhältnisse und Krankenmord im nationalsozialistischen Deutschland 1939–1945.* München: Oldenbourg Verlag, 2003.

von Alten, Henning. *Recht oder Unrecht: Der Verwaltungsrechtsstreit des Staatssekretärs a.D. Prof. Dr. Dr. h.c. Franz Schlegelberger um seine beamtenrechtlichen Versorgungsbezüge.* Norderstedt: Herstellung und Verlag GmbH, 2009.

Wildt, Michael. *Generation des Unbedingten: Das Führungskorps des Reichssicherheitshauptamtes.* Hamburg: Hamburger Edition, 2003.

5 The normality of going to war

Aspects of symbolic violence in participation and perpetration in civil war

Daniel Bultmann

Introduction

For many if not most combat soldiers, fulfilling the role of the one who must carry out the fighting is perceived as normal due to their position in society. This chapter argues that most become soldiers mainly due to the symbolic violence of belonging to the lowest stratum of society. The state of war and their own roles as soldiers serving on the front line are both perceived as *facts* beyond their own agency and possible influence. The bulk of rank-and-file soldiers simply take the existence of war and their task of fighting the enemy for granted. The issues and causes of war are more or less unreal to them. This chapter asks which role is played by aspects of symbolic violence in civil war participation and perpetration. It maintains that symbolic violence, in which socially constructed orders are interpreted as having been given by nature, constitutes a factor that is not studied enough but explains important aspects of civil war participation and the willingness to fight and kill. This 'banality of perpetration' has been largely overlooked in the literature, which above all focuses either on a hunt for exceptional circumstances, or on psychological traits that can be dug up from the abyss of a perpetrator's soul, or tries to prove that they actually are 'ordinary men' (Browning 1992). The current discourse proves incapable of making sense of the fact that many combat soldiers, in the course of doing their 'dirty jobs,' simply believe that they are ordinary men doing ordinary things during extraordinary times.

This chapter traces how insurgent movements reproduce the social structure of a society and how rank-and-file soldiers adapt to the 'necessities' of being a soldier in wartime. Although it is 'a normal thing' for most (e.g. amongst the rural poor) to become soldiers and merely a 'necessity' to engage in battles, they nevertheless need to overcome their fears and reluctance to kill others in combat. Even though soldiers on the front line believe that it is simply their role as 'ordinary men' to do the fighting, combat is still difficult. Indeed, in contradiction to this belief, soldiers apply various disciplinary techniques to make themselves docile, to establish a certain routine and to overcome emotional barriers on the front line. At the same time, they make use of 'lines of flight,' through which they try to bypass combat and orders from above. Therefore, a wide range of practices comes to the fore, highlighting the complexity of obedience to command in armed groups. Soldiers

100 *Daniel Bultmann*

do not simply become obedient or try to evade command (e.g. through defection, refusal of orders or the staging of combat) but, in fact, take part in their own subjugation under a man-made but naturalized order while trying to accommodate perpetration. The social order of an armed group and the task of fighting the enemy go unquestioned, and perpetrators accommodate to this ultimately arbitrary, but naturalised imposition using techniques of self-rectification.

Among other sources, this chapter makes use of dozens of qualitative interviews conducted with members of the tripartite Cambodian insurgent movement called the Coalition Government of Democratic Kampuchea (CGDK), which fought against Vietnamese occupation during the 1980s and 1990s: The groups involved included the National Army of Democratic Kampuchea (NADK, better known as the Khmer Rouge), Khmer People's National Armed Forces (KPNLAF) and the Armée Nationale Sihanoukiste (ANS). Soldiers and commanders were interviewed regarding the course of their lives, their understanding of good leadership and soldierhood and the use of disciplinary techniques to deal with command and combat reluctance (cf. Bultmann 2014, 2015). Section one of the chapter explains how armed groups reproduce the social structure of the society they are part of and how perpetrators within the lowest ranks take up positions homologous to the ones they have in society. Perpetrators thus assume the role of being in charge of perpetration mainly due to their position in society and in certain social networks. The second section explores symbolic violence as an explanation of why that is the case – namely why, aside from their motives, the threat of force, etc., people *accept* their positions as perpetrators in combat. The third section describes how powerful symbolic violence is, in that it is maintained by the perpetrators themselves, and how it helps to explain the ways that people accommodate being in charge of perpetration.

To start with, preliminary definitions of 'combatants,' 'perpetration' and 'perpetrators' are needed. 'Perpetration,' as the term is used within this chapter, is a regular, collectively and, to certain degrees, centrally organised activity that is allocated to the lowest rank of the military's hierarchy, namely the rank-and-file soldiers. Hence, so-called *lone-wolf violence* drops out of consideration here, as the violent activities discussed in this chapter are not simply individual aggression writ large but, rather, are collective and organised (cf. Tilly 2003). This also means, in turn, that 'combatants' are not 'perpetrators' by nature, but mainly by role attribution within societies and warring organisations in particular. This role attribution becomes constantly reinforced by observers, commanders and combatants alike, when assuming that there is a hidden will to kill for a certain cause, an innate bloodlust or simply greed driving people into perpetration in civil wars, thereby directly or indirectly *naturalising* an arbitrary allocation of lower social milieus to combatant positions within armed groups.

The social structure of armed groups

Armed groups largely reproduce socio-political differentiations inherent to the societies they are part of. Most positions within the internal structure of these

The normality of going to war 101

groups are homologous with pre-existing societal hierarchies (e.g. with a military and political elite forming the upper ranks, their patrimonial network within the mid-range command and lower social milieus forming the rank and file). Biographies of the top command and of first movers starting a rebellion usually refer to dissent within the military and political elite, pointing toward elite politics as a/the major source for internal conflict (cf. Tilly 2003, Schlichte 2009). Within the threefold hierarchy of an armed group, the mid-range in command has so far received the least academic attention, though it is oftentimes decisive in running a rebellion, implementing command and even in finding peaceful solutions to conflict (Alden 2002).

Armed groups are social fields in which access to positions, resources, institutions and activities becomes socially mediated (Bultmann 2015). Within the leadership and mid-range, for example, political, intellectual and military elite networks are not recruited in a literal sense; rather, old loyalties are reconstituted and militarised (Hoffman 2007). A small portion of positions within the leadership and mid-range are filled with recruits from lower social milieus who have risen in rank due to an increased value of battle bravery and combat strength in societies at war. The symbolic value of a warrior ethos makes vertical mobility within the ranks of the military apparatus possible. However, at the same time, these status gains are rather seldom seen – mostly occurring during early stages of conflict – and remain highly field-bound and volatile (cf. Bultmann 2014).

While the reconstitution of elite networks has not often been scrutinised by scholars, the process of becoming a perpetrator within the rank-and-file of an armed group is maybe one of the most-studied topics in academia dealing with the emergence of internal conflict. Countless studies have tried to understand the motives and mindset of perpetrators within the lowest ranks and the reasons why they participate in rebellions. Most are puzzled by the question of why an individual would risk his or her own life in combat. Which incentives, emotions, structural factors or discursive formations push people into armed groups, killing fellow human beings and risking their own deaths? For more than a decade, the discussion revolved around whether conflicts are caused either by grievances among justice-seeking ethnic, political or religious groups (Gurr 1970; Cederman et al. 2013) or greed, in which economic circumstances make participation in collective violence perfectly rational and beneficial for the individual (Collier 2000; Fearon and Laitin 2003; Collier and Hoeffler 2004). Greed theories have tried to calculate the conditions under which it becomes rational for an individual to personally engage in collective violence; this as opposed to staying away from the violence and simply hoping for a group to succeed in its striving for justice or to deliver public goods (the so-called free rider problem; for a critique, compare Kalyvas and Kocher 2007).

However, perpetrators in civil wars are not just young, unemployed men in search of economic profit with nothing to lose – or "loose molecules" as Robert D. Kaplan (2001) famously called them. By contrast, current research points to the complexity of motives and processes leading to civil war participation. Within the latest micro-political turn, studies have not speculated upon motives

102 *Daniel Bultmann*

of rebels by analysing macro-sociological and economic data. Instead, they have used surveys and qualitative interviews with former belligerents in order to better understand their motives and the logic behind different patterns of violence (most notably Kalyvas 2006; Weinstein 2007; Weinstein and Humphreys 2008). Instead of uncovering an all-encompassing cause, current research increasingly points toward a multiplicity of motives for and drivers of collective violence, which may change over the course of a conflict and which differ from region to region (cf. Kalyvas 2006; Sanín 2012; Guichaoua 2012b).

At this time, scholars have dissected how economic motives intersect with grievances from marginalised groups and with attempts to gain political recognition, honour and respect or simply to attain a perspective for their own future (Wood 2003; Dietrich Ortega 2012; Kruglanski et al. 2014). Others are driven by the prospect of a better life, by the hope of achieving social security through membership in armed groups or by the desire to protect their own property (Kalyvas 2006: 173). Many are also driven by a perceived threat against their community and consider themselves protectors of themselves, their families and the local or national community (Sanín 2012; Chelpi-den Hamer 2012: 37–8). The desire for protection of one's own community is usually not just an abstract fear; rather, it is born out of the experience of state repression or outright violence.

For a long time, theorists did not take war into account as a cause for recruitment, though few members of armed groups are recruited when a war is not already in full swing (cf. Arjona and Kalyvas 2012). For many perpetrators within the rank-and-file, the experience of violence within their local communities as well as their own family and the wish to retaliate is of major importance (Fujii 2009; Balcells 2010). Others enter armed groups for their own physical protection. In times of war, an armed group might be the safest place to be (Nordstrom 1992: 271; Kalyvas and Kocher 2007). Instead of reflecting deeply felt commitment to the official cause, entry into an armed group is oftentimes driven by a desire to survive the exigencies created by the war itself or to receive essential social, economic or even medical goods (Guichaoua 2012b). The exigencies of war thereby create conditions through which war becomes perpetuated, leading to its own escalation. The exigencies of civil war also call a too narrow focus on individual motives into question. One simple reason for this is that, in many conflicts, forced recruitment and even abduction is common. This factor has long been ignored (cf. Weinstein and Humphreys 2008). Quite often, these recruits are minors whose abduction is part of a close-knit socialisation into violence (Borzello 2009: 152–3).

Therefore, it is not just the individual's motive to join that is decisive but also his or her respective *mode of access*. Recruitment into armed groups does not always consist of a centrally coordinated policy from above that is met by a rational decision made by socially 'loose molecules' from below after profound deliberation. First, in many conflicts the line between being a full-time member of a rebellion, a part-time supporter, combatant, mercenary or someone joining for a brief period only (or who, at least, believes their membership is temporary) is difficult to draw (cf. Guichaoua 2012a). Second, rebellions do not merely make use of religious, political, communal and ethnic networks (Giustozzi 2008: 43–69)

The normality of going to war   103

but consist of and reproduce them. Usually armed groups consist of whole social networks that become militarised, not just at the top but also within lower ranks (Hoffman 2007; Staniland 2014). These networks can differ from one another heavily in terms of institutionalisation and possible peer group pressures at their disposal, which may include sport clubs, political circles, religious and ethnic groups or networks of friends and families. Many perpetrators refer to friends, contacts within association or clubs or a lengthy warrior history within their own family as their main reasons for joining an armed group (cf. Argo 2009; Schlichte 2014). Close solidarity bonds within the recruit's social milieu regulate access to armed groups. The networks lay out trajectories of access and also some basic patterns of disciplinary techniques securing loyalty to 'the cause.' People fight not just out of solidarity for their military unit or the overarching goals of the organisation but also for the members of their close social environment, whom they do not want to disappoint, whose pressure they feel, in whose (at least self-perceived) tradition they stand and whose norms and values they strive to support and protect.

Ana Arjona and Stathis Kalyvas (2012) conducted a study in which they compared the motives of perpetrators for joining Colombian insurgent groups as opposed to those joining the incumbent state military. The surprising result was that the motives do *not* differ significantly. Arjona and Kalyas tested whether motives would differ in terms of classical explanations for joining an armed rebellion (such as, for example, economic incentives or communal grievances). What they found instead was that spatial and social proximity is a very good predictor of whether someone joins a certain group and not another. The possibility and mode of access are decisive, i.e. whether a group's networks and institutions reach into the social milieu of a recruit or, quite simply, are within a spatial reach. According to Arjona and Kalyvas (2012), more than half of the perpetrators within the lowest ranks stated that they knew somebody within that group before joining who helped them to access the group – either the state military or the insurgency. Arjona and Kalyvas (2012) believe that the existence of an access route via one's close social milieu is a strong predictor for joining a particular military faction over another.

In this way the social structure of an armed group reproduces within its ranks the structure of the society they are part of, not only its different levels of institutionalisation and basic modes of securing loyalty but also its internal hierarchies. It is not by chance that positions within these groups are homologous with the position of the respective recruit within the society at large – no matter how socially revolutionary these groups appear (a comparison of a royalist, a republican and a communist insurgent group can be found in Bultmann 2015). The top command is filled with the military and political elite of the respective society, and the lowest ranks are filled with lower milieus accordingly. Thus, an important factor in why someone becomes a rank-and-file soldier – meaning one who is in charge of front-line perpetration – is his or her respective position within certain networks as well as the society at large. To use the words of Pierre Bourdieu (1986), it depends on one's cultural, economic and social capital and its symbolic valuation when accessing a group and, to a very limited degree, while being a

104 *Daniel Bultmann*

member of that group (e.g. through further training within a military school or the accumulation of symbolic capital as a strong, battle-hardened warrior).

Aspects of symbolic violence in participation and perpetration

But why do recruits accept their inferior social position as perpetrators within an armed group on top of risking their lives on the front line? Only a few join in order to kill or to be killed. And many studies point to the fact that the lowest ranks are usually the least ideologically firm members of these groups, with some only paying lip-service to the official, major cause of their side (cf. Kilcullen 2009). But nevertheless, most join and believe that they are simply the ones who 'somehow have to do it.' The reasons for this are manifold, but one of the least-mentioned is *symbolic violence*. According to this concept, ordinary perpetrators on the front line do not take up the inferior position of the ones who must do the fighting simply because they believe so strongly in the cause of the war and the goals of their leadership, because they are willing to die for the cause or because they hope to gain an economic benefit worth the risks. In fact, many regard it as somehow self-evident that it is their responsibility as 'ordinary men' to do it, as a result of their (essentially random) position within society.

For Pierre Bourdieu, symbolic violence means a complicity of the social agent in his own subjugation under power. Social agents mistakenly perceive the arbitrariness of social orders as naturally given and unchangeable: "Symbolic violence is misrecognised obedience in that symbolic power is accepted as legitimate rather than as an arbitrary imposition" (Swartz 2013: 83; cf. Bourdieu and Wacquant 1992). The soldier, for example, believes that it is normal for someone 'like him' to be the one to fight and that he has 'no choice' but to comply by dealing with his own reluctance and fears in combat. Power, here, is exercised not through physical force or a powerful disciplinary apparatus – such are often weakly developed in non-state armed groups – but through a symbolic order that is arbitrary but seen as legitimate and is therefore adhered to. The soldier makes himself obedient because he believes that he is an 'ordinary man' who is not in a position to question authority. Fears and reluctance are normal but must be dealt with in private. Being in a subjugate position is normal for many because, as a rank-and-file soldier phrased it in an interview with the author, they are just 'pedals' of power anyway (Interview with a KPNLAF section commander, cited in Bultmann 2015: 145). Or as another respondent put it: "We [as 'ordinary soldiers'] simply followed what we were meant to be" (Interview with a KPNLAF rank-and-file soldier, August 9, 2015, Battambang, Cambodia).

Even commanders are sometimes puzzled by how easy it is to recruit soldiers to fight for their cause since, as a regimental commander for the CGDK stated, for the rank-and-file soldiers, "because it is wartime (.) it is normal that they are recruited (.) to be a soldier of the resistance (.) to be a soldier of the resistance movement (1) so (.) there is no problem at all, you know," adding that it was simply "a logical choice" for them (Interview with a KPNLAF regimental commander, word by word transcription with each set of parentheses indicating a breathing pause and its duration, cited in Bultmann 2015: 136). In the end, becoming a soldier and engaging in perpetration is, in many cases, not perceived

The normality of going to war   105

as a personal choice at all but a necessary act that comes into being due to one's social status and the mere fact of living in a society at war. During interviews conducted by the author with soldiers of the CGDK, many stated that it was "just normal" to become a soldier and that the exigencies of war drove them into the insurgency: For example, they ended up in an armed group by chance during their flight to a refugee camp along the Thai-Cambodian border; they were tricked into joining; they saw no alternative besides joining due to the fact that this was the only way to receive food and shelter [this is especially the case for men in refugee settlements]; they were forced or pressured to join; or friends brought them in. Almost nobody in the lowest ranks even mentioned the official nationalist purpose (to fight the Vietnamese occupying Cambodia during the 1980s) or any personal hatred against ethnic Vietnamese as a motive for joining the resistance movement (Bultmann 2015: 136–8). War is not just embedded in an ongoing normality. Instead, it *is* that normality: one in which everyone takes up his position in the everyday life of a society at war (cf. Koloma Beck 2012).

In a famous study by Stouffer et al. (1949) on American soldiers serving in World War II, the scholars also pointed toward aspects of symbolic violence in which frontline soldiers similarly took the existence of war and their task to fight the enemy for granted:

> The combat soldier [. . .] was likely to feel that the war was worth fighting, though this does not mean that ideological considerations were often in the forefront of his mind. While he might express feelings of hatred toward the enemy, depending partly on which enemy he was fighting, his hatred was not particularly stable or consistent and does not appear to have been central to his motivation. In his everyday concerns, the combat man mostly took the existence of the war and the general task of fighting the enemy for granted. His position in the Army gave him no real choice. The issues behind the war were singularly unreal to him in contrast to the issues and exigencies of his day-to-day existence.
>
> (Stouffer et al. 1949: 167)

Or as Tarak Barkawi argued, citing Field Marshall Lord Wavell, it is time to decolonise our concept of war and perpetration, since: "many battles and campaigns have been won by men who had little idea of why they were fighting, and, perhaps cared less" (Barkawi 2015: 24).

With regard to a state military, such as the US Army that is fighting for a cause that 'we' as observers regard as a good and legitimate one, most would accept the existence of symbolic violence as one possible explanatory factor. However, this would be regarded as a poor excuse with regard to non-state military organisations in the so-called Global South fighting for a cause that seems illegitimate in the eyes of the beholder (e.g. terrorist networks, groups known for indiscriminate or mass violence). Depending on the legitimacy of the cause, symbolic violence and statements by perpetrators that they are not in the 'position' to question authority and therefore 'just followed orders' or have been 'cogs in a machine' become more or less accepted as an explanatory factor. However, this explanation

106   *Daniel Bultmann*

is usually regarded as too flat and banal; there must be a deeper reason for obedience in illegitimate non-state or 'bad' armed groups than symbolic violence, than symbolic complicity among rank-and-file perpetrators believing that it is self-evident that they should be the ones who kill and die on the front line. The question, however, is whether this might be a matter of perspective, albeit to a varying degree. Parts of it might be attributed to the ethics of the scholar rather than the actual motivation of the perpetrator.

The role of a legitimate, symbolic order in perpetration is also exemplified within Stanley Milgram's (1974) classical study on obedience. Milgram invited volunteers to participate in a study of learning at Yale University. In a laboratory, the participants were told to administer electronic shocks to a student every time he failed to memorise a word pair. With each failure, the participant was told to increase the voltage, starting with 15 and ending with as many as 450 volts. The device used to administer the shocks did so through electrodes attached to the students' arms. These electrodes carried warnings such as *extreme intensity shock* (at 255 volts), *danger: severe shock* (at 375 volts), culminating in *X X X* (at 435 to 450 volts). The student was sitting on a chair behind a glass pane. The participant, however, did not know that the student was actually a confederate of Milgram; the student was only simulating increasing desperation and screams of severe pain. If the participant refused to administer a shock, a 'scientist,' who was watching from the back, was to give a series of 'prods' to ensure the participant continued (e.g. "please continue" or "the experiment requires you to continue"). Two-thirds (65 per cent) of the participants continued to administer shocks up to the highest level of 450 volts. One of the decisive factors ensuring obedience within this experimental setting is the legitimacy of the situation and the demands made by the scientists (cf. Haslam and Reicher 2012). The number of compliant participants, for example, was lower in a setting in which two 'scientists' were attending the experiment and started to argue with each other about whether it was justifiable to carry on, with one leaving the laboratory and the other staying and prodding the participant to continue.

However, while obeying until the end, Milgram's participants very often showed signs of discomfort and reluctance to deliver the shocks. Although they went on and, thus, conformed to authority, many asked the scientists whether it was really necessary to continue; others trembled and sweated heavily, expressed discomfort or even tried to avoid giving shocks by helping the student in secret or by pretending to administer shocks. Many also remarked that the responsibility lay with the scientists and made clear that they were only following orders, thereby relieving themselves from psychological distress, emotional barriers and moral reluctance. These strategies come to the fore through the concept of symbolic violence. Perpetrators use strategies of noncompliance to circumvent authority at certain points and, in a seeming paradox, to make themselves docile in order to deal with their own position within the order of violence that – in its fundamentals – goes unquestioned. Perpetrators use manifold strategies to make themselves docile and to relieve themselves from moral and psychological reluctance. These are not just moral excuses but also *strategies of self-discipline*. Perpetrators thereby take

The normality of going to war   107

part in their own subjugation under an arbitrary but naturalised symbolic order. The same can be found with soldiers serving on the front line who are in charge of combat perpetration.

Making yourself docile: self-discipline

While combat is frightening, a widespread stereotype of soldiers is that of loyal automatons who, when properly drilled, become disciplined and obedient machines that (re-)act without a thought during battle. However, the official US army historian S.L.A. Marshall made a much-disputed discovery during World War II: Although faced with life-threatening danger in the dugout, most of the soldiers were reluctant to fight or even to make use of their weapons (Marshall 1947). According to Marshall, only up to 25 per cent of soldiers actually shot their weapon at least once – and not necessarily in the direction of the enemy. Fear and incompetence are constant companions on the battlefield. All of a sudden, actual combat becomes an unlikely event: Soldiers do not fight fiercely and desperately for their own survival, nor do they react like drilled automatons after long-term professional training in the US army. In the field of 'combat studies,' this revelation of the "human element" (Grossman 1995; Bourke 1999) instigated a lengthy debate with further elaborations, criticisms and sometimes even outright rejections of the findings as a complete fabrication (primarily by US veterans, as one might expect). Even though Marshall's barely testable estimates might not be empirically correct, the core problem for state as well as non-state armed groups remains: How can soldiers be made to fight?

Even with a high level of motivation, the act of violence itself poses a major problem for the agents, not just during war but also in smaller violent incidents. Randall Collins' micro-sociological approach to violent situations clarifies many 'myths' regarding violent encounters (2008: 10–19). The situation overwhelms the agent, particularly if he or she has no previous fighting experience. For the most part, violent situations are short in duration due to the fears of all persons involved and their incompetence in dealing with the situation. Even military battles tend to be short, and most participants try to get out of the situation as soon and as safely as possible. Most people, however, have not encountered violent situations in their lives and refer to images from movies when thinking of battles and skirmishes as lengthy. Our picture of a battle tends to be structured by myths regarding its intensity, duration, and the willingness of people to engage in fighting. Lengthy violent situations, if they do occur, are staged similarly to movies and follow well-known scripts and behavioural norms that each agent acknowledges and follows in detail (for example, in meetings between hooligans, each hooligan knows the rules regarding when, how and for how long to attack). Hence, fear of the unexpected is reduced by ritualisation.

Violence, as Collins puts it, is 'hard' and characterised by fear and incompetence, which is why basing explanations of violent behaviour on an agent's motivation is short-sighted: "My objection across the board is that such explanations assume violence is easy once the motivation exists. Micro-situational evidence, to

108 *Daniel Bultmann*

the contrary, shows that violence is hard" (Collins 2008: 20). Therefore, conflict cannot fully explain violence and its emergent dynamics: "Conflict, even quite overtly expressed conflict, is not the same as violence, and taking the last step is not at all automatic" (ibid.). Against greed or grievance theories, Collins holds that even though a group might have a motivation (e.g. oppression or money), violence does not necessarily follow. Oftentimes, conflicting parties exchange threats in order to avoid violent situations. Lust for violence, as Collins suggests (in line with Milgram), increases with the distance between the perpetrator and the victim, and people on the 'home front' tend to depict their enemies in a much more inhuman manner than soldiers would (Collins 2008: 66).

Perpetrators in settings of organised violence need to overcome emotional barriers, moral reluctance and fear during perpetration. Whereas disciplinary systems designed to make soldiers obedient are already well-studied, self-disciplinary techniques that silently maintain power within armed groups of all sorts have seldom been explicitly scrutinised. The fact that many non-state armed groups possess disciplinary apparatuses that are only weakly developed, if at all, shows that obedience, and with it resistance, are always the product of an interplay between individual motives, the disciplinary apparatus within the respective group and self-disciplinary techniques that are enacted in order to accommodate being a perpetrator in a setting of collective violence. The remainder of this chapter sketches some of the many possible techniques used to discipline the perpetrator's self.

Routinisation

Possibly the most effective technique to discipline the self is routinisation: exposing oneself to combat again and again in order to develop a combat routine. To do so, it may be enough to just shoot randomly, pulling the trigger without looking and without the intent to hit any target. A rank-and-file soldier for the CGDK phrased it as follows:

INTERVIEWER: How did you deal with your fear?
RESPONDENT: Shooting! Shooting back and forth! Although I did not even know whether I would hit any target.

> (Interview with a KPNLAF company commander,
> cited in Bultmann 2015: 140)

In the long run, combat becomes a habit, as another soldier stressed:

RESPONDENT: To avoid fear, I shot. After a while of shooting, we were no longer afraid. Without randomly shooting for a while, we couldn't calm ourselves down.
INTERVIEWER: Were you still afraid later on?
RESPONDENT: Not anymore. I don't know why. At first I was very afraid. But after shooting for a while, I wasn't anymore. I became so brave.

> (Interview with a KPNLAF battalion commander,
> cited in ibid.: 140–1)

The normality of going to war 109

Perpetrators who have not received much preparation or training rely heavily upon self-routinisation. However, while routinisation is a well-known phenomenon among perpetrators in general, many soldiers on the front line make use of the effect specifically to lower their fears.

Drugs

Some groups use drugs to lower the reluctance of their soldiers and to foster their dependence on their leaders (this is especially the case with children, cf. e.g. Honwanda 2006: 49–74). However, this is not just a disciplinary trick used by the leadership; drugs are also widely used by soldiers to deal with their fears during perpetration. Front-line perpetrators report that they use drugs specifically to numb themselves and, thus, make themselves able to face all kinds of danger. A CGDK combatant, for example, reported the following:

> We drank wine until we were able to see [i.e. to face and fight] all kinds of giants. That made us extreme. Without wine, we could not do it. [. . .] I always carried rice wine with me. No matter what happened, I had some with me.
> (Interview with a KPNLAF section commander,
> cited in Bultmann 2015: 146)

Not surprisingly, quantitative studies reveal that drugs are widely used and significantly increase the readiness of combatants to fight (cf. Hecker and van der Haer 2015).

Spiritual discipline

Spiritual and religious techniques are also used for self-rectification. Spiritual teachings and magical objects may lower fears and help to reduce moral scruples in killing others. While many perpetrators possess certain magical items, such as tattoos, handkerchiefs or talismans, and believe in magical spells and chants of all sorts, these oftentimes go hand in hand with disciplinary rules or codes of conduct (cf. Ellis 2001). Many combatants believe that the effectiveness of these items depends on the possessor's adherence to certain behavioural rules. In the end, it is not merely the item itself but adherence to personal ethics and even to certain diets and hygiene that make a warrior powerful and strong:

> All rebels wore cotton strings around the wrist and around the neck and shoulder. They all displayed black tattoos on the arm, slightly below the shoulder. They believed that any person who wore these talismans and tattoos, and strictly adhered to the laws of not eating pumpkin, having sex, touching lime and taking a bath, could not be killed in battle by enemy fire.
> (Cited in Ellis 2003: 1)

Only those who possess magical items and who, at the same time, constantly adhere to specific codes of conduct connected with these items (including rather

110 *Daniel Bultmann*

worldly rules, such as what to eat or touch) are bulletproof. Those who die despite possessing powerful items simply did not follow the code of conduct properly, thereby negating its effectiveness and protective powers. This was outlined by a CGDK combatant thusly:

> There was a guy, who was bulletproof. But later on he cursed me, so I said he would not live much longer. I only said that. One day, he betrayed the commander and pointed the gun at [name of commander], so our group chased him and shot him dead in spite of having tattoos all over his body. This means that only as long as he was strictly obedient to the rules, he was bulletproof.
>
> (Interview with an ANS rank-and-file soldier, cited in Bultmann 2015: 149)

Morals of killing

Though the perpetrators may not question the reasons for war or their own role within it, killing still clashes with most of their personal ethics. Many develop certain morals of killing that are there to guide their perpetration and to make them believe in their own moral superiority despite being the ones in charge of killing others. Within these morals of killing, as Harald Welzer (2005) termed them (*Tötungsmoral* in German), it is possible to prove decency and personal quality while having to kill others. Welzer exemplifies this morale with a famous quote by Heinrich Himmler, who was in charge of the *Schutzstaffel* (Protection Squadron, SS) within the Nazi regime:

> I believe gentlemen that you know me well enough to know that I am not a bloodthirsty person; I am not a man who takes pleasure or joy when something rough must be done. However, on the other hand, I have such good nerves and such a developed sense of duty – I can say that much for myself – that when I recognise something as necessary, I can implement it without compromise.
>
> (English translation as cited in Longerich 2003: reference 19.17, cf. Welzer 2005: 23)

The point here, according to Welzer, is that this morale includes scruples regarding the killing of others. These scruples, however, do not prevent the act of killing but morally elevate the perpetrator, proving their personal decency. Scruples, disgust and shame become part of a heroic gesture that – and this is the main point – still does not prevent the perpetrator from perpetration. Much to the contrast, it supports its execution.

Whereas Himmler's ethics are reflected within the Nazis' genocidal morals, combat soldiers oftentimes develop morals of killing that seem to conflict with the organisational goals and ethics of the armed group to which they belong. However, these serve the same function: enabling the individual to kill people while still believing in his or her own moral superiority. Some, for example, point toward their rule of sparing certain groups of possible victims (e.g. children;

civilians; members of certain social, religious or ethnic groups; or those who are afraid). This, in their own view at least, sets them above others who are more brutish. Their actions are pure(r) in comparison:

> Some commanders were so brutal. When an enemy got shot in his leg and might even survive with some help by others, they would shoot them right away. For me, by contrast, I would ask the wounded whether they are Khmer or Vietnamese. If he was Khmer, I would help him to survive. If he wasn't, I wouldn't help. That was my approach.
>
> (Interview with a KPNLAF group commander, cited in Bultmann 2015: 142)

Sparing Khmer soldiers diverted the perpetrator's attention away from the fact that they were killing others toward an act of mercy that was demonstrative of the personal quality of the perpetrator. By guiding their behaviour through ethics like these, perpetrators use a technique of self-rectification: They lower their reluctance to kill certain people by sparing others who are not worth it or who could not be properly identified as either Khmer or Vietnamese in the heat of combat. On the one hand, they are, to an extent, resisting orders to fight the enemy, thereby correcting minor wrongs of the larger order of which they are part of. On the other hand, they are not questioning the general task of perpetration within the naturalised order, and their ethics of mercy help to foster their willingness to kill others. Sparing some potential victims to prove one's decency leads to both the refusal of and the compliance with orders.

Refusal of orders – and their dialectics

Having said this, it remains nevertheless clear that soldiers are not powerless pedals of power. The most evident and probably most common form of noncompliance would be defection. Defection is not necessarily a means for soldiers to secure themselves a better life outside of an armed group; however, many defect in order to improve their conditions as a soldier, hence defecting only to a different commander. In so doing, they do not alter their position within the lowest rank of the military and within the wartime order of society, but they aim to improve their living conditions as rank-and-file combatants. Mobility within the military field remains horizontal.

Besides defection, perpetrators use various micro-strategies to bypass orders and to accommodate commands that they regard as unacceptable. While refusing orders in front of a commander can be dangerous – as is defection – many perpetrators opt for more or less invisible acts of noncompliance. For example, soldiers may shoot in the air instead of shooting at the enemy. They may hide in fear during combat (Grossman 1995: 18–40). Some may even stage combat when they meet someone on the other side whom they know:

INTERVIEWER: Did you ever face a situation where you did not want to shoot your enemy during combat situations?

112   *Daniel Bultmann*

RESPONDENT: When we met someone we knew, we did not shoot.
INTERVIEWER: What could you do to avoid shooting him?
RESPONDENT: We simply shot into the sky.
INTERVIEWER: Weren't you afraid that it could be revealed?
RESPONDENT: No. You might wonder, how could we know whether somebody else knew whether we were actually fighting? They only knew through their radio transmitters. Both sides [one's own unit and the enemy's unit] knew that, so we both just shot into the sky.

> (Author's interview with a KPNLAF battalion commander
> at Borvel, Cambodia, March 4, 2012)

Sometimes the disciplinary apparatus of armed groups is too tightly knit, leaving only drastic measures as options to avoid combat. A former Khmer Rouge combatant, for example, reported that he tried to hurt himself:

> I was trying to shoot myself in the lap in a way that would not hurt the bone. I checked myself over. The bullet could hit the flesh, but not the bone because it could cause amputation. I shot myself in the lap like this. The bullet did not get through my flesh. It did not hurt me. Therefore, I thought to myself that I had to find another way to hurt myself. I starved myself for three days.

> (Suoy 2011)

Power is never exhaustive. Absolute obedience remains a chimera. However, such strategies of noncompliance are "weapons of the weak" (Scott 1985) that do not alter the position of the perpetrator but – at best – ameliorate the worst effects of power on his or her daily life. In so doing, they leave the individual's role as the perpetrator unquestioned, thereby fostering obedience to command.

Discussion

Within the context of collective violence, not many people who strive for perpetration do so because they are especially willing to die or kill or because they are very different from 'ordinary' people. Instead, as this chapter has argued, symbolic violence is an important factor for why people end up being in charge of perpetration. Armed groups reproduce the internal hierarchy of the society they are a part of and, more specifically, of social networks that are being militarised. People within these networks do not take up their positions as perpetrators simply because they crave money or want to kill people they hate. They also do it because they come from lower social milieus from which it is rather *normal* to be recruited as combat soldiers within the lowest spheres of an armed group. Symbolic violence here means misrecognised obedience whereby an arbitrarily imposed symbolic power and the resulting social order are accepted as legitimate or simply beyond one's own agency.

Though the social order of an armed group and the task of fighting the enemy oftentimes go unquestioned, perpetrators accommodate this ultimately arbitrary

The normality of going to war   113

but naturalised imposition using techniques of self-rectification. Part of this self-rectification is also to idealise being battle-hardened and not to show signs of 'improper' idealism:

> The core of the attitude among combat men seemed to be that any talk that did not subordinate idealistic values and patriotism to the harsher realities of the combat situation was hypocritical, and a person who expressed such ideas a hypocrite. The usual term by which disapproval of idealistic exhortation was invoked was 'bullshit', which conveyed a scornful expression of the superiority of the combat man's hard-earned, tough-minded point of view.
>
> (Stouffer et al. 1949: 150)

Attitudes like these idealise the inferior position of the combat soldier at times of war and, amongst other effects, help to accommodate perpetration.

To look for deeply hidden motives or a certain discourse among perpetrators in societies at war, therefore, might be a misplaced exercise as long as one expects to gather 'the' motive or even *the* reason for war. Perpetrators in armed groups are very different from those who might be called 'lone-wolf perpetrators.' By contrast, in order to understand the formation and the maintenance of an armed group, the whole organisation with its tripartite hierarchies, its trajectories of access for diverse social milieus and the whole course of conflict with its different stages need to be taken into account. Current research has already started to dissect the inner workings of armed groups, providing ever greater insight into the complex structure and dynamics of organisations at war. The concept of symbolic violence adds nothing more and nothing less than the basic principle of social structuration on which all of this operates: the glue that keeps these organisations together and allocates people to the positions that they are 'entitled to.' It is not decisive to speculate on what people actually are (ordinary or extra-ordinary in any sense), but that they are perceived as and perceive themselves as 'ordinary people – doing ordinary things during extra-ordinary times.' To a certain degree, their participation as perpetrators of violence becomes a matter of an ascribed and incorporated status within lower segments of society: nothing special, just 'normal people' – a caste that is in charge of doing the polluted, the 'dirty' work of warfare.

References

Alden, Chris. "Making Our Soldiers Fade Away: Lessons from the Reintegration of Demobilized Soldiers in Mozambique." *Security Dialogue* 33, no. 3 (2002): 341–56.

Argo, Nichole. "Why Fight? Examining Self-Interested Versus Communally-Oriented Motivations in Palestinian Resistance and Rebellion." *Security Studies* 18, no. 4 (2009): 651–80.

Arjona, Ana M., and Stathis N. Kalyvas. "Recruitment into Armed Groups in Colombia." In *Understanding Collective Political Violence*, edited by Yvan Guichaoua, 143–71. New York: Palgrave Macmillan, 2012.

Balcells, Laia. "Rivalry and Revenge: Violence Against Civilians in Conventional Civil Wars." *International Studies Quarterly* 54, no. 2 (2010): 291–313.

114 *Daniel Bultmann*

Barkawi, Tarak. "Subaltern Soldiers: Eurocentrism and the Nation-State in the Combat Motivation Debates." In *Frontline: Combat and Cohesion in the Twenty-First Century*, edited by Anthony King, 24–45. Oxford: Oxford University Press, 2015.

Borzello, Anna. "The Challenge of DDR in Northern Uganda: The Lord's Resistance Army." In *Reintegrating Armed Groups After Conflict: Politics, Violence and Transition*, edited by Mats Berdal and David H. Ucko, 144–77. New York: Routledge, 2009.

Bourdieu, Pierre. "The Forms of Capital." In *Handbook of Theory and Research for the Sociology of Education*, edited by John G. Richardson, 241–58. New York: Greenwood Press, 1986.

Bourdieu, Pierre, and Loïc J. D. Wacquant. *An Invitation to Reflexive Sociology*. Chicago and London: University of Chicago Press, 1992.

Bourke, Joanna. *An Intimate History of Killing*. London: Granta Books, 1999.

Browning, Christopher. *Ordinary Men: Reserve Police Battalion 101 and the Final Solution in Poland*. New York: HarperCollins, 1992.

Bultmann, Daniel. "Analyzing the Cambodian Insurgency as a Social Field." *Small Wars & Insurgencies* 25, no. 2 (2014): 457–78.

Bultmann, Daniel. *Inside Cambodian Insurgency: A Sociological Perspective on Civil Wars and Conflict*. Burlington, VT and Farnham: Ashgate, 2015.

Cederman, Lars-Erik, Kristian S. Gleditsch, and Halvard Buhaug. *Inequality, Grievances, and Civil War*. Cambridge: Cambridge University Press, 2013.

Chelpi-den Hamer, Magali. "Militarized Youth in Western Côte d'Ivoire: Who Are They? Why Did They Fight?" In *Understanding Collective Political Violence*, edited by Yvan Guichaoua, 21–45. New York: Palgrave Macmillan, 2012.

Collier, Paul. "Doing Well Out of Civil War: An Economic Perspective." In *Greed and Grievance: Economic Agendas in Civil Wars*, edited by Mats Berdal and David M. Melone, 91–111. Boulder, CO and London: Lynne Rienner, 2000.

Collier, Paul, and Anke Hoeffler. "Greed and Grievance in Civil War." *Oxford Economic Paper – New Series* 61, no. 1 (2004): 1–27.

Collins, Randall. *Violence: A Micro-Sociological Theory*. Princeton, NJ: Princeton University Press, 2008.

Dietrich Ortega, Luisa Maria. "Gendered Patterns of Mobilization and Recruitment for Political Violence: Experiences from Three Latin American Countries." In *Understanding Collective Political Violence*, edited by Yvan Guichaoua, 84–104. New York: Palgrave Macmillan, 2012.

Ellis, Stephen. "Mystical Weapons: Some Evidence from the Liberian War." *Journal of Religion in Africa* 31, no. 2 (2001): 222–36.

Ellis, Stephen. *Young Soldiers and the Significance of Initiation: Some Notes from Liberia*. Leiden: Afrika-Studiecentrum, 2003.

Fearon, James, and David Laitin. "Ethnicity, Insurgency and Civil War." *American Political Science Review* 97, no. 1 (2003): 75–90.

Fujii, Lee A. *Killing Neighbors: Webs of Violence in Rwanda*. Ithaca, NY: Cornell University Press, 2009.

Giustozzi, Antonio. *Koran, Kalashnikov and Laptop: The Neo-Taliban Insurgency in Afghanistan*. New York: Columbia University Press, 2008.

Grossman, Dave. *On Killing: The Psychological Cost of Learning to Kill in War and Society*. New York: Back Bay Books, 1995.

Guichaoua, Yvan. "Circumstantial Alliances and Loose Loyalties in Rebellion Making: The Case of Tuareg Insurgency in Northern Niger (2007–2009)." In *Understanding Collective Political Violence*, edited by Yvan Guichaoua, 246–66. New York: Palgrave Macmillan, 2012a.

The normality of going to war   115

Guichaoua, Yvan. "Introduction: Individual Drivers of Collective Violence and the Dynamics of Armed Groups." In *Understanding Collective Political Violence*, edited by Yvan Guichaoua, 1–18. New York: Palgrave Macmillan, 2012b.

Gurr, Ted. *Why Men Rebel*. Princeton, NJ: Princeton University Press, 1970.

Haslam, S. Alexander, and Stephen D. Reicher. "Contesting the 'Nature' of Conformity: What Milgram's and Zimbardo's Studies Really Show." *PLOS Biology* 10, no. 11 (2012): 1–4.

Hecker, Tobias, and Roos van der Haer. "Drugs Boosting Conflict? A Micro-Level Test of the Linkage Between Substance Use and Violence." *Terrorism and Political Violence* 27, no. 2 (2015): 205–24.

Hoffman, Danny. "The Meaning of Militia: Understanding the Civil Defence Forces of Sierra Leone." *African Affairs* 106, no. 425 (2007): 639–62.

Honwanda, Alcinda. *Child Soldiers in Africa*. Philadelphia: University of Pennsylvania Press, 2006.

Kalyvas, Stathis. "The Urban Bias in Research on Civil Wars." *Security Studies* 13, no. 3 (2006): 160–90.

Kalyvas, Stathis, and Matthew A. Kocher. "How 'Free' Is Free Riding in Civil Wars? Violence, Insurgency, and the Collective Action Problem." *World Politics* 59, no. 2 (2007): 177–216.

Kaplan, Robert. *Coming Anarchy: Shattering the Dreams of the Post Cold War*. New York: Vintage Books, 2001.

Kilcullen, David. *The Accidental Guerrilla: Fighting Small Wars in the Midst of a Big One*. Oxford: Oxford University Press, 2009.

Koloma Beck, Teresa. *The Normality of Civil War: Armed Groups and Everyday Life in Angola*. Frankfurt and New York: Campus, 2012.

Kruglanski, Arie W., Michele J. Gelfand, Jocelyn J. Belanger, Anna Sheveland, Malkanthi Hetiarachichi, and Rohan Gunaratna. "The Psychology of Radicalization and Deradicalization: How Significance Quest Impacts Violent Extremism." *Advances in Political Psychology* 35, Supplement S1 (2014): 69–93.

Longerich, Heinz. *Hitler's Role in the Persecution of the Jews by the Nazi Regime*. Electronic Version. Lewis H. Beck Center for Electronic Collections: Emory University Atlanta, 2003.

Marshall, Samuel. *Men Against Fire: The Problem of Battle Command in Future War*. New York: Combat Force Press, 1947.

Milgram, Stanley. *Obedience to Authority: An Experimental View*. London: Tavistock, 1974.

Nordstrom, Carolyn. *The Paths to Domination, Resistance, and Terror*. Berkeley: University of California Press, 1992.

Sanín, Francisco G. "The Dilemmas of Recruitment: The Colombian Case." In *Understanding Collective Political Violence*, edited by Yvan Guichaoua, 175–95. New York: Palgrave Macmillan, 2012.

Schlichte, Klaus. *In the Shadow of Violence: The Politics of Armed Groups*. Frankfurt and New York: Campus, 2009.

Schlichte, Klaus. "When 'The Facts' Become a Text: Reinterpreting War with Serbian War Veterans." *Revue de synthèse* 135, no. 4 (2014): 1–24.

Scott, James. *Weapons of the Weak: Everyday Forms of Peasant Resistance*. New Haven, CT: Yale University Press, 1985.

Staniland, Paul. *Networks of Rebellion: Explaining Insurgent Cohesion and Collapse*. New York: Cornell University Press, 2014.

Stouffer, Samuel A., Edward A. Suchman, Leland C. DeVinney, Shirley A. Star, and Robin M. Williams, Jr. *The American Soldier: Combat and Its Aftermath*. Vol. II. Princeton, NJ: Princeton University Press, 1949.

116 *Daniel Bultmann*

Suoy, Lat. *Interview by Dany Long, Documentation Center of Cambodia, Interview Series, no. 3.* 18 May 2011.

Swartz, David. *Symbolic Power, Politics, and Intellectuals: The Political Sociology of Pierre Bourdieu.* Chicago and London: University of Chicago Press, 2013.

Tilly, Charles. *The Politics of Collective Violence.* Cambridge: Cambridge University Press, 2003.

Weinstein, Jeremy. *Inside Rebellion: The Politics of Insurgent Violence.* Cambridge: Cambridge University Press, 2007.

Weinstein, Jeremy, and Macartan Humphreys. "Who Fights? The Determinants of Participation in Civil War." *American Journal of Political Science* 52, no. 2 (2008): 436–55.

Welzer, Harald. *Täter. Wie aus ganz normalen Menschen Massenmörder werden.* Frankfurt am Main: S. Fischer, 2005.

Wood, Elisabeth Jean. *Insurgent Collective Action and Civil War in El Salvador.* Cambridge: Cambridge University Press, 2003.

6 "We no longer pay heed to humanitarian considerations"

Narratives of perpetration in the Wehrmacht, 1941–44

David Harrisville

Introduction

In the aftermath of the Second World War, the legacy of the Wehrmacht – the German military – survived relatively unscathed. Veterans and their defenders insisted that the armed forces had fought honorably and avoided participation in Nazi crimes. Over the past several decades, however, this version of events, now known as the myth of the 'clean Wehrmacht,' has crumbled under intense scrutiny. Nowhere has this been more apparent than in the case of Germany's invasion of the Soviet Union, where the largest number of its soldiers fought. Historians now characterize the conflict as a war of extermination aimed at destroying 'Jewish-Bolshevism' and securing a vast empire in the East. In pursuit of these goals, the army deliberately starved to death over three million Soviet POWs, executed political functionaries, reduced thousands of villages to ashes, and terrorized the local population, whom the Nazis considered racially inferior and therefore expendable. Army units were also instrumental in carrying out the Final Solution. The Wehrmacht is now understood as a willing partner of the Nazi regime, one that eagerly waged a criminal war in accordance with Hitler's plans.

There is a vast literature on the subject of perpetrators in the Third Reich, from doctors who assisted in euthanasia programs to concentration camp guards. It is only fairly recently, however, that scholars have focused their attention on the killing fields in the East, where the majority of the regime's victims met their fate (Snyder 2010). Much of this interest has been generated by the work of Christopher Browning and Daniel Goldhagen, who studied the practice of genocide within an SS reserve police battalion tasked with murdering Jews in Poland (Browning 1992; Goldhagen 1996). Whereas Goldhagen cited a tradition of hate-filled antisemitism among the killers, Browning emphasized the importance of group dynamics and authority structures that led 'ordinary men' to engage in barbarism. More recent scholarship on the Wehrmacht has continued to highlight situational factors while also citing Nazi racial ideology as perhaps the single most powerful factor in explaining soldiers' willing participation in crimes (Bartov 1985, 1991; Heer and Naumann 2000; Wette 2006; Beorn 2014). Research on Wehrmacht perpetrators, however, has been hampered by a lasting focus on upper-level decision makers and a lack of attention to how individual soldiers reflected on their actions during the war.

118 *David Harrisville*

Social psychologists have also been active in the debate over the dynamics of criminal violence. Most have rejected an emphasis on personal predispositions in favor of a situationist model that holds that anyone could become a killer under the right circumstances (Miller 2004). Such an approach, however, tends to discount the role of ideas, as well as historical forces, and frequently overlooks the issue of perpetrators' self-understanding. Another method has been to investigate how individuals rationalize their behavior and insulate their moral identities. Albert Bandura and others (1996), for instance, have identified several "mechanisms of moral disengagement," including the demonizing of victims and denial of personal responsibility, that help individuals deal with the effects of cognitive dissonance. Similarly, Claude Steele (1988) has argued that as long as they maintain an affirmative self-concept, individuals can violate social norms with few psychological consequences. These theories offer a promising line of inquiry into perpetrator psychology but have not been examined in a wartime context.

This chapter explores perpetrators and criminal violence in the Wehrmacht during Germany's war with the Soviet Union from 1941 to 1944. Rather than focus on the much-studied question of why soldiers took part in crimes, I combine the close empirical study of historical sources, social-psychological theories centered on moral rationalization, and an attention to the role of ethics and morality to investigate how Wehrmacht perpetrators thought and wrote about their actions and what they thought about themselves. Without dismissing the importance of situational factors or the role of ideology, I argue that in order to understand soldiers' descent into complicity it is crucial to understand the moral and psychological processes by which they managed to exonerate themselves from any sense of guilt, as well as how they attempted to maintain identities as 'decent men.' This chapter is divided into three parts, each devoted to a distinct area of inquiry: how soldiers rationalized a range of specific crimes from theft to mass murder, how they justified the war of extermination as a whole, and, finally, how they constructed and presented their moral identities.

In order to explore these questions, this chapter draws from a sample of 2,000 letters written by thirty Wehrmacht soldiers, as well as several diaries. Most of these materials are housed in the *Museumsstiftung Post und Telekommunikation*, managed by the *Museum für Kommunikation* in Berlin, and have not yet been examined by scholars. They represent a fraction of the roughly forty billion letters sent between the German front and home front (Fritz 1995). Unlike other letter collections, the *Museumsstiftung* has preserved a large number of letters for each writer, allowing for a deeper look into individual attitudes and experiences. From its corpus, I selected a sample of low-ranking soldiers from all sectors of the Eastern Front that captured the diversity of economic, social, religious, and political backgrounds present in the Wehrmacht. Not every man in this chapter can be considered a perpetrator in the strictest sense – defined here as having personally taken part in actions that violated German or international law – but as members of an organization that dutifully carried out Hitler's will, all can be considered complicit to various degrees in his genocidal project, and all but a few described personally witnessing or committing atrocities. Studying their writings does not

Perpetration in the Wehrmacht   119

necessarily provide a direct window into soldiers' motives, particularly since they sought to preserve a certain self-image for their readers and because their letters were censored for signs of defeatism or political unreliability. However, these sources offer a means to study the rationalizations perpetrators adopted and the narratives they presented to the German homeland.

Legitimating atrocities

Despite their awareness of the army's censorship, many German soldiers were relatively open in describing the crimes their side committed, and even occasionally admitted their personal involvement. This section explores what Wehrmacht perpetrators wrote to their loved ones about these atrocities. It demonstrates that perpetrators offered their families a diverse range of explanations for why they and their comrades joined in criminal activity on the micro level. Though some soldiers invoked racial hierarchies, most rationalized specific atrocities with arguments based on less ideological factors, including local circumstances, the actions of their enemies, military imperatives, and personal need. Their rationalizations helped the perpetrators overcome moral and psychological inhibitions, dehumanized victims, and diminished any sense of personal guilt while at the same time presenting their loved ones in the homeland with a distorted narrative of the Wehrmacht's actions in Russia.

From the euphoric weeks of early German victories to the catastrophic defeats of the war's final years, Wehrmacht perpetrators frequently represented their side's atrocities as legitimate responses to what they dubbed illegal or immoral enemy actions. For instance, they regularly depicted the murder of prisoners – a relatively common practice on the Eastern Front – as retaliation for the ferocity of enemy resistance or crimes they attributed to the Red Army. A few weeks into the invasion, Fritz F.,[1] on the road to Smolensk with the 7th Panzer Division, revealed to his wife that he and his comrades shot every political functionary they captured.[2] By way of explanation, he expressed his disgust that Soviet officials lived well while their population suffered, and added that they frequently attacked German troops after pretending to surrender.[3] A month later, private Hans Albring described to a friend in uniform how he had twice witnessed how German troops led captured Soviet snipers to a ditch and shot them one by one in the back of the head. Albring found the murders disturbing but hinted that the victims had deserved this treatment because of their misdeeds, writing, "[t]his is a . . . just end, when one knows the events that led up to it, however much one can argue about the methods."[4]

In subsequent years, German perpetrators in uniform turned to similar arguments in order to rationalize the murderous tactics they employed as they battled partisans behind the lines. These included rounding up and executing any civilians deemed suspicious, especially Jews, and responding to resistance activity with 'collective punishments' that included the wholesale destruction of entire communities. Most soldiers portrayed Soviet insurgents as little more than common criminals, 'bandits' who threatened the security of the entire region. Artilleryman Hans-Peter

120   *David Harrisville*

Eckener described them as a "plague" that constantly harried German soldiers.[5] In this context, he noted approvingly when fifteen partisans were hanged[6] and offered his parents a chilling description of the Germans' tactics: "While combing through the land in pursuit of such gangs entire villages are torched and all women and children completely wiped out," he explained.[7] His letters suggest that he, like other troops, considered this extreme use of violence a justifiable response to a dangerous and illegitimate partisan threat.

As they closed in on Moscow, Germany's men-at-arms ransacked whatever supplies they could find from already-impoverished local inhabitants, whom they also frequently pressed into service as forced laborers. Although racism was a major factor in their behavior, soldiers tended to favor other explanations when they wrote to their relatives. One common argument was that exploiting the population was the only means to survive, since supplies and manpower were often scarce. In the winter of 1941, Harald H., a private in the 23rd Infantry Division, described how he and several comrades entered a hut, where they stole the last potatoes of a woman and her children and then forced her to clean for them. Harald wrote that he was deeply disturbed by the scene that transpired, but cited his unit's lack of supplies: "[i]t was really terrible, but we also had to eat," he explained.[8] The Wehrmacht did occasionally suffer critical supply shortages, largely due to logistical difficulties, poor planning, and the determination by Nazi and army leaders that soldiers would "live off the land" rather than receive food from Germany (Müller 1984; Bartov 1991; Latzel 1998; Kay 2006). However, Wehrmacht perpetrators continued to take advantage of the defenseless population even when they were adequately supplied.

During the winter of 1941, the Red Army launched massive counterattacks to dislodge German forces from their positions outside Moscow. For many soldiers, the rest of the war consisted of desperate defensive battles and long retreats, during which they burned Russian settlements to the ground in "scorched-earth" actions and continued to employ violence against civilians or exploit their labor. Wehrmacht perpetrators justified these measures as the product of military necessity, claiming, as German military thinkers had long done, that any action was acceptable if it brought them closer to victory. In the winter of 1942, Johannes H. wrote his brother Willy that it had been necessary to drive the entire civilian population from their homes in his sector because doing so would deprive the partisans of necessary support,[9] while Rolf D. told a female acquaintance that the city of Orel had been "razed to the ground" so nothing could fall into enemy hands as the Germans retreated.[10] In the minds of perpetrators, the aim of winning the war was enough to justify any means.

Racism occasionally surfaced in soldiers' accounts as a rationale for German crimes, particularly when it came to the mistreatment of prisoners or the massacre of Jews. Employing language that echoed Nazi propaganda, Kurt N., who several times observed how starving POWs were packed onto open boxcars, described the captives as a lice-ridden "horde" who deserved no sympathy.[11] Willy S. explained to his love interest that because the Soviets fought so fanatically, he and his comrades "no longer pay heed to humanitarian considerations." Later on, after

Perpetration in the Wehrmacht 121

the death of several comrades, he asserted that the Russians deserved no mercy, "[s]ince they are in most cases beasts in human form."[12] Thinking of the enemy as biologically or culturally inferior helped ease the crossing of moral boundaries.[13]

As recent scholarship has shown, Wehrmacht units took an active role in the Final Solution (Wette 2006; Beorn 2014). When soldiers wrote about crimes against Jews, which they did only rarely, they invoked a combination of antisemitism and an insistence on their victims' guilt. In May of 1942, Heinz Sartorio approvingly informed his sister that "hundreds of thousands of Jews" had been executed in the East. A staunch anti-Semite, he admitted that the killings were shocking, "but when one thinks about the big idea, then one must say to oneself that it was necessary," he insisted.[14] After witnessing mass graves outside the Warsaw Ghetto in March, 1942, Kurt N. accused the victims of imaginary crimes: "they did not deserve any better," he penned, "since they murdered the Germans by the thousands."[15]

As months turned into years, Wehrmacht perpetrators wrote less and less about the atrocities their side committed. Although some had initially displayed shock, most eventually came to accept these occurrences as routine practice that no longer demanded explanation (Heer 2000). Günter Koschorrek, newly drafted in the war's second year, recalled in his memoirs that one of his more experienced comrades, Meinhard, shot Soviet prisoners out of hand. Meinhard explained to the newcomer that "this is the way of war," and that the Soviets did the same thing.[16]

Whether they accepted criminal violence as routine or expressed moral misgivings, the language German soldiers employed in their letters throughout the conflict made it easier for them to spin a narrative in which their enemies appeared worthy of punishment and their own responsibility retreated into the background. Euphemisms helped to mask the reality of the war of extermination: food was "organized" or "found" rather than stolen, "civilian" and "partisan" became interchangeable, and enemies were described as gangsters or animals rather than legitimate combatants. Such terminology served to dehumanize victims and obscure the harm they suffered, a strategy that has long been recognized by scholars of violence.

In addition, troops rarely admitted direct personal culpability for reprehensible behavior; instead, they laid the responsibility elsewhere, whether at the feet of other soldiers or the SS. Perpetrators wrote more openly of relatively minor acts of theft or the mistreatment of civilians while avoiding the subject of sexual violence or large-scale atrocities, even though the latter were widespread (Mühlhäuser 2010). They also tended to confine their rationales to whatever they believed their readers would find most comprehensible – instead of citing sadistic motives, for instance, they insisted that their actions were the product of sober judgment.

Their letters and diaries indicate that perpetrators in the Wehrmacht on the Eastern Front employed a broad spectrum of rationalizations to make sense of the crimes in which they were complicit. The validations they turned to, only a few of which are discussed here, accord well with practices social psychologists have identified as common in peacetime situations, and included blaming or dehumanizing the victims, construing violence as a necessary means to a desired

122 *David Harrisville*

end, and negating any sense of personal responsibility. The version of events they offered to their relatives at home obscured the extent of the army's criminal activity and their own involvement. Although many soldiers at first displayed a certain level of discomfort with the way the war was being waged, their writings suggest that Wehrmacht perpetrators proved adept at justifying their crimes and came to view atrocities as a 'normal' part of the war (Heer 2000). Significantly, only one soldier in this sample fell back on the excuse of "following orders" that would become prevalent in the postwar period.[17] Most Wehrmacht troops, it appears, had already convinced themselves of the legitimacy of their actions, as well as any orders behind them.

Justifying a criminal war

The invasion of the Soviet Union was a naked war of aggression against a country with which the Reich had concluded a peace accord just two years earlier. Having largely embraced Hitler's vision, German generals informed their troops that its purpose was to annihilate the Soviet regime, reduce its population to a state of servitude, and put an end to an imaginary Jewish danger. In spite of the knowledge that international law and humanitarian concerns would be cast aside, the men of the Wehrmacht swiftly came to the conclusion that the war was a legitimate and even noble undertaking. As motorcycle courier Franz Siebeler opined to his parents and siblings in late 1941, "this war against the criminal work of Bolshevism is the battle for a just cause."[18] Four years later, as the Wehrmacht retreated after having murdered millions of Soviet POWs and civilians, Willy H. still insisted that "[w]e must win, because we fight for the more worthy cause."[19]

As this section will illustrate, Wehrmacht perpetrators convinced themselves that the war of extermination they waged was both necessary and morally justified. Throughout the conflict, they relied on a diverse set of rationales to shore up this assertion, some based on official pronouncements and Nazi ideology, others derived from personal experience or long-held beliefs. These intellectual constructs facilitated soldiers' willing cooperation by redefining a criminal war as a righteous act or an existential struggle in which the ends justified the means. In the end, soldiers of all backgrounds, including true believers as well as skeptics of Nazism, arrived at ways of making sense of the war of extermination. And, as Stephen Fritz has argued, they justified the war not only as a means to annihilate dangerous enemies but also as a path to a brighter future (Fritz 1996).

According to the Nazi regime's official pronouncements, the invasion was a defensive measure to forestall the devastating attack on Germany that Moscow had supposedly been planning (Pietrow-Ennker 2011). This 'preemptive strike' rationale was repeated ad nauseam in the mainstream and army presses, as well as in the messages generals handed down to their men. Although it was little more than a fairy tale, a large proportion of the Wehrmacht's rank-and-file took this version of events at face value. Typical of many soldiers, Franz Siebeler declared to his family hours before the invasion that the Russians had violated the nonaggression pact and "only waited for the best opportunity to pounce on us."[20]

Perpetration in the Wehrmacht 123

As the conflict went on, the men who waged an aggressive war continued to insist on its defensive quality. In 1943, as the Red Army steadily drove the invaders back, sergeant Wilhelm A. told his family that, "it is still a thousand times better that we are here in Russia than if Bolshevism had overrun Germany."[21] The myth of its preventive nature retained widespread currency among veterans and the German public even long after the guns fell silent (Pietrow-Ennker 2011).

The Third Reich's leaders openly admitted, however, that staving off an ostensible Soviet attack was not the invasion's only purpose. They declared that the German nation needed to seize *Lebensraum* (living space); enslave or kill the "racially inferior" inhabitants of the Soviet Union; and destroy communism, which Hitler insisted was the centerpiece of a Jewish bid for world domination (Messerschmidt 1969; Bartov 1991; Wette 2006). Within Nazi ideology, then, the war figured as a legitimate act of conquest that would win the Reich new economic resources. It was also an existential conflict in which Germany would either eliminate dangerous racial enemies or be annihilated. Having spent much of their lives in Hitler's Germany, many soldiers embraced the Nazi view of the war, in whole or in part (Bartov 1991; Fritz 1995; Latzel 1998). Wilhelm Moldenhauser, for instance, agreed that the Germans faced a "Jewish-Bolshevik" threat. He told his wife that he envisioned "Ukraine and the borderlands of Russia" as "colonial possessions," and that the invaders would have to be stern masters.[22] Others compared the Russian people to "animals"[23] and registered their approval of the Final Solution.[24]

Religious justifications also played a role in how soldiers made sense of the invasion. Protestant and Catholic leaders in Germany often framed the war as a conflict between Christian Europe and "godless communism," as well as a chance to return religion to the USSR. The roughly one thousand chaplains who served in the Wehrmacht followed suit (Bergen 2001; Faulkner Rossi 2015). Although Nazi officials had little interest in a re-Christianized Russia, they tacitly encouraged a "crusade" mentality in their bid to generate public support (Wette 1984). It is not surprising, then, that devout soldiers often saw religious meaning in the war. Heinz Rahe, a former Protestant pastor who served in an armored division, wrote to his wife of his "hope . . . that in a free Ukraine perhaps also Christian preaching would be possible again. This wish is also a goal for me," he added, "for which it is worth fighting."[25] Although the Nazis increasingly restricted religious practice in the army, many soldiers continued to take comfort in the belief that they had a religious duty to put an end to the atheist regime.

Some of the most powerful justifications originated from soldiers' experiences over the course of four years in the Soviet Union. In their letters home, troops described a land of crushing poverty and state oppression that bore little resemblance to the "paradise of workers and farmers" of which its rulers had boasted. Kurt N., who like many others referred to Russia sarcastically as the "Soviet paradise," declared that Germans would be shocked if they witnessed the "conditions and the hand-to-mouth life of the inhabitants." He went on to remark that, "among us in Germany the stables are better than the houses here."[26] Hans-Peter Eckener agreed that "the fate of [the] Russian people is tragic and

124 *David Harrisville*

lamentable" and described them as "oppressed . . ., plundered, and left in poverty and ignorance" by Soviet leaders.[27] Witnessing social and economic conditions in the USSR proved, in the minds of many Wehrmacht servicemen, that the invasion had been fully justified, since only military force could put an end to Stalinist misery and prevent it from spreading to Germany. Many soldiers interpreted the poverty they encountered as a sign that the country was filled with threatening "sub-humans," as Nazi leaders had predicted. Some emphasized the welcome they received from certain quarters of the population and even began to entertain the notion that the German Army had come as a liberating force to lift the burden of communist tyranny.[28] This justification deviated sharply from Nazi ideology – Nazi authorities insisted that soldiers treat non-Aryans only as slaves – but in spite of this incongruity, styling themselves as heralds of freedom helped some perpetrators come to terms with their participation. Other justifications received further impetus from experience. Encountering the overwhelming might of the Red Army convinced many soldiers that the USSR had indeed been planning to attack. Walking the aisles of churches the Soviets had turned into movie theaters constituted ample proof that the enemy had nothing but contempt for religion.

Toward the war's end, the multiplicity of rationales that soldiers had clung to gave way to a singular concern with protecting the German homeland. The army's own actions had in fact created the very scenario its leaders had most feared: a massive Soviet force was now advancing toward Germany's border, eager to take revenge for four years of Wehrmacht atrocities on Russian soil. By 1943 and 1944, soldiers wrote overwhelmingly of the need to protect their homes and families from the Red juggernaut and insisted that a Soviet victory would mean the complete downfall of the German nation. "We will take care that the enemy cannot come to Germany, in order to lay waste to everything," Johannes H. assured his younger brother in October 1943.[29]

Understandably, historians have focused their attention on the 'negative' justifications for the war, particularly the Nazi call to destroy and conquer supposedly inferior races. Though many soldiers indeed relished the thought of laying waste to "Jewish-Bolshevism," a close examination of their writings throughout the conflict suggests that even more preferred to focus on 'positive' rationales for the conflict (Fritz 1996). Against all the evidence, they insisted that war was the only way to preserve the German nation and secure a better future for themselves and their families. "From the life-struggle that we now wage, our children will harvest," wrote Wilhelm Moldenhauser. "All sacrifices that we make, we make for our children."[30] The war "is about more than us," echoed Walter Neuser, "[w]e are now the generation that will bring the Reich a happy future."[31] Borrowing language that frequently appeared in propaganda, soldiers also spoke of the war as necessary for ensuring the survival of European civilization. Like many soldiers, former theology student Hans Wilhelm S. considered himself above all to be fighting for his nation, but he speculated that "through the blood shed mutually in battle" by Germany and her allies, "a Europe will be welded together" whose future he and his generation would shape.[32] In short, soldiers

Perpetration in the Wehrmacht 125

who yearned to find meaning in their sacrifices desperately held onto the illusion that the war would somehow make the world a better place.

The case of the Wehrmacht in Russia underscores the psychological importance of such illusions for the perpetrators of mass atrocities, illusions that framed the war as a noble act or an existential conflict in which any means were acceptable. Even though the invasion of the USSR had been totally unprovoked, and although it was waged as much against defenseless civilians as it was against an armed enemy, Wehrmacht soldiers managed consistently to justify their complicity and maintain a sense of self-righteousness mission. The rationales they clung to were as numerous as they were diverse, including not only the Nazi-inspired racism that has attracted the most scholarly attention, but also religious justifications and arguments regarding the injustice of the Soviet system. Soldiers of all backgrounds found myriad ways to make sense of their participation, whether they identified as avid Nazis or displayed little interest in ideology. In whatever form they took, the power of these intellectual constructs helps explain why, with the exception of a handful of individuals who began to question the German cause,[33] few veterans ever admitted wrongdoing.

Constructing 'decency'

Scholarly work over the past decade has made great advances in our understanding of the army's complicity in Nazi crimes. All too often, however, Wehrmacht historians have assumed that soldiers unequivocally embraced their role as conquerors and agents of genocide. In contrast, several Third Reich scholars, building in part on Hannah Arendt's thesis of the "banality of evil," have shown that many perpetrators continued to see themselves as civilized and normal individuals (Arendt 1963; Lifton 1986; Schroer 2012). Their observations accord with the work of social psychologists who have argued that the affirmation of one's feeling of self-worth can provide a sense of moral license and that the desire to defend one's self-image can become an occasion for violence (Steele 1988; Crocker et al. 2004; Merritt et al. 2010).

A close examination of the writings they left behind indicates that despite their widespread participation in crimes, Wehrmacht servicemen consistently viewed themselves not as criminals but as upright individuals who retained important aspects of their prewar selves even as they did Hitler's bidding. This image was grounded above all in an array of 'military virtues' and the cultivation of an insular moral community, in which Wehrmacht perpetrators directed kindness toward one another and the homeland, and savagery toward outsiders (Kühne 2006). Although the experience of war took a psychological toll, the killers found comfort in playing out accepted social roles and styling themselves not just as 'ordinary men' but also men of moral stature. Cultivating a sense of decency while casting themselves as valued members of a community helped soldiers to overcome any qualms they may have felt about their participation and led them to strike out all the more viciously against their victims.

126   *David Harrisville*

During four years of war with the Soviet Union, the Wehrmacht carefully worked to instill its men with a constellation of military values, values that had long been part of the army's tradition but were now employed to ensure that soldiers would unhesitatingly execute the Führer's genocidal vision (Schilling 2002; Mineau 2004). The infamous loyalty oath that every soldier was required to take glorified unquestioning obedience to the Führer and held up death on the battlefield as the highest ideal. Publications distributed to the troops entwined the army's traditional code of honor with the imperatives of Nazi ideology. A 1940 training manual explained that the soldier's duties "are sustained by National Socialist spirit and built upon old soldierly traditions." It went on to declare that, "[c]onfident and at the same time modest, upright and loyal, God-fearing and sincere, discrete and incorruptible, the soldier shall be an example of manly strength for the entire Volk."[34] Army propagandists claimed that German soldiers had the right to violate the property and life of their supposedly sub-human victims while insisting that, as the High Command's official propaganda leaflet declared, the perpetrators were "decent guy[s]" who exemplified the moral superiority of German culture.[35]

Many soldiers incorporated these values and assumptions into their self-image. In doing so, they retreated from moral responsibility and insulated their identities from the barbaric practices in which they were engaged. By embracing the virtues of loyalty and obedience, soldiers waived their right to judge the rightness and wrongness of their actions for themselves. Germany's leaders, above all Adolf Hitler, would serve as the nation's conscience (Gross 2007). "Up to this point our Führer has managed everything, and he will certainly also continue to do things correctly," wrote Johannes H. on the eve of the invasion.[36] The concept of duty, another central military value, transformed mass murder into a job that had to be done, even if it was unpleasant (Heer 2000). The only thing that mattered was that he performed it; the actual contents of the soldier's actions were irrelevant. Hans Simon put it this way in a letter to his mother: "I do my duty, so that I can stand before my conscience and my comrades and I try to do it gladly for myself. That makes things much easier."[37] The importance of duty was also bound up with German ideas of masculinity: to be a good man was to be a faithful, courageous, and effective soldier (Schilling 2002; Kühne 2006). This meant being the master of one's emotions and doing what had to be done, no matter the cost.

As soldiers pledged to do their manly duty, they also took the time to celebrate the virtues of heroism and sacrifice when their brothers-in-arms fell in battle. Simon noted that many of his old friends had perished by late 1942, but he prayed that "their sacrifices [would] not [be] in vain. . . . It is, however, good to know that one dies for a better and beautiful Germany."[38] This aspiration helped reassure soldiers that their deeds would be remembered and that they put their lives on the line for worthy ideals. Of course, not all soldiers embraced the values the Wehrmacht claimed to uphold, especially as the tides of war shifted. However, these concepts still provided a powerful means for soldiers to absolve themselves of moral responsibility and redefine even the most heinous crimes as laudable acts of obedience or heroism.

Perpetration in the Wehrmacht 127

As they developed a self-conception grounded in virtues like duty and honor, Wehrmacht perpetrators also cultivated a strong sense of in-group morality that extended to the circle of their immediate comrades and their loved ones in the homeland. The army had long emphasized the importance of 'comradeship,' the mystical connection between brothers-in-arms, and the Nazis held up this concept as an ideal model for the national racial community they sought to create (Kühne 2006). The bonds between comrades on the Eastern Front were constantly nurtured through propaganda, shared experience, and social interaction. Officers arranged parties so their men could share jokes and allow alcohol to help them forget the horrors of combat. Propaganda troops provided entertainment, including film viewings and centers where the rank-and-file could relax between operations. Soldiers regularly shared food, cigarettes, and the contents of packages they received from home.[39] They made music together, celebrated birthdays and promotions, and visited each other's families on leave.[40] Even in the midst of heavy fighting during frigid Russian winters, they organized Christmas celebrations to solidify their connections to each other and to the homeland. In 1943, Hans-Peter Eckener and his comrades set up a small Christmas tree in a bunker, listened to speeches by officers, sang holiday carols, and organized a special dinner. "[I]t could hardly look more extravagant at home!" he opined.[41] The army's chaplains held worship services that reinforced the Wehrmacht's sense of soldierly community. Funerals and memorial celebrations ritualistically brought soldiers together to honor the sacrifices of their fallen comrades, whose deaths, so their officers told them, obligated the survivors to continue the struggle. High losses and the inflow of thousands of new recruits made it difficult to form stable bonds as the war intensified. In the end, however, soldiers still viewed themselves as faithful comrades and members of a selfless community. Within the group, the sense of personal responsibility easily retreated, just as it had behind the fog of military values the army promoted.

Soldiers also did their best to maintain identities as decent men by keeping constant contact with relatives and friends in Germany, to whom they directed unflagging generosity. They sent home Christmas, Mother's Day, and birthday cards, sometimes decorated with flowers or hand-made illustrations.[42] When conditions permitted, they shipped chocolate to their children and sent extra food, soap, cigarettes, and portions of their paycheck to family members experiencing wartime shortages.[43] Despite the deprivations of life on the front, Walter Neuser proudly informed his parents that he and his comrades had started a collection for the Winter Relief Fund, one of the Third Reich's largest charities.[44] Continuing to play their peacetime social roles as best they could, soldiers offered financial advice to wives who were now running the family business and admonished their children to behave in their absence.[45] Gestures like these helped them to assure themselves and their loved ones that even in the face of vast distances and the horrors of the Eastern Front they remained loving fathers, devoted husbands, and obedient sons. "Your children are happy to have you as parents and ask God that He give you many, many more healthy years," wrote Johannes H. to his parents on the occasion of their 25th anniversary. "What father participated in from 1914–18,

128 *David Harrisville*

two sons are experiencing today."[46] The act of letter-writing itself served to retain whatever could be salvaged from prewar identities and assure soldiers and their readers that they had not turned into monsters.

However much they clung to identities as 'good men,' perpetrators in the German army still worried that the war experience and the crimes in which they took part were slowly but surely severing them from civilization. Some noted that they no longer felt like themselves, that they had become callous and cold, unable to feel sympathy for their fellow human beings (Heer 2000). In a chilling reflection on the effects of war, Harald H. wrote his aunt that "one ceases to emphasize morality, above all one gets to know oneself as 'sub-human.'"[47]

As their writings indicate, in the final years of the war, following a catastrophic defeat at Stalingrad, the men of the Wehrmacht often jettisoned their initial delusions of heroism. Uninterrupted combat with a numerically superior Red Army, the experience of punishing environmental conditions, a lack of supplies, and the loss of countless comrades led many to think of themselves more as victims than perpetrators. "Ultimately we have gotten to know nothing but need and suffering," wrote Heinz Sartorio to his sister in August, 1943, the same month the Wehrmacht lost a key battle at Kursk.[48] Soldiers worried that they were losing the best years of their lives. They blamed their opponents, traitors in the homeland, and the workings of fate, but rarely renounced their faith in the Führer.

Wehrmacht perpetrators styled themselves not as sadists or the 'willing executioners' of Goldhagen's formulation, but as men both ordinary and decent. Over the course of four years of war, soldiers for the most part understood themselves as loving fathers and selfless comrades who honorably sacrificed for the greater good while doing a job that was perhaps disagreeable but ultimately necessary. Ordinariness, banality, and decency, however, were not simply static properties. They had to be constantly reasserted in the face of the soldiers' own barbaric practices. The production and protection of this identity, with its accompanying sense of self-righteousness, made it easier to dismiss violent crimes as mere aberrations in otherwise honorable lives, or to recast them as heroic deeds. Further, Wehrmacht servicemen's moral horizons rarely extended beyond their community, which included both their fellow soldiers and their 'racial comrades' on the home front. Ultimately, the cultivation of this community became an engine for violence against outsiders, who were labeled as existential threats (Kühne 2006).

Conclusion

Examining the writings of the more than two dozen soldiers in this chapter offers insight into how German men from all walks of life came to accept their role in a war that violated all moral boundaries in service to Hitler's genocidal goals. These sources confirm the results of previous scholarship regarding the importance of ideology and social factors. In addition, they demonstrate that investigating how perpetrators overcome their moral inhibitions, how they narrate their crimes, and how they construct their moral identities are also valuable keys to understanding how 'ordinary' people become killers.

Perpetration in the Wehrmacht 129

The road to the Wehrmacht's participation in genocide was paved with a thousand small rationalizations to which perpetrators turned in order to assert the legitimacy of the war and short-circuit their own inhibitions toward criminal violence. Their acceptance and continued cooperation were not foregone conclusions, or the result of a purely passive reception of orders or political mantras, but the product of ongoing moral and intellectual work. Each soldier nurtured a particular set of rationales to justify his behavior. Some were supplied by the regime, in the form of racial ideology or the notion that Germany had been forced to launch a preemptive strike. Others were developed on the individual level and involved appeals to traditional moral argumentation, such as an insistence on the need to destroy a supposedly evil foe. Through modes of justification such as these, German troops managed to reframe the war as a righteous cause and present the atrocities committed by their side as necessary actions, both to themselves and to the recipients of their letters.

Their writings also reveal that the men of the Wehrmacht rarely saw themselves as perpetrators, despite their routine employment of criminal violence. This finding accords with the observations of social psychologists, as well as the conclusions of Third Reich historians regarding other perpetrator groups, but has not been fully recognized in the case of the Wehrmacht. Participation in atrocities did take a psychological toll. Nevertheless, the men of the Wehrmacht consistently cultivated identities as decent men, loving family members, and respected members of a soldierly community by embracing military values and through their interactions with comrades and relatives. By the war's end, many had even come to view themselves as the conflict's true victims. Understanding this mentality helps to explain why so few veterans ever acknowledged guilt. The self-absolving narratives they constructed would go on to exercise a powerful influence on German memory for decades after the Third Reich's collapse (Wette 2006).

Notes

1 Soldiers' last names have been abbreviated in accordance with archival regulations, except in cases where they have already been published elsewhere. If a name is unknown, a pseudonym has been used.
2 The execution of commissars was actually the result of orders issued by Hitler and the High Command.
3 Fritz F. to wife, 19 July, 1941, Bundesarchiv-Militärarchiv (hereafter: BA-MA) MSG 2/4048.
4 Hans Albring to Eugen Altrogge, 30–31 August, 1941, *Museumsstiftung Post und Telekommunikation* (hereafter: MSPT) 3.2002.0211.
5 Hans-Peter Eckener to father, 6 June, 1942, in *Lieber Vater. Mein lieber Per. Hans-Peter Eckener Briefwechsel mit zu Hause 1940–1944* (Stuttgart: Selbstverlag, 1998), MSPT 3.2002.0307.
6 Hans-Peter Eckener to parents, 1 March, 1942, MSPT 3.2002.0307.
7 Hans-Peter Eckener to parents, 21 November, 1942, MSPT 3.2002.0307.
8 Harald H. to parents and Marion (sister), 15 November, 1941, MSPT 3.2002.0382.
9 Johannes H. to Willy (brother), 4 January, 1942, MSPT 3.2002.7169.
10 Rolf D. to Hilde, 6 August, 1943, MSPT 3.2002.7236.

130 *David Harrisville*

11 Kurt N. to Hanni (wife) and Lieselotte (daughter), 14 and 19 October, 1941, MSPT 3.2008.1750.

12 Willy S. to Wandelgard, quotations from 21 July and 27 March, 1942, respectively, MSPT 3.2002.0326.

13 For the role of racism in a different context, America's war with Japan, see John Dower, *War without Mercy: Race and Power in the Pacific War* (New York: Pantheon Books, 1986; 7th printing).

14 Heinz Sartorio to Elly (sister), 20 May, 1942, MSPT 3.2002.0827.

15 Kurt N. to wife, 10 March, 1942, MSPT 3.2008.1750.

16 Günter K. Koschorrek, *Blood Red Snow: The Memoirs of a German Soldier on the Eastern Front* (Minneapolis, MN: Zenith Press, 2005), 68–70; quotation from 69.

17 See Rolf D. to Hilde, 22 February, 1944, MSPT 3.2002.7236.

18 Franz Siebeler to parents and siblings, 23 November, 1941, MSPT 3.2002.1285.

19 Willy H. to Kressen (sister of a fallen comrade), 3 September, 1944, MSPT 3.2002.7234.

20 Franz Siebeler to parents and siblings, 21 June, 1941, MSPT 3.2002.1285.

21 Wilhelm A. to father and sister, 12 September, 1943, MSPT 3.2002.0201.

22 Wilhelm Moldenhauser to Erika (wife), 20 March, 1942, *Im Funkwagen der Wehrmacht durch Europa: Balkan, Ukraine, Stalingrad. Feldpostbriefe des Gefreiten Wilhelm Moldenhauser 1940–1943*, ed. Jens Ebert (Berlin: trafo Verlagsgruppe, 2008).

23 See Heinz Sartorio to Elly (sister), 4 August, 1942, MSPT 3.2002.0827.

24 See Anton Böhrer to sister, 21 December, 1941, and to sister and parents, 25 December, 1941, MSPT 3.2002.0889.

25 Heinz Rahe to Ursula (wife), 18–20 July, 1941, MSPT 3.2002.0985.

26 Kurt N. to Johanna (wife) and Lieselotte (daughter), 14 May, 1942, MSPT 3.2008.1750.

27 Hans-Peter Eckener to parents, 9 June, 1942, MSPT 3.2002.0307.

28 See Eugen Altrogge to Hans Albring, 18 July, 1942, MSPT 3.2002.0210.

29 Johannes H. to Otto, 5 October, 1943, MSPT 3.2002.7169.

30 Wilhelm Moldenhauser to Erika (wife), 8 December, 1941, *Im Funkwagen der Wehrmacht*.

31 Walter Neuser to parents, 6 February, 1942, MSPT 3.2002.0947.

32 Hans Wilhelm S. to parents and sisters, 8 October, 1942, MSPT 3.2002.1271.

33 For a soldier who began to question his side's cause after viewing the barbaric treatment of Soviet POWs, see *Reluctant Accomplice: A Wehrmacht Soldier's Letters from the Eastern Front*, ed. Konrad H. Jarausch (Princeton, NJ: Princeton University Press, 2011).

34 Reibert, *Dienstunterricht im Heer, Ausgabe für den Kanonier* (Berlin: Verlag E.S. Mittler & Sohn, 1940), 31–2.

35 Quotation from "Das ist der deutsche Soldat," *Mitteilungen für die Truppe*, Nr. 117, July, 1941, BA-MA RW 4/357.

36 Johannes H. to parents, May, 1941, 3.2002.7169.

37 Hans Simon to mother, 12 October, 1942, MSPT 3.2002.1288.

38 Hans Simon to parents and sister, 21 November, 1942, MSPT 3.2002.1288.

39 See Wilhelm A. to father and sister, 15 February, 1942, MSPT 3.2002.0201.

40 See for example Hans Wilhelm S. to parents and sisters, 26 July, 2 October and 23 October, 1942, MSPT 3.2002.1271.

41 Hans-Peter Eckener to mother, 26 December, 1943, MSPT 3.2002.0307.

42 See for example Hans Wilhelm S. to family, 1 September, 1942, MSPT 3.2002.1271.

43 See Johannes H. to parents, 19 September, 1943, MSPT 3.2002.7169.

44 Walter Neuser to parents, 3 March, 1942, MSPT 3.2002.0947.

45 Wilhelm Moldenhauser to Erika (wife), January 10 and May 21, 1942, *Im Funkwagen der Wehrmacht*; Kurt N. to wife, 12 August, 1942, MSPT 3.2008.1750.

46 Johannes H. to parents, 16 June, 1944, MSPT 3.2002.7169.

47 Harald H. to Hertha, 27 August, 1941, MSPT 3.2002.0382.

48 Heinz Sartorio to Elly (sister), 7 August, 1943, MSPT 3.2002.0827.

References

Arendt, Hannah. *Eichmann in Jerusalem: A Report on the Banality of Evil.* New York: London: Penguin Books, 1963.

Bandura, Albert, Claudio Barbaranelli, Gian Vittorio Caprara, and Concetta Patorelli. "Mechanisms of Moral Disengagement in the Exercise of Moral Agency." *Journal of Personality and Social Psychology* 71, no. 2 (1996): 364–74.

Bartov, Omer. *The Eastern Front 1941–45: German Troops and the Barbarisation of Warfare.* London: Macmillan, 1985.

Bartov, Omer. *Hitler's Army: Soldiers, Nazis, and War in the Third Reich.* New York: Oxford University Press, 1991.

Beorn, Waitman. *Marching into Darkness: The Wehrmacht and the Holocaust in Belarus.* Cambridge, MA: Harvard University Press, 2014.

Bergen, Doris. "Germany Military Chaplains in the Third Reich." In *In God's Name: Genocide and Religion in the Twentieth Century,* edited by Omer Bartov and Phyllis Mack, 123–38. New York: Berghahn Books, 2001.

Browning, Christopher. *Ordinary Men: Reserve Police Battalion 101 and the Final Solution in Poland.* New York: HarperCollins, 1992.

Dower, John. *War Without Mercy: Race and Power in the Pacific War.* 7th Printing. New York: Pantheon Books, 1986.

Faulkner Rossi, Lauren. *Wehrmacht Priests: Catholicism and the Nazi War of Annihilation.* Cambridge, MA: Harvard University Press, 2015.

Fritz, Stephen. *Frontsoldaten: The German Soldier in World War II.* Lexington: University Press of Kentucky, 1995.

Fritz, Stephen. "'We Are Trying . . . to Change the Face of the World' – Ideology and Motivation in the Wehrmacht on the Eastern Front: The View from Below." *The Journal of Military History* 60, no. 4 (October 1996): 683–710.

Goldhagen, Daniel. *Hitler's Willing Executioners: Ordinary Germans and the Holocaust.* New York: Alfred A. Knopf, 1996.

Gross, Raphael. "Loyalty in National Socialism: A Contribution to the Moral History of the National Socialist Period." *History of European Ideas* 33, no. 4 (2007): 488–503.

Heer, Hannes. "How Amorality Became Normality: Reflections on the Mentality of German Soldiers on the Eastern Front." In *War of Extermination: The German Military in World War II,* edited by Hannes Heer and Klaus Naumann, translated by Roy Shelton, 239–344. New York: Berghahn Books, 2000.

Herr, Hannes, and Klaus Neumann. *War of Extermination: The German Military in World War II,* translated by Roy Shelton. New York and Oxford: Berghahn Books, 2000.

Jennifer Crocker, Shawna J. Lee, and Lora E. Park. "The Pursuit of Self-Esteem: Implications for Good and Evil." In *The Social Psychology of Good and Evil,* edited by Arthur G. Miller, 271–302. New York: The Guilford Press, 2004.

Kay, Alex J. *Exploitation, Resettlement, and Mass Murder: Political and Economic Planning for German Occupation Policy in the Soviet Union, 1940–1941.* New York: Berghahn Books, 2006.

Kühne, Thomas. *Kameradschaft. Die Soldaten des nationalsozialistischen Krieges und das 20. Jahrhundert.* Göttingen: Vandenhoeck & Ruprecht, 2006.

Latzel, Klaus. *Deutsche Soldaten – nationalsozialistsicher Krieg? Kriegserlebnis – Kriegserfahrung 1939–1945.* Paderborn: Ferdinand Schöningh, 1998.

Lifton, Robert Jay. *The Nazi Doctors: Medical Killing and the Psychology of Genocide.* New York: Basic Books, 1986.

132 *David Harrisville*

Merritt, Anna, Daniel Effron, and Benoît Monin. "Moral Self-Licensing: When Being Good Frees Us to Be Bad." *Social and Personality Psychology Compass* 4, no. 5 (2010): 344–57.

Messerschmidt, Manfred. *Die Wehrmacht im NS-Staat. Zeit der Indoktrination.* Hamburg: Von Decker, 1969.

Miller, Arthur G. "Introduction and Overview." In *The Social Psychology of Good and Evil*, edited by Arthur G. Miller, 1–17. New York: The Guilford Press, 2004.

Mineau, André. *Operation Barbarossa: Ideology and Ethics Against Human Dignity.* Rodopi: Editions Rodopi B.V., 2004.

Mühlhäuser, Regina. *Eroberungen. Sexuelle Gewalttaten und intime Beziehungen deutscher Soldaten in der Sowjetunion 1941–1945.* Hamburg: HIS Verlag, 2010.

Müller, Rolf-Dieter. "Das 'Unternehmen Barbarossa' als wirtschaftlicher Raubkrieg." In *'Unternehmen Barbarossa.' Der deutsche Überfall auf die Sowjetunion 1941. Berichte, Analysen, Dokumente*, edited by Gerd R. Ueberschär and Wolfram Wette, 173–96. Paderborn: Schöningh, 1984.

Pietrow-Ennker, Bianka (ed.). *Präventivkrieg?: Der deutsche Angriff auf die Sowjetunion.* Frankfurt am Main: Fischer Taschenbuch Verlag, 2011.

Schilling, René. *'Kriegshelden': Deutungsmuster heroischer Männlichkeit in Deutschland 1813–1945.* Paderborn: Schöningh, 2002.

Schroer, Timothy L. "Civilization, Barbarism, and the Ethos of Self-Control Among the Perpetrators." *German Studies Review* 35, no. 1 (2012): 33–54.

Snyder, Timothy. *Bloodlands: Europe between Hitler and Stalin.* New York: Basic Books, 2010.

Steele, Claude M. "The Psychology of Self-Affirmation: Sustaining the Integrity of the Self." In *Advances in Experimental Social Psychology*, edited by L. Berkowitz, 261–302. Vol. 1. San Diego: Academic Press, 1988.

Wette, Wolfram. "Die propagandistische Begleitmusik zum deutschen Überfall auf die Sowjetunion am 22. Juni 1941." In *'Unternehmen Barbarossa.' Der deutsche Überfall auf die Sowjetunion 1941. Berichte, Analysen, Dokumente*, edited by Gerd R. Ueberschär and Wolfram Wette, 122–3. Paderborn: Schöningh, 1984.

Wette, Wolfram. *The Wehrmacht: History, Myth, Reality*, translated by Deborah Lucas Schneider. Cambridge, MA: Harvard University Press, 2006.

7 Gender and genocide
Assessing differential opportunity structures of perpetration in Rwanda

Evelyn A. Gertz, Hollie Nyseth Brehm and Sara E. Brown

Introduction

When Rwanda plummeted into genocide in April of 1994, Kristen was a 21-year-old woman living with her parents, regularly attending prayer services at her local church, and specializing in sewing at a nearby trade school. After the violence reached her small farming village, however, Kristen wittingly became an accomplice to murder. She joined a mob that chased a Hutu "traitor" to the brink of the Nyabarongo River, threw him in, and watched him drown. Today, Kristen is serving a 12-year sentence for perpetration of genocide.

Kristen is one of tens of thousands of women who participated in the 1994 genocide in Rwanda, which took the lives of over 800,000 Tutsi and Hutu moderates in just over three months. Like many other instances of mass violence throughout history, women participated in the genocide in assorted ways, ranging from organizing and inciting violence to exposing their neighbors or looting their homes. Despite this, women's participation in genocide is often ignored or sensationalized by scholarship focusing on the particularly grotesque cruelty[1] of well-known individuals like the Nazi Isla Koch or the first woman convicted of genocide by the International Criminal Tribunal for Rwanda, Pauline Nyiramasuhuko.

In light of this lacuna, this chapter systematically examines women's participation in the 1994 genocide in Rwanda. Using newly available data from the Rwandan National Service of *Gacaca* Jurisdictions, we analyze cases involving women across types of genocidal crime. We supplement these data with 25 in-depth interviews with Rwandan women perpetrators,[2] which complement the macro-level court data by elucidating some of the social contexts relevant to women who participated in the violence.

After reviewing scholarship on women perpetrators, we explain how sociological criminology enables us to theorize genocide as a form of social action.[3] We then discuss women's status in pre-genocide Rwanda, followed by an overview of the *Gacaca* trials that found women guilty of perpetrating genocide. Finally, we draw upon interview data to analyze participation in genocide as situated action, illustrating how women's perpetration of genocide cannot be theorized outside the constraints of structural inequality.

Women perpetrators of genocide

Throughout history, women have participated in genocide. Although many women have been silent bystanders legitimating perpetrators' actions through providing a social context of approval and justification, women have also played integral administrative functions contributing to the massive scale of genocidal violence (Smeulers 2015: 3). Raul Hilberg (1985: 1024) clarifies that during the Holocaust, for example, "It must be kept in mind that most of the participants [of genocide] did not fire rifles at Jewish children or pour gas into gas chambers. . . . Most bureaucrats composed memoranda, drew up blueprints, talked on the phone, and participated in conferences. They could destroy a whole people by sitting at their desk." During World War II, an estimated 12 million women worked for National-Socialist organizations in these types of capacities (Smeulers 2015: 3).

Although the Holocaust is perhaps a particularly salient example of women's involvement in mass violence as supporting personnel, it is far from the only one. African Rights documents that during the genocide in Rwanda, women sang and cheered as men hunted Tutsi (African Rights 1995; Smeulers 2015). Chris Coulter (2009) likewise finds that in Sierra Leone, women soldiered, looted, and engaged in domestic sex slavery. Finally, Amnesty International's reports regarding the ongoing genocide in Sudan indicate that women have acted as cheerleaders while troops commit crimes (Amnesty International 2004; Smeulers 2015: 4).

Women have also directly participated in numerous genocides. At various times, they have been profiteers, thieves, traitors, spies, prison guards, murderers, and sex offenders. Several women Nazi concentration camp guards perpetrated acts of sexual violence against their prisoners, while Biljana Plavšsić – acting president of the Serb Republic in 1992 and again from 1996 to 1998 – spearheaded the Serbian genocidal rape strategy (Sjoberg 2011: 25–6). In Smeulers' (2015: 11) words, when it comes to the preponderance of mass violence across time and space, "there seems to be no role women haven't played."

Despite the indisputable evidence of women's involvement in atrocities, scholarship on the perpetrators of genocide has overwhelmingly focused on men. Foundational studies like Chris Browning's (1992) examination of a police battalion responsible for the massacre of Polish Jews and Scott Straus' (2006) interviews with Rwandan perpetrators exclusively investigate men's roles, as do other high-profile studies, such as Michael Mann's (2000) analysis of Holocaust perpetrators and Philip Verwimp's (2006) study of Rwandan killers. Though men often represent the majority, this singular focus contributes to the pervasive assumption that women are inherently more peaceful than men. Indeed, portrayals of women's roles in genocide in academic scholarship remain obscured by intransigent assumptions of women's passivity and an oversimplified notion of women as victims and men as perpetrators (Sjoberg and Gentry 2007; MacKenzie 2009; Smeulers 2015).

Further, perhaps as a result of such assumptions, violence committed by women is typically framed as involuntary, defensive, or due to a mental illness (Vronsky 2007: 5–6). As Laura Sjoberg and Caron Gentry (2007) demonstrate, violent women ranging from suicide bombers in the Middle East and Chechnya,

Gender and genocide 135

genocidaires in Bosnia and Rwanda, and military personnel at Abu Ghraib, are typically categorized into three discursive paradigms – mother, monster, or whore – each of which reflects an archaic stereotype that the femininity of women offenders is somehow flawed.

This portrayal stands in stark contrast to the enduring finding that men who perpetrate genocide are 'normal' and do not display a pattern of personal sociopathy (e.g. Straus 2006; Peter B. Owens et al. 2013). Several studies have accordingly attempted to prove not only that women do perpetrate genocide but that they, too, are 'normal.' This includes research on the thousands of women SS guards who supervised the Nazi death camps from 1939 to 1945 (Smith 1994; Sarti 2011; Lower 2013), the tens of thousands of Cambodian women who served as *Mekongs* (leaders) and *Yotears* (guards) in labor camps during the late 1970s (Smith 1994) and – the focus of this chapter – the Rwandan women who organized extermination campaigns; hacked Tutsi men, women, and children to death with machetes; and exposed Tutsi in hiding (African Rights 1995; Sharlach 1999; Adler et al. 2007; Brown 2014).

Without question, hundreds of thousands of women and girls perpetrated direct and indirect genocidal violence in numerous cases of genocide over the twentieth century. The sheer prevalence of so many women perpetrators counters erroneous claims of women perpetrator abnormality. Ignoring these women, treating them as aberrant, or assuming passivity does disservice to a more thorough understanding of the causes and processes of genocide.

Situated action

In this chapter, we employ a constructivist approach to understanding women's participation in genocide (see also Sharlach 1999), placing greater emphasis on the socialization of women and the social situations in which they act rather than the biological or psychological determinants of participation. Specifically, we focus on women perpetrators' 'constrained agency,'[4] meaning that we consider both their decisions to participate in violence as well as social structures and other external limitations to participation (Brown 2014).

For instance, many of the women perpetrators mentioned in the previous section exerted agency in their decisions to act. Some killed more than others, and some participated solely of their own volition. Yet, this agency was constrained by entrenched gender norms and expectations that limited women's exposure to violence and, in turn, opportunities to perpetrate harm. Wendy Lower (2013) and Roger Smith (1994) discuss structural constraints facing women in 1940s Germany, who were expected to devote the majority of their efforts toward raising patriotic Aryan children. Likewise, hierarchical gender norms in 1994 Rwanda socialized women to spend the majority of their time in and around the home, tending to their farms and overseeing the housework and childcare (Sharlach 1999; Hogg 2010).

A model of situated action therefore informs our analysis of women perpetrators of genocide in Rwanda. To be clear, situated action frameworks have typically

136 *Evelyn A. Gertz et al.*

been applied toward understanding women's participation in crime.[5] Jody Miller (2002), for instance, highlights and extends previous work (e.g. Messerschmidt 1993; see also Garfinkel 1967; Kessler and McKenna 1978; West and Zimmerman 1987; Connell 1987) to illustrate how women's involvement in street crime should be construed as situated action, suggesting that theories of women's participation in criminal activity must account for women's agency and their structural positionality. Specifically, Miller argues that men and women *choose* to perform one of several masculinities and femininities to which they are exposed. Differing social contexts, such as gang membership or genocide, allow for, encourage, or preclude the enactment of particular gender norms.

Recognizing gender as fluid and context-dependent is critical to account for the nature and diversity of women's criminal offenses. Further, it allows for conceptual disaggregation of agency and structural constraints. Women do not commit fewer violent criminal acts because they are the passive recipients of static, deterministic gender roles. Rather, with every social act, women draw from a multitude of gender schemas (Sewell 1992)[6] that are limited by restricted occupancy of hierarchical social positions and unequal access to resources (Sewell 1992; Miller 2002). In this sense, gender is a powerful factor that structures all social action, including perpetration of crime and, in our case, the crime of genocide.

Thus, we argue that it is particularly productive to examine how gender differentially influences the ways men and women participate in genocide. Gender norms in every country, as Sjoberg (2010: 181) articulates, reflect "socially assigned, expected roles on the basis of perceived membership in implicitly natural sex groups" (Smeulers 2015). To assess how notions of gender in Rwanda may have uniquely affected women's opportunities to participate in the genocide, we turn to a brief discussion of women's status in the country in the years leading up to the violence.

Women in 1994 Rwanda

During the colonial period and throughout the 1900s, Rwanda was a patriarchal, agrarian society. Despite a historical reverence for certain women (like the Queen Mother), Rwandan proverbs such as, "In a home where a woman speaks, there is discord" (Agahozo 1999: 32) and "Woman's only wealth is a man" (Hogg 2010: 72) vividly convey women's inequality within the family as well as within the economic and political spheres (Hogg 2010). The Rwandan woman, symbolic of "fertility and weakness," was generally subordinate to the Rwandan man, symbolic "of strength and protection" (UNFAO 1991: 7; Hogg 2010).

Accordingly, women and men held distinct duties within and outside of the household (Hogg 2010). Women's responsibilities included educating children, welcoming visitors, and maintaining traditions (Hogg 2010). They were also charged with digging, planting, and harvesting. Men, by contrast, provided for the family and engaged in heavy labor (Jefremovas 1991; Burnet 2012: 46). This gendered division of work began at an early age, as boys shepherded livestock and girls fetched water and conducted household chores. Boys often trained for

Gender and genocide 137

combat, while girls helped their mothers and learned obedience, respect, and submission (Hogg 2010).

Economically, women were marginalized and were often poorer than men and illiterate (UNFAO 1991; Hogg 2010). Although women conducted much of the agricultural work, they generally did not possess or control natural, economic, or social resources (Hogg 2010). Furthermore, the Family Code of 1992 officially designated husbands the head of households. Women could not inherit property, open a bank account, engage in commerce, or enter into a legal agreement, and they were also marginalized in the education system. Likewise, Rwandan women occupied second-class roles in the political sphere. Prior to 1990, there were no women in the executive branch, and afterwards they comprised a mere 5 per cent. As of 1994, there were also no women mayors or prefects (Sharlach 1999).

While this paints a picture of women as marginalized across many spheres of life, there were also exceptions. For instance, 22 per cent of rural households were women-headed households (MINAGRI 1991: 48; Hogg 2010). The Prime Minister of Rwanda in 1994 was also a woman, though she and other women in positions of power were consistently marginalized by the reigning political party (Brown 2017). Thus, on the eve of the genocide, "The majority of Rwandan women . . . adhered to the traditional expectations of homemaking, childrearing, and creating community between households," while men were responsible for "protecting their families and defending their communities" (Adler et al. 2007: 216).

Women perpetrators in Rwanda

Although the scope of this chapter precludes a more nuanced analysis, myriad factors precipitated the 1994 genocidal violence, including decades of strife between the two ethnic groups, a civil war, an economic downturn, and recurring government repression. Then, on 6 April 1994, the plane carrying President Habyarimana was shot down on descent into Kigali. Immediately, Hutu extremists seized power in the capital and began systematically hunting down and murdering Tutsi and Hutu moderates. Although government leaders were largely responsible for orchestrating the genocide, there was vast popular participation. Over the span of a few months, at least 800,000 individuals were killed;[7] millions were displaced; and many others were the victims of sexual violence, property attacks, and torture.[8]

New data from Rwanda's *Gacaca* courts shed light on women's participation in this violence. *Gacaca* courts were local-level courts instituted throughout the country to try those who participated in the violence (for more details on the *Gacaca* courts, see Clark 2010; Bornkamm 2012; and Nyseth Brehm et al. 2014). Those tried at *Gacaca* courts were categorized into one of the following groups:[9]

- *Category 1:* People accused of planning, organizing, or supervising the genocide; people who acted in positions of authority or leadership at high levels; people who incited genocide; and people who committed acts of rape or sexual torture.[10]

- *Category 2:* People or accomplices who intentionally killed someone or injured someone through acts intended to kill her or him; people who committed dehumanizing acts on the dead, torture, and other criminal acts against other people.
- *Category 3:* People who committed offenses against property, such as looting.

For a separate project, access to all court data were obtained and compiled into a database of trials (see Nyseth Brehm et al. 2014 and Nyseth Brehm et al. 2016 for more information).[11] Notably, this is a database of trials, not people. If a person was accused of a Category 2 and a Category 3 crime, he or she was tried in two separate cases. Similarly, if people were accused of crimes in more than one region, they were tried in separate cases in each region.[12]

The dataset includes 1,678,881 trials (excluding appeals trials and trials missing data on the defendant).[13] Of these, 147,148 trials involved a woman defendant, indicating that 8.8 per cent of all trials involved women (prior to appeal). Approximately 87 per cent of these trials resulted in a guilty verdict, and 8.8 per cent of the trials with guilty verdicts involved women. Thus, these data clearly indicate that the clear majority of people who participated in the genocide were men, in line with other studies. Yet, over 130,000 trials involved a woman who was found guilty of participating in genocide, illustrating that the violence was not only perpetrated by men.

The *Gacaca* data also reveal that women's participation varied across the three categories. As seen in Figure 7.1, upwards of 2,000 Category 1 trials, which were designated for people in positions of power and authority who planned, organized, and supervised the genocide, ended with a guilty verdict for women. This category includes prominent women affiliated with the interim government, as well as those who broadcasted inflammatory anti-Tutsi propaganda on *Radio-Télévision Libre des Mille Collines* (RTLM) (African Rights 1995; Alison Des Forges 1999).

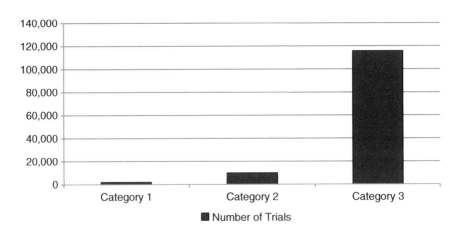

Figure 7.1 Gacaca court trials in which women were found guilty

Nonetheless, many women in this category were unusual in terms of the amount of power they wielded. Structural factors precluding women's attainment of power and authority prior to the genocide likely resulted in fewer opportunities for leadership among the genocide planners, organizers, and supervisors. For instance, none of Rwanda's 145 communes or 12 prefectures was led by a woman in 1994, and only a few women had risen to prominence within the national government.

A larger share of Category 2 trials – over 10,000 – arrived at guilty verdicts for women. This category included the individuals who committed murder or aided in violence against people. Such violence was typically committed in groups, some of which had formed before the genocide. For instance, after the Rwandan Patriotic Front (RPF) invasion in 1990, political leaders urged civilians to form self-defense groups. These groups recruited men, capitalizing on gendered notions of a man's duty to defend the country. Partially as a result of this gendered dynamic, women comprise a relatively small percentage of the defendants in this category, though we again see women who killed people and many others, such as Kristen, who aided genocidal murder by encouraging men to act or exposing a Tutsi in hiding.

Finally, while this is a database of cases, it is nonetheless evident that the majority of women who participated in the genocide were involved in crimes against property (Category 3) rather than crimes directly targeting people (Categories 1 and 2). Over 90 per cent of trials convicting women were Category 3 trials (see Figure 7.2), totaling over 115,000. As African Rights (1995) and numerous others explicate, women looted bodies and households for valuables, including household items such as pots, pans, and clothing, as well as livestock and parts of houses, like corrugated iron sheets used for roofing.

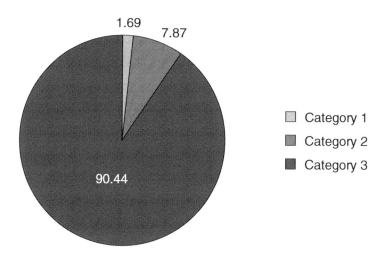

Figure 7.2 Percentage of Gacaca trials with a guilty verdict for women, by category

140 *Evelyn A. Gertz et al.*

The majority of trials of men – 76 per cent – were also in Category 3, though a much higher percentage of men were found guilty of Category 2 crimes. This reveals more about social norms in Rwanda during the genocide than it does about inherent discrepancies in violent tendencies between men and women, however. Political elites who organized the genocide launched a vicious propaganda campaign that justified the violence as necessary to protect the country from civil war and dangerous outsiders. Men and women grew up with different exposure to violence and expectations of combat, and it was men who were called to defend the country with physical force. Regardless of any natural (or unnatural) predisposition to perpetrate violence, women were presented with fewer opportunities to do so. Their participation in the genocide thus reflects reactions to a weakened social fabric, which provided specific types of opportunities for deviation from normative femininity.

Situating women perpetrators' actions

The *Gacaca* court data provide much information about the broader patterns of perpetration, though they cannot shed light on the immediate social situations that influenced actions. Existing research on Rwandan perpetrators likewise cannot fully illuminate the situations in which women acted, as much of this scholarship focuses exclusively on the motivations of men who committed murder (Category 2). For example, through interviews with 210 such individuals, Straus (2006) found that most perpetrators did not describe hostile relations or deep beliefs in racist culture. Instead, strong intra-group pressure associated with authority and motivated by fear or anger influenced participation (Straus 2006: 151).[14]

To better understand the decisions of women who participated in the violence, including the social situations in which they acted, we turn to interviews with 25 women who were convicted of participating in the genocide. These 25 women were each found guilty of a Category 2 crime, which again includes murder and other violence against people. We focus on this category because of our general interest in women perpetrators (e.g., not the women in Category 1 who often wielded unrepresentative amounts of power) and because perpetration of murder and bodily harm is a starker departure from social norms for women prior to the genocide. Our focus on Category 2 also falls in line with existing research on men perpetrators (e.g., Straus 2006).

Interviews were conducted with these 25 women in 2011, 2012, and 2014.[15] Respondents were selected through a random sampling process and were interviewed in seven community service facilities commonly referred to as TIG (Travaux d'Interet General or "works of public interest") camps. All interviews were conducted with a translator in a semi-structured style, using probing questions to ascertain in detail the experiences of the individual. Generally, questions covered life before, during, and after the genocide, with a focus on the woman's mobilization, participation, and impressions.[16]

Interviewees' names were changed to pseudonyms with a random name generator in order to protect the anonymity of participants. As seen in Table 7.1, the

Gender and genocide 141

Table 7.1 Interviewee characteristics

Name	Crime	Age	Acceptance of Guilt
Amy	Associated with *Interahamwe*	20	Yes
Cindy	Participated in mob violence	29	Limited acceptance
Deena	Participated in militia violence	38	Limited acceptance
Laura	Exposed a person in hiding	20	Yes
Agnes	Exposed people in hiding	38	No
Lucy	Exposed people in hiding	41	Yes
Rebecca	Identified people for killing	Not known	No
Rose	Exposed a person in hiding	22	Not known
Suzanne	Helped her daughter kill her grandson	67	No
Jennifer	Gathered stones for killing	28	Yes
Cassie	Sounded an alarm for her husband to commit a killing	32	Yes
Lynn	Witnessed a killing	23	Yes
Sally	Sounded an alarm for a killing	24	Yes
Tanya	Collected stones for a killing	47	Yes
Elaine	Exposed someone in hiding	28	No
Gloria	Participated in militia violence	45	Limited acceptance
Kathleen	Killed an infant	42	No
Kristen	Participated in militia violence	21	Limited acceptance
Charlotte	Killed two children and their grandmother	51	No
Alexa	Complicit in killing a 13-year-old she was supposed to rescue	25	Limited acceptance
Sylvia	Participated in mob killing	43	No
Vanessa	Participated in *Interahamwe* violence and helped kill multiple women and children	26	Limited acceptance
Julie	Inflammatory language	44	No
Tracy	Exposed people in hiding	42	Limited Acceptance
Polly	Exposed someone in hiding	27	Limited Acceptance

Note: The ages of the women at the time of the genocide are approximate. "Limited acceptance" means that the women switched back and forth during the interview, at times admitting their guilt and at times denying aspects of it.

interviewees' approximate ages ranged from 20 to 67 at the time of the violence. Sixteen were married in 1994, and 11 had children. All 25 women identified as Christian and were affiliated with Catholic, Protestant, Seventh Day Adventist, or Pentecostal churches. Only Kristen had completed primary school, and she was also one of just two women who did not identify herself as a farmer prior to incarceration.

As we analyze these women's accounts of their actions, we conceptualize gender as a dynamic yet constraining structural factor and assess women perpetrators'

142 *Evelyn A. Gertz et al.*

actions as situated. In doing so, we shift the focus from the individual to the sometimes mercurial nature of the individual's behavior. We thus begin by examining women perpetrators' agency – which we understand as a woman's conscious choice to take action or to not act (albeit within a deeply patriarchal context) – followed by an examination of the structural constraints and opportunities that influenced these choices and actions.

Agency

The agency exerted by these 25 women falls across a spectrum, with some women exerting relatively unconstrained agency and others holding relatively little ability to make their own choices. Starting with the former, it is evident that several women perpetrators chose to participate in the killing. Amy, for example, readily described her participation in *Interahamwe* meetings and actions with the intent to kill Tutsi. She reflected, "During the genocide, I participated. I kind of helped someone who participated in genocide, so I was accused during the *Gacaca*."

Tanya likewise displayed agency by choosing to participate in the violence, albeit for a surprising reason. When *Interahamwe* militias came to her property to look for volunteers, she was hiding a Tutsi in her home. She explains, "When they came to collect us and mobilize us to go and pick the stones . . . I didn't want them to come in the house, so I went outside when they said 'Come out!'" In order to save a young Tutsi man and to protect her family, Tanya then joined the *Interahamwe* and gathered rocks for an assault on a nearby church.

In contrast, some women assert they were forced to participate. For Laura, sheer physical discrepancies in size, strength, and number influenced her decision to expose someone in hiding. She emphasizes women's lack of choice, explaining that many women,

> got involved in the same way I got involved. Not because you wanted someone to be killed, but sometimes they would come and torment you or torture you and you would give in. You wouldn't want really someone you have been going to church with to be killed but because sometimes you didn't have a choice, we were forced to give in.

Jennifer – who was sentenced 12 years for collecting stones to throw at a person drowning in a well – likewise reveals,

> They forced me to bring the stones. . . . The reason why I'm here is because during the genocide I was at home and then I heard an alarm. . . . I found they [the *Interahamwe*] had thrown a person in the well and they were throwing stones at that person. . . . I was ordered by the men who were throwing stones at the person in the well who was drowning – they ordered us to bring stones. So I went to bring the stones. That's why I'm accused, that's why I'm here.

As this narrative indicates, Jennifer felt forced to participate, suggesting that her own agency was compromised. It is noteworthy, however, that even in situations of limited agency, Jennifer and others were able to exercise *some* degree of control over their actions. For instance, Jennifer first went to the well because she heard people shouting and wanted to "see what was going on." In other words, Jennifer chose to leave her home and travel to the well out of curiosity. Only then was she, in her own words, forced to participate at the behest of the killers.

The other women perpetrators fall along the spectrum, each illustrating some degree of agency yet also illustrating the complexities of participation in genocide. For example, Cassie was sentenced to 12 years for alerting her husband to the presence of Tutsi children. She explains that these unfortunate events unfolded when she called her husband to help her carry fish that she had been selling along a main road. After handing him her wares, she continued ahead without him. Then, "They collided. My husband was coming to pick the stuff that was left at the roadside and also these kids were also coming. They kind of met, and that's why they were killed." Accordingly, Cassie suggests that the fact that her actions resulted in the murder of Tutsi children at the hands of her husband was an unhappy coincidence and not a result of a decision she made.

Of course, some of these women likely deny their agency in order to deny their participation in crimes of genocide. Kristen, for instance, was convicted of joining a militia that drowned a man in the river. While she admitted to participating in the militia, she also suggested that this was her only role in the violence. Her account, however, was challenged at her *Gacaca* court trial. One witness testified that he heard Kristen referring to Tutsi as snakes and calling for their persecution. A number of other witnesses confirmed that Kristen would intimidate and torture a neighboring Tutsi family, deny Tutsi access to the local well, and sing encouragement to the *Interahamwe* militias. These corroborated stories suggest that Kristen's involvement may have been more consequential than she articulated in her interview. As this demonstrates, attributing agency to perpetrators' post-hoc accounts of their genocidal crimes is difficult because this attribution often depends on the authenticity of their narratives, which must be kept in mind when analyzing results and would, if anything, likely lead to downplaying agency.

Nevertheless, these interviews represent a range of instances in which women made a series of choices to perpetrate violence. While other actors may have coerced some of their behavior, the frequency and severity with which many of these women participated were clearly sometimes of their own volition. In many of these women's interpretations, agency is present, though analyzing agency as situated action necessitates further investigation into the structural constraints and opportunities relevant to women during the genocide.

Structural constraints and opportunity

As detailed above, gender norms in this agrarian, patriarchal society prescribed that women remained at home, on the farm, or otherwise removed from the public sphere. These established patriarchal customs continued to influence the spaces women were allowed to occupy, even during the genocide. In turn, this meant that women's agency was limited, whether they sought to avoid or perpetrate violence.

144   *Evelyn A. Gertz et al.*

A number of women referenced their relegation to the private sphere and their limited options to participate in or even witness the genocide. Rose, who was 22 in 1994, was sentenced to 12 years for exposing a Tutsi hiding on her farm to the *Interahamwe*. When asked about the pre-genocide mobilization efforts, she explained, "When you are a girl, what you do is, you know, you stay home, you eat, you do what you're doing told. . . . I didn't really focus on really putting my concentration on radio or what." In other words, Rose suggests that as a young woman or girl, she was precluded from participating in mobilization efforts.

Cassie concurs and explains that during the genocide, "Most of the time I was at home. . . . Where we used to stay, I didn't see any women participate, most of them stayed home." Elaine likewise shares, "Most of the time I was home and I was pregnant. I had kids, so all I could do is go in the garden close to home [and] get a few things." As a result of their limited access to the public sphere, Elaine and Cassie claim ignorance as to the details of the genocide in their area.

As these accounts indicate, some women felt removed from the genocide as a result of their limited mobility and access to the public sphere wherein the genocide occurred. Even as the chaos of the genocide overtook their area, a certain element of 'normalcy' continued to structure their days. Despite the genocide raging around them, these women still viewed their domestic duties, including caring for the home, farm, and children, as their primary obligation. Even though the genocide weakened social norms and created a space for women to participate in violence, certain gendered practices and restrictions remained intact. Many women thus filled their days much as they had before the genocide: with gendered duties in and around their households and in line with gendered practices and expectations in Rwanda.

In a similar vein, when describing the immediate context that precipitated their perpetration of a crime, many of the interviewees are quick to paint a binary picture of their environment. In their eyes, men often instigated the killing and either physically coerced women into participating or created a 'legitimating' environment in which it was understood that it was appropriate for the women to partake in the violence. Suzanne, for instance, initially took sole responsibility for her crime, explaining, "The reason why I'm here is because I'm accused, I actually killed my grandson, one of my grandkids during the war." Only later did she explain that she was gathering food when her daughter and husband took the child out of the home, killed him, and buried the body. When Suzanne came home, she realized the child was gone, questioned her husband as to the fate of the murdered grandson, and was quickly admonished. She concluded, "You know, from that, I couldn't add any questions. I just kept silent." Since he was her husband and the head of the household, she did not challenge him further or protest the murder of her grandson. Instead, she persisted in questioning her daughter, a woman, and encouraged her to confess her crimes.

Broadly, structural constraints patterned women's involvement in the genocide by generating discrete circumstances and conditions that uniquely influenced women's actions. For many women, the daily opportunity to participate in the violence was simply constrained. For instance, Elaine was found guilty of providing information to killers about a Tutsi in hiding, though she claims she was tricked into believing she was speaking to fellow rescuers. She explains, "I didn't see people killing, I just used to hear people talking about [it] . . . I knew there were people moving up and down and people running and hiding, and then at one point we heard bullets and shootings and we ran but after some time we came back." This account tellingly reveals Elaine's limited awareness of the organization and perpetration of the genocide, illustrating how this limited awareness may have influenced women's relatively lower levels of participation.

Lucy also describes witnessing chaos in the community but draws a sharp distinction at actually seeing murder. She states, "I used to hear during the war that there were killings where I was staying. I didn't see people being killed. . . . Sometimes I would hear people screaming and running around, but I never saw exactly. But I was hearing that there were killings, through news, that people are killing each other, stuff like that." In line with Elaine and Lucy, the majority of the interviewees describe hearing screaming and shouting from groups on the street and being aware of mass chaos in their communities. Yet, they claim that they did not witness the violence firsthand. Though this may be part of a strategy of denial, it is also illustrative of women's perceptions of opportunities to participate in the violence and thus warrants consideration.

Indeed, even in instances of more direct involvement, women claim to have been less privy to the actual act of violence. Amy was sentenced 12 years in prison for associating and plotting massacres with the *Interahamwe*. In response to the question of whether she witnessed any killings, she explains,

> We weren't going to a killing or planning, we were going to see other members in the group. So I was with them. I was with a group of people . . . to plan a massacre. We were basically planning what we were going to do next. So I went with them one time. And then, they decided to go back. So that is the only time that I was involved.

In other words, Amy was with a group of people who were going to participate in the violence, though the group decided not to commit a murder at that time. Amy later shared that she would have participated in a murder had the group decided to proceed with the killing, however, the opportunity did not present itself.

The distinction between 'hearing' about killings and 'seeing' killings suggests differential opportunity structures for men and women to perpetrate crimes. Some women discuss hearing anti-Tutsi propaganda on the radio. Many reference hearing the firing of guns on the street, hearing about (and occasionally seeing) houses set ablaze by others, and hearing groups discussing killing in churches. What they surprisingly do not mention, despite the extraordinary number of people who lost their lives, is seeing any direct violence occur, or even deceased bodies. Again, like many people accused of committing a crime, many of these women may deny seeing violence in order to deny participating in it, thereby absolving themselves of blame. Regardless of their exposure to killing, this rhetoric reflects these women's *perceptions* of limited access and opportunity, which sheds light on the social situations in which they acted.

Conclusion

Throughout history, women have perpetrated mass violence. In the twentieth century alone, hundreds of thousands of women participated in genocide. Yet, while scholarship has primarily focused on perpetrators as 'ordinary men,' the few accounts of women who perpetrate genocide often paint them as aberrant, flawed, or unhuman. The sheer number of women who have participated in modern genocides undermines this assumption, however, and indicates the disservice this gendered narrative does to a fundamental understanding of the crime of crimes.

This chapter presents a novel framework for understanding women's perpetration of genocide. The model of situated action shifts the focus from the psychology or biology of the individual perpetrator to the social situation in which he or she behaves. With every act of violence, there are aspects of the behavior that reflect ascription to normative gender performance as well as unique movement away from it. Discerning between the two allows for increased focus on the immediate social contexts that engender perpetration. Situated action, therefore, allows for contemplation of why and how women participated (or did not participate) in the violence.

Further, the framework presents a means of understanding differential opportunity structures in Rwanda. From a young age, Rwandan boys trained for combat while girls learned obedience and submission. Additionally, after the RPF invaded the country in 1990, men were recruited to form civilian self-defense groups, which later comprised, in part, the groups that hunted Tutsi. Thus, when the country plummeted into genocide, men were equipped with the knowledge and training to participate. Women, in contrast, often continued to perform their domestic obligations and were neither exposed to the violence to the same extent nor expected to make the violence the center of their lives. The daily circumstances and conditions associated with the lives of men and women varied significantly.

Women did participate in the violence, though their participation typically took the form of Category 3 property crimes rather than the more serious crimes tried in Categories 1 and 2. This likely reflects social norms in Rwanda prior to the genocide and says little about women's natural predispositions to perpetrate violence. Women were typically confined to the home and the private sphere, and departing from this space remained a stark departure from normative gender performance. The social upheaval weakened hierarchical gender boundaries and created new methods for expression of women's autonomy, but the genocide still occurred in the context of a rigidly patriarchal system. It was in this context that we must locate, analyze, and understand women's participation in genocide.

Notes

1 This emphasis on malice may emerge from attempts to counter essentialist arguments suggesting that women are naturally more inclined to protect life.
2 We conceptualize women perpetrators as women who participate in acts of direct and indirect violence during a genocide. Direct violence includes person-to-person violence, such as murder, assault, or looting. Indirect violence includes planning, organizing, and inciting violence perpetrated by others (see Brown 2017). Both direct

Gender and genocide   147

and indirect violence are crimes of genocide as outlined by international law, and both forms of violence occur during genocide.

3 See also Nicole Rafter (2016).

4 Much literature debates the dynamic nature of agency, though this goes beyond the scope of this chapter. For our purposes, agency is the conscious choice to take action (or inaction), albeit within a deeply patriarchal context.

5 We do not propose that genocide is equal to street crime, though genocide *is* a crime. There are also numerous similarities between genocide and other types of crime (see Nyseth Brehm et al. 2016).

6 Jody Miller (2001), for example, finds that in majority male street gangs, women strive to be "one of the guys," which can sometimes be accomplished through the perpetration of violent crime.

7 Estimates range from 800,000 to 1.2 million individuals.

8 For more on the history of the genocide, please see René Lemarchand (1970), Catharine Newbury (1988), Des Forges (1999, 2011), Helen M. Hintjens (1999), Mahmood Mamdani (2001), Jan Vansina (2005), Timothy Longman (2011), Straus (2006), André Guichaoua (2010), Verwimp (2013).

9 The courts were originally designed with four categories of crime.

10 Those in the higher levels of this category who were not sent to the International Criminal Tribunal for Rwanda – which tried those who were thought to be key orchestrators of the violence – were tried in the regular court system. Those tried in the *Gacaca* included people who supervised or incited violence, people at some levels of power within the government (such as mayors), and people who committed rape and sexual torture.

11 Note that the second author worked with Dr. Gasanabo to analyze these data and that here we summarize findings presented elsewhere.

12 These data are official data and thus subject to the constraints that come with all official data, as they do not include those who were not tried and surely include some people who were found guilty but were actually innocent.

13 A small percentage of trials are missing data on the sex of the defendant. Additionally, a little over one thousand trials had nonsensical data entered for the sex of the defendant (e.g., zero).

14 Alternatively, Adam Jones (2002) suggests that the Rwandan genocide was organized by elites as a mechanism to engage and thus abate the threat of a large swath of young, unemployed male youth.

15 Interviews were conducted by the third author, Sara Brown, as part of her dissertation work. See Brown's book *Gender and the Genocide in Rwanda* for additional information on the sampling strategy and interview process.

16 There are clear are limitations to the use of oral histories to understand perpetrators' actions. For instance, some participants are reluctant to admit the full scope of their actions during the genocide. This could be due to a lapse in memory due to the passage of time, interviewer race and nationality, the perceived ethnicity of the translator, or an effort on the part of the participant to misrepresent herself in some way (Brown 2017). Thus, Brown randomly selected nine perpetrator testimonies and checked them against their Gacaca Courts transcribed records. Of the nine cases reviewed, translated, and compared to the testimony provided during the interviews, six had substantial inconsistencies.

References

Adler, Reba N., Cyanne E. Loyle, and Judith Globerman. "A Calamity in the Neighborhood: Women's Participation in the Rwandan Genocide." *Genocide Studies and Prevention* 2, no. 3 (2007): 209–33.

148   *Evelyn A. Gertz et al.*

African Rights. *Not So Innocent: When Women Become Killers.* London: African Rights, 1995.

Agahozo, Avega (Association of Genocide Widows). *Survey on Violence Against Women in Rwanda.* Kigali, 1999.

Amnesty International. *Sudan: Darfur: Rape as a Weapon of War – Sexual Violence and Its Consequences.* Amnesty International Report, 18 July 2004.

Bornkamm, Paul Christophe. *Rwanda's Gacaca Courts: Between Retribution and Reparation.* New York: Oxford University Press, 2012.

Brown, Sara E. "Female Perpetrators of the Rwandan Genocide." *International Feminist Journal of Politics* 16, no. 3 (2014): 448–69.

Brown, Sara E. *Gender and the Genocide in Rwanda: Women as Rescuers and Perpetrators.* London: Routledge, 2017.

Browning, Chris. *Ordinary Men: Reserve Police Battalion 101 and the Final Solution in Poland.* New York: HarperCollins, 1992.

Burnet, Jennie E. *Genocide Lives in Us: Women, Memory, and Silence in Rwanda.* Madison: University of Wisconsin Press, 2012.

Clark, Philip. *The Gacaca Courts, Post-Genocide Justice and Reconciliation in Rwanda: Justice without Lawyers.* Cambridge: Cambridge University Press, 2010.

Connell, Raewyn. *Gender and Power.* Stanford, CA: Stanford University Press, 1987.

Coulter, Chris. *Bush Wives and Girl Soldiers: Women's Lives through War and Peace in Sierra Leone.* Ithaca, NY: Cornell University Press, 2009.

Des Forges, Alison. *'Leave None to Tell the Story': Genocide in Rwanda.* New York: Human Rights Watch, 1999.

Des Forges, Alison, and David S. Liebhafsky. Newbury. *Defeat Is The Only Bad News: Rwanda under Musinga, 1896–1931.* Madison: University of Wisconsin Press, 2011.

Garfinkel, Harold. *Studies in Ethnomethodology.* Englewood Cliffs, NJ: Prentice Hall, 1967.

Guichaoua, André. *Rwanda, de la Guerre au Génocide: Les Politiques Criminelles au Rwanda (1990–1994).* Paris: La Découverte, 2010.

Hilberg, Raul. *The Destruction of the European Jews.* New York: Random House, 1985.

Hintjens, Helen M. "Explaining the 1994 Genocide in Rwanda." *The Journal of Modern African Studies* 37, no. 2 (1999): 241–86.

Hogg, Nicole. "Women's Participation in the Rwandan Genocide: Mothers or Monsters?" *International Review of the Red Cross* 92, no. 877 (2010): 69–102.

Jefremovas, Villia. "Loose Women, Virtuous Wives, and Timid Virgins: Gender and the Control of Resources in Rwanda." *Canadian Journal of African Studies* 25, no. 3 (1991): 378–95.

Jones, Adam. "Gender and Genocide in Rwanda." *Journal of Genocide Research* 4, no. 1 (2002): 65–94.

Kessler, Suzanne J., and Wendy McKenna. *Gender: An Ethnomethodological Approach.* New York: Wiley, 1978.

Lemarchand, René. *Rwanda and Burundi.* New York: Praeger Publishers, 1970.

Longman, Timothy. *Christianity and the Genocide in Rwanda.* New York: Cambridge University Press, 2011.

Lower, Wendy. *Hitler's Furies: German Women in the Nazi Killing Fields.* Boston: Houghton Mifflin Harcourt, 2013.

MacKenzie, Megan. "Securitization and Desecuritization: Female Soldiers and the Reconstruction of Women in Post-Conflict Sierra Leone." *Security Studies* 18, no. 2 (2009): 241–61.

Gender and genocide 149

Mamdani, Mahmood. *When Victims Become Killers: Colonialism, Nativism, and the Genocide in Rwanda*. Princeton, NJ: Princeton University Press, 2001.

Mann, Michael. "Were the Perpetrators of Genocide 'Ordinary Men' or 'Real Nazis'? Results from Fifteen Hundred Biographies." *Holocaust Genocide Studies* 14, no. 3 (2000): 331–66.

Messerschmidt, James W. *Masculinities and Crime: Critique and Reconceptualization of Theory*. Lanham: Rowman & Littlefield, 1993.

Miller, Jody. *One of the Guys: Girls, Gangs and Gender*. New York: Oxford University Press, 2001.

Miller, Jody. "The Strengths and Limits of 'Doing Gender' for Understanding Street Crime." *Theoretical Criminology* 6, no. 4 (2002): 433–60.

Ministry of Agriculture (MINAGRI) Report as cited in *Re'seau des Femmes, Profil Socio-Economique de la Femme Twandaise*. Kigali, May (1991): 48.

Newbury, Catharine. *The Cohesion of Oppression: Clientship and Ethnicity in Rwanda, 1860–1960*. New York: Columbia University Press, 1988.

Nyseth Brehm, Hollie, Christopher Uggen, and Jean-Damascéne Gasanabo. "Genocide, Justice, and Rwanda's Gacaca Courts." *Journal of Contemporary Criminal Justice* 30, no. 3 (2014): 333–52.

Nyseth Brehm, Hollie, Christopher Uggen, and Jean-Damascéne Gasanabo. "Age, Gender, and the Crime of Crimes: Toward a Life-Course Theory of Genocide Participation." *Criminology* 54, no. 4 (2016): 713–43.

Owens, Peter B., Yang Su, and David A. Snow. "Social Scientific Inquiry into Genocide and Mass Killing." *Annual Review of Sociology* 39, no. 1 (2013): 69–84.

Rafter, Nicole. *The Crime of All Crimes: Toward a Criminology of Genocide*. New York: New York University Press, 2016.

Sarti, Wendy Adele-Marie. *Women and Nazis: Perpetrators of Genocide and Other Crimes During Hitler's Regime, 1933–1945*. Palo Alto, CA: Academica Press, 2011.

Sewell, William H. "A Theory of Structure: Duality, Agency, and Transformation." *American Journal of Sociology* 98, no. 1 (1992): 1–29.

Sharlach, Linda. "Gender and Genocide in Rwanda: Women as Agents and Objects of Genocide." *Journal of Genocide Research* 1, no. 3 (1999): 387–99.

Sjoberg, Laura. "Reconstructing Women in Postconflict Rwanda." In *Women, War, and Violence: Personal Perspectives and Global Activism*, edited by Robin M. Chandler, Lihua Wang and Linda K. Fuller, 171–86. New York: Palgrave Macmillan, 2010.

Sjoberg, Laura. "Women and the Genocidal Rape of Women: The Gender Dynamics of Gendered War Crimes." In *Confronting Global Gender Justice: Women's Lives, Human Rights*, edited by Debra Bergoffen, Paula Ruth Gilbert, Tamara Harvey and Connie L. McNeely, 21–35. New York: Routledge, 2011.

Sjoberg, Laura, and Caron E. Gentry. *Mothers, Monsters, Whores: Women's Violence in Global Politics*. London: Zed Books, 2007.

Smeulers, Alette. "Female Perpetrators – Ordinary and Extra-Ordinary Women." *International Criminal Law Review* 15, no. 2 (2015): 207.

Smith, Roger W. "Women and Genocide: Notes on an Unwritten History." *Holocaust and Genocide Studies* 8, no. 3 (1994): 315–34.

Straus, Scott. *The Order of Genocide: Race, Power, and War in Rwanda*. Ithaca, NY: Cornell University Press, 2006.

United Nations Food and Agriculture Organization (UNFAO). La Place de la Femme Dans Les Projets de De'veloppement Rural: Le Projet d'Intensification agricole de Gikongoro au Rwanda, Etude de Cas, F.A.O., Rome, (1991): 7.

Vansina, Jan. *Antecedents to Modern Rwanda: The Nyiginya Kingdom*. Madison: University of Wisconsin Press, 2005.

Verwimp, Philip. "Machetes and Firearms: The Organization of Massacres in Rwanda." *Journal of Peace Research* 43, no. 1 (2006): 5–22.

Verwimp, Philip. *Peasants in Power: The Political Economy of Development and Genocide in Rwanda*. New York: Springer, 2013.

Vronsky, Peter. *Female Serial Killers: How and Why Women Become Monsters*. New York: Berkley Books, 2007.

West, Candace and Don H. Zimmerman. "Doing Gender." *Gender & Society* 1, no. 2 (1987): 125–51.

8 Perpetrators of sexual violence in armed conflict

Inger Skjelsbæk

Introduction[1]

When Antony Beevor (2002) published his book *Berlin: The Downfall 1945* one aspect that received much attention was his documentation of the rape committed by Russian soldiers in Berlin during the final days of World War II.[2] According to his research, Russian soldiers raped as many as two million German women in total, half of whom were gang-raped. The Berlin rapes are thought to have been perpetrated against about 130,000 women, 10,000 of whom are believed to have committed suicide (Summers 2002). Many historians have written about this and have had access to a wide variety of sources – from archives to interviews with victims and former military officials. Perhaps the most reliable sources of documentation, however, were two main hospitals in Berlin, whose records suggest that about 6 percent of the female population in Berlin were raped (Wood 2006: 309–10). Moreover, a more personal perspective is given in the book *Eine Frau in Berlin – Tagebuchaufzeichnungen vom 20. April bis 22. Juni 1945*, which depicts the anonymous diary entries of a woman in her thirties who writes with poignant and insightful precision about the Soviet takeover and the mass rape, of which she, too, was a victim. The author writes that in her apartment building alone at least 12 women were raped. Beevor, who has written the foreword to the Norwegian translation of the book, claims that based on the unique characteristics of this manuscript he has no reason to doubt the woman's accounts of these events. Elisabeth Jean Wood (2006: 310) wonders whether the Soviet troops committed these acts in retaliation for rapes committed by German troops, or as a form of reward. It could well have been for both reasons.

Most importantly for the context of this chapter, though, all of these crimes were committed with complete impunity; the perpetrators were never brought to justice. This was partly because at the time these deeds were not seen as part of the repertoire of political violence, nor were there legal norms constituting them as a criminal offence. Today this is no longer the case. The approach and attitude towards perpetration of sexual violence crimes in times of armed conflict have changed immensely in policymaking, as well as in both the legal and academic fields.

But how can the perpetration be explained? The objective of this chapter is not to provide a causal explanation, but rather to illustrate how institutions mandated

152   *Inger Skjelsbæk*

to deal with these crimes seek to make sense of them. Given that perpetrating acts of sexual violence in armed conflict is now prosecuted by national and international courts, it asks how the motivation behind it is explained in these fora. More precisely, it discusses how perpetrators of sexual violence in armed conflict are narrated in the legal proceedings of the International Criminal Tribunal for the Former Yugoslavia (ICTY), in particular in its sentences and judgments (see also Skjelsbæk 2015). Against this backdrop, it illustrates how the narratives about the perpetrators situate the individuals in question along a continuum of normal to abnormal behavior. In other words, this chapter explores if and how – in the eyes of the court – sexual violence in war is seen as normal military behavior.

The prosecution of perpetrators of sexual violence is a rather recent development. Although after World War II the Nuremberg and Tokyo trials were the first courts to prosecute major war crimes, sexual violence was no *corpus delicti*, nor was it documented to any significant extent. This failure to bring crimes of sexual violence in war to court is puzzling for, as de Anne-Marie L.M. Brouwer (2005) and Nicola Henry (2011) show, there would have been ample leverage within the law at both tribunals. There are many possible reasons for this, such as lack of evidence,[3] lack of legal will or lack of (female) lawyers and judges who pursued this particular agenda. Another possible explanation might be that sexual violence was not considered to be a criminal offence at the time. Sönke Neitzel and Harald Welzer's (2011: 13) extraordinary analysis of conversations between German soldiers reveals that acts of extreme brutality such as rape, killings and bombings were commonplace elements within the daily conversations of these soldiers. Acts of rape and sexual violence were the *modus operandi* in war and were accordingly not treated with particular attention; they were nothing special. The trials, however, were set up to prosecute extraordinary crimes, not 'normal' ones. Accordingly, stories of sexual violence failed to become part of the collective memory of World War II through these trials, even if these actions were an integral part of a behavioral repertoire of German, Axis and Allied soldiers alike (Lily 2007).

Since the end of World War II, attitudes towards sexual criminal behavior in war have changed dramatically, accompanied by significant changes in how legal institutions, policymakers and scholars seek to understand how victims, communities and perpetrators are affected by these types of crimes (Skjelsbæk 2012a), and not least seek to bring perpetrators to justice. Both supranational and national criminal prosecutions of perpetrators of sexual violence are now taking place in several courts around the world. The ICTY was the first to systematically prosecute crimes of sexual violence committed during armed conflict. The central principle of the ICTY is the same as that of the proceedings in Nuremberg and Tokyo: to hold individuals, as opposed to states, responsible for crimes committed in times of war. However, with the ICTY's added focus on sexual violence, the crimes for which individuals are held accountable have changed. Work that has been carried out since the establishment of the ICTY has altered the perceptions of crimes of sexual violence in ways that were unimaginable some decades ago.[4]

Researching perpetrators of sexual violence in armed conflict

There is an emerging body of literature on perpetrators of sexual violence crimes in war (Baaz and Stern 2013; Cohen et al. 2013; Leiby 2009; Nordås 2013). Whereas early studies primarily focused on the impact on victims (Skjelsbæk 2001), there is now a shift towards analyzing perpetrators. This shift is a response to a general lack of empirical knowledge about perpetrators, increased attention by the United Nations Security Council[5] on how to prosecute and prevent perpetration, and the lack of a conceptualization of perpetrators of sexual violence as opposed to other crimes committed by soldiers in wartime.

One example of the quantitative approach is the work of Dara Kay Cohen et al. (2013), who take as their point of departure a set of preconceptions regarding sexual violence in war, a sub-set of which relate to perpetrators. These include that the perpetrators are always men; that sexual violence is more common among rebel groups than state militaries; that given an opportunity men will rape; and that sexual violence is always perpetrated by combatants. Through their large-N analysis the authors make an important point in showing that there is a great degree of variation in the perpetration of sexual violence: not all perpetrators are men, state actors are no less involved in these crimes than other military groups, not all men will rape if the opportunity arises and not all perpetrators in armed conflicts are combatants. Maria Eriksson Baaz and Maria Stern (2009, 2013), in contrast, based their perpetrator research on extensive fieldwork and qualitative interviews in the Democratic Republic of Congo. Based on a discourse analysis of interviews with 193 people in 43 group interviews, Baaz and Stern (2009) differentiate between different motivations for sexual violence among perpetrators: lust rapes (which were seen as more 'normal,' i.e. not linked to the conflict pattern) and evil rapes (which happened in conjunction with other forms of war violence in the armed conflict), providing important insights into how "perpetrators, themselves, understand their violent crimes" (Baaz and Stern 2009: 496).

Michele Leiby (2009) provides yet another insight into the perpetration of sexual violence in Guatemala and Peru. The basis for her work is a quantitative coding of the published reports from the truth and reconciliation commissions which she supplements by fieldwork. Her focus is on the state as perpetrator, and more specifically on how the "state either explicitly encouraged, condoned, or at the very least had knowledge of the crimes being committed" (Leiby 2009: 456). In concluding her work, she asks whether there are differences "in rebel groups – such as their size, their proximity to civilian populations, their resource base or their politico-military strategy – that make some more likely to commit these kinds of human rights abuses? Do these factors in turn make the state more likely to use sexual violence?" (Leiby 2009: 466). As can be seen from these examples from the emerging literature on sexual violence perpetrators, methods, analyses and scholarly aims vary, but together they bring new empirical insights and debates to the conceptualization of the military sexual violence perpetrator.

There are moreover several studies on the legal discussions pertaining to sexual violence crimes in armed conflicts (de Brouwer et al. 2013; Fineman and Zinsstag

154   *Inger Skjelsbæk*

2013; Henry 2011; Houge 2008). From a methodological perspective, through the legal dialogue in the international courtroom, and assessment of the criminal actions, a picture of the accused emerges based on a bifocal view of the person and the crimes, and a discussion of normality and abnormality linked to the person and the situation underpins the court transcripts. As Leiby shows (2009), there is ever-growing data which lends itself to substantive new analyses of the sexual violence perpetrator in armed conflicts: truth commissions as well as indictments, court transcripts and judgments from various criminal courts provide a wealth of material which can and should be analyzed. While Leiby's research used quantitative coding of the transcripts from the truth commissions in order to establish an overview of "the type of sexual violence and the context under which it occurred" (Leiby 2009: 453), official texts from truth commissions and criminal courts can also be subject to an analysis along the lines of Baaz and Stern (2009). Such texts can provide insight into qualitative questions about how perpetrators of sexual violence situate their actions, behavior and ultimately their identities within a narrative/the narrative. In doing so, we gain an understanding not only of how they are situated within testimonies, but also of the reactions from the court/truth commission/others towards them.

Though much of the social science research on sexual violence perpetrators in armed conflict has been dominated by political science and international relations scholars, it is clear that the field of psychology has something unique to offer this field of knowledge. The conceptualization of the individual in a socio-political context is at the core of social and political psychological scholarship, and a narrative gaze at how non-psychological scholars use psychological language in their assessments of sexual violence perpetrators in armed conflicts helps us better understand how these perpetrators can be placed along a normal to abnormal behavioral continuum.

Regarding perpetration more generally, as reflected in this volume, there is a large and rich body of scholarly literature that analyzes international crimes, mass atrocities and genocidal actions in armed conflict. Some contributions situate perpetration along an axis of normal versus abnormal behavior. James Waller, a leading expert on genocide behavior, sums this distinction up by stating that the:

> social construction of cruelty – buttressed by professional socialization, group identification, and binding factors of the group – envelops perpetrators in a social context that encourages and rewards extraordinary evil. It reminds us that the normal reaction to an abnormal situation is abnormal behavior; indeed, normal behavior would be an abnormal reaction to an abnormal situation. We must borrow the perspective of the perpetrators and view their evil not as the work of 'lunatics' but as actions with a clear and justified purpose – so defined by a context of cruelty.
>
> (Waller 2007: 271)

Alette Smeulers adds to this understanding by arguing that "within a malignant governmental system, military organizations or police units, it is those who do not

Perpetrators of sexual violence 155

break the rules but those who *abide* by the rules who become perpetrators" (2008: 236–7). Hannah Arendt's (2006 [1963]) infamous elaborations of the Eichmann case fit into this assertion. Eichmann acted and saw himself as a bureaucrat. The fact that he was a bureaucrat of genocide is part of Arendt's conceptualization of the banality of evil; it becomes an everyday practice. How this transformation takes place is what several scholars attempt to understand from a vast array of different data material. Leigh A. Payne, for instance, has gone through confessions of state violence in various court and truth commissions from Argentina, Chile, Brazil and South Africa. These confessions do not, the author points out, disclose the truth but are "merely accounts, explanations and justifications for deviant behavior, or personal versions of a past" (Payne 2008: 2). Ronald D. Crelinsten (1995: 39) also makes this point by stating that "the language of torture is one that replaces the world of cruelty with euphemisms" and through this we can conclude that the truth about the reasoning of the individual perpetrator at the moment of action cannot be uncovered. We can only come close to an understanding by examining narrative construction in hindsight. What this literature has in common is a focus on international crimes and torture, but not on sexual violence crimes exclusively. My aim, therefore, is to add to this literature by examining the narratives on sexual crimes (and the criminals), in the context of mass atrocities.

Narratives on the perpetration of sexual violence at the ICTY

The narrative turn has opened a vast array of analyses that focus on the content and form of how life histories form social constructions of selves. According to Theodore Sarbin (1986: 23), "in giving accounts of ourselves or of others, we are guided by narrative plots [. . .] whether for formal biographies or autobiographies, for psychotherapy, for self-disclosure, or for entertainment, we do much more than catalog a series of events." Rather, we transform the events into a story. The ways in which narrative data are gathered and analyzed varies. In this chapter, I undertake a thematic analysis of the elements of the court cases which pertain to perpetrators of sexual violence sentenced by the ICTY, and untangle how the themes raised in relation to perpetration create a narrative account that situates the perpetrator along a normal to abnormal continuum as discussed earlier by Waller. The narratives analyzed are organized according to themes in the stories rather than by the way in which the stories are told.

The international criminal proceedings in this chapter lend themselves exceptionally well to such a narrative approach because the proceeding can, and ought to be, seen as narrative constructions of people and events for legal purposes.[6] In the ICTY's assessments of individuals and their crimes, the court is obliged to consider the "appropriate punishment in relation to the individual as well as the crime."[7] For the process of sentencing does more than simply punish perpetrators: it also involves an assessment of the individuals concerned – providing narratives about them – in relation to the law. In this context May-Len Skilbrei argues that the application of law is an inscription of norms because "[t]he law is not only the result of cultural norms; it is also a political and formal process whereby public

156 *Inger Skjelsbæk*

concern and international obligations are translated into law" (Skilbrei 2010: 42). The judgments of the ICTY thus reflect the normative shift by the international community from impunity regarding crimes of sexual violence in armed conflict to their prosecution, giving these criminal acts a different meaning.

In total, 30 individuals have been convicted of crimes of sexual violence by the ICTY, nine as principal perpetrators. For the purpose of my narrative analysis the judgments of the principal perpetrators proved to be most informative for they discuss acts of sexual violence at the greatest length and hence provide the richest material about these crimes.[8] The sentencing judgments were carefully analyzed by means of coding the descriptions of sexual violence within a narrative structure as described earlier. This non-chronological coding devoted special attention to episodic elements such as the ways in which the *settings* in which sexual violence occurred were described. In this process, it was the voices of the victims, perpetrators and others who were called as witnesses (and who are referred to in the sentencing judgments) that were coded. The coding was done by looking at how the violence was carried out: in detention facilities, in connection with other kinds of war violence or in a 'recreational' setting, and the ways in which the victims was seen (e.g. prisoners or not). Further, it was essential to map out the *role of the perpetrator* and in this effort it was primarily the discussions between the defense council, the prosecutor and to some extent the perpetrators themselves which were coded (also from the sentencing judgments) according to: if the crimes were carried out by one or several perpetrators, comments made by the perpetrators to victims/others at the moment of the criminal action, role of perpetrator in the military setting and how the crimes were carried out. Finally, the *assessment of the judges* was coded according to the ways in which aggravating and mitigating circumstances were discussed (explicitly or indirectly) in each case. Aggravating circumstances considered by the court included the role of the accused, whether the victims were particularly young, the duration of the crimes, whether more than one victim was involved, whether more than one perpetrator was involved, the vulnerability of the victims, and whether there had been widespread and systematic persecution that involved sexual violence in inhumane conditions.[9] Mitigating circumstances that were discussed were a guilty plea, expressing remorse, voluntary surrender, and cooperation with the Office of the Prosecutor.

Nine convicted principal perpetrators were found guilty of crimes of sexual violence against 32 identified women and five identified men. In addition, one of the individuals was convicted of raping and sexually assaulting an unidentified number of women and girls in a classroom in Foča. For these and other crimes, the perpetrators received prison sentences ranging from five years (Milan Simić) to 28 years (Dragoljub Kunarac). Three of the men in the group pleaded guilty to crimes of sexual violence (Miroslav Bralo, Milan Simić and Dragan Zelenović).

This group contains two particularly historic judgments in relation to the criminal prosecution of crimes of sexual violence. The first comprises the judgments against Hazim Delić and Esad Landžo, who were prosecuted together in what is referred to as the Mucić *et al.* case, in which rape was recognized as torture, a grave breach of the Geneva Conventions and a violation of the laws and customs

Perpetrators of sexual violence   157

of war. In addition, the case against Kovač, known as the Kunarac *et al.* case, was the first case in which sexual enslavement was classified as a crime against humanity.

Three narratives along a normal–abnormal continuum

As introduced earlier, the different narratives were organized along a continuum of normal to abnormal regarding how the actions of the perpetrators in times of war were explained. Three different perpetrator narratives could be identified which drew a clear link between sexual violence, militarism and masculinity.

First, the *notions of chivalry* and militaristic identities are strongly interlinked (Young 2007) and the masculine protector can be seen as the archetypical soldier (Enloe 1989; Elshtain 1987). As an example, consider the following passage from the Kunarac *et al.* case. It is Kunarac himself whose voice is heard:

> *JUDGE MUMBA: Is it your position, accused, that DB seduced you?*
>
> I did not give her a pretext for having sexual intercourse. I didn't say I wanted it at that moment; I had sexual intercourse with her against my will. I mean, without having a desire for sex. I will explain this later. She did this quite consciously for other reasons that I was not aware of at that moment.
>
> *Q. I shall remind you, Mr. Kunarac, of the following: During her statement, during her testimony, this witness, Witness DB, said that she was not sure that there would have been sexual intercourse if she had not taken an active role. What can you say as far as this claim is concerned?*
>
> I assert that had she not started doing all of this, I would have not – I would not have done a thing. I did not have any ideas about doing anything to her or sexually abusing her. I said that this behavior of hers really took me by surprise. I cannot say that I was raped. She did not use any kind of force, but she did everything. The way she acted was that she did not give me any manoeuvring space. As a man, I accepted her behavior and I did not refuse her as a woman. I did have sexual intercourse with her.
>
> (Kunarac *et al.* transcript, 6 July 2000, pp. 4541–2)

Bearing in mind that Kunarac has been given the most severe (crimes against humanity) and longest (28 years) sentence for sexual violence crimes to date, reading this passage is chilling. He admits having had sexual intercourse with the victim, but does in no way see himself as a perpetrator. Acts of sexual violence, particularly against young girls, by military men in times of war will not enhance their masculinity in the eyes of the court, rather the contrary. Yet sexual violence against young girls by men in uniform does lend itself to an attempted conceptualization of chivalrous behavior by the Defense Counsel. The soldiers had sex with the girls as a response to alleged infatuation and seduction in addition to claiming that the involuntary sexual behavior was not so bad because it

158   *Inger Skjelsbæk*

could have been worse, presumably if committed by others. Vuković, who was also convicted at the same trial of raping a girl the same age as his own daughter (FWS-50, aged 16 at the time), is said to have told the victim that "she was lucky in that she was the same age as his daughter, otherwise he would have done much worse things to her and that she was lucky about this conscience" (Kunarac et al. sentencing judgment, 22 February 2001, para. 814, p. 255). In other words, he is portrayed as cautious or 'protective' by being less violent than he could have been. The defense argued further that his acts had been committed out of "sexual urge, not out of hatred" (Kunarac et al. sentencing judgment, 22 February 2001, para. 816, p. 256), thereby suggesting that the acts were disconnected from the war, somewhat in contrast to the perpetrator's own accounts of various forms of protection in the war situation. Sexual behavior is conceptualized as a masculine issue along the lines of the boys-will-be-boys argument; the acts were seen as an expression of sexual lust which needed an outlet, in other words as normal male behaviour, triggered by the young age and innocence of the victims. In the discussions of the factors relevant for sentencing for the various crimes, the young ages of the victims were commented upon in the following ways: "this further increases the gravity of the crimes committed against her" (Zelenović sentencing judgment, 4 April 2007, para. 39, p. 13); "offences were committed against a particularly vulnerable and defenseless girl" (Kunarac et al. sentencing judgment, 22 February 2001, para. 879, p. 279); "the youthful age [. . .] and very young age are aggravating circumstances [. . .] against particularly vulnerable and defenseless girls and a woman" (Kunarac et al. sentencing judgment, 22 February 2001, para. 874, p. 278); and "the youthful age of certain of the victims of the offences [. . .] is considered an aggravating factor" (Kunarac et al. sentencing judgment, 22 February 2001, para. 864, p. 276). In three of the four formulations regarding age as an aggravating circumstance the judgment also made specific mention of the fact that these were young girls.

As young girls, these victims were both children and adolescents and had come to a stage in their lives when they would be maturing both emotionally and physically. Witness FWS-191, who was 17 years old when the relevant events occurred, "told him she was a virgin and Dragoljub Kunarac said that he would then be the first" (Kunarac et al. sentencing judgment, 22 February 2001, para. 259, p. 95). At this crucial time, they were molested by multiple men, twice their age and over extended periods of time, under terrifying conditions. What this has done to the victims was not discussed at any length in the judgments, but from other studies we know that fears of being unattractive and unmarriageable and feelings of shame caused by such events can often be overwhelming (Skjelsbæk 2012a).

If we see the chivalrous narrative as one which defines the perpetrator as a soldier who is driven by a protection rationale and normal sexual desires, then the second *narrative of opportunism* can be said to do the opposite. War provides opportunities to commit sexual violence crimes with impunity, but not all soldiers will take advantage of this situation. A closer look at what the court labeled "opportunistic perpetrators" reveals a second conceptualization of the military

Perpetrators of sexual violence 159

perpetrator, one in which sexual violence sets the perpetrator apart from fellow soldiers in a non-chivalrous way. These cases relate to crimes of sexual violence committed by soldiers who worked in a range of different detention facilities. One example is Milorad Radić, who worked as prison guard shift leader at the Omarska concentration camp. In this camp a relatively small number of detainees, approximately 36 according to the ICTY, were women. The oldest of these were in their 60s, and only one of them was particularly young (Radić sentencing judgment, 2 November 2001, para. 98, p. 31), but they were all considered to be threats to the Serb regime (Radić sentencing judgment, 2 November 2001, para. 19, p. 7). In their testimonies, several of the women told of multiple rapes that were committed against them in a somewhat orderly fashion, whereby they would be taken out of the rooms where the women were being held to a different location. There they would be raped by several men, before typically being sent back to the rooms where the women were being kept. Under these circumstances, in addition to the direct traumas caused by individual acts of sexual violence, the women at the camp were continually traumatized by each other's experiences, as they would never know who would be next in line. This, the court commented, created a constant atmosphere of fear and terror for all. Ultimately, Milorad Radić was sentenced to 20 years' imprisonment for acts that included crimes of sexual violence at the Omarska camp in central Bosnia. In its assessment of the charges and evidence regarding Radić's involvement in crimes committed at the camp, the court stated:

> The Trial Chamber heard compelling evidence that Radić was personally involved in the sexual harassment, humiliation, and violation of women in Omarska camp. He would call particular women out from their place of detention and when these women returned, it was apparent to the other women that something terrible had happened to them. Typically, they did not speak to or look at the other women.
>
> (Radić sentencing judgment, 2 November 2001, para. 546, p. 153)

The sexual violence perpetrators in this group were all found guilty of having committed sexual crimes against women who were imprisoned and who were subjected to criminal sexual violation on multiple occasions in these detention facilities. What sets these three sexual violence perpetrators apart from the three perpetrators in the previous category is that they exercised a different power and control. All victims were held in different detention facilities and the perpetrators all had different levels of superior responsibilities in these facilities. In addition, they had different levels of professional training. This context is different from the homes in which the sexual violence victims in the former category were allegedly placed. The fact that the perpetrators had a formal training which should have prepared them to act responsibly in a prison setting is seen as particularly aggravating. In addition, their position of authority meant that their behavior set an example to others. Further, while the perpetrators in the former category were conceptualized as committing acts of sexual violence to boost their military status,

160   *Inger Skjelsbæk*

the court is much more focused on sadistic aspects of the crimes committed by the perpetrators in the present category. One example of this is the case of Hazim Delić, who was found guilty of raping two women in the Čelebići prison camp that had been set up close to the town of Konjic in southwestern Bosnia, where Serb prisoners were held by Croat (and Bosnian) defense council HVOxiv soldiers. Hazim Delić was the deputy commander at the camp from May to November 1992, and was alleged to have also been in charge during the last month before the camp was closed down in December 1992. Women held at the camp (the exact number of whom is not stated in the sentencing judgment) were housed in a separate building, but were taken to a separate room where they were held together for interrogation. One of the victim witnesses, Mrs. Grozdana Ćećez, said that she had been raped by Hazim Delić and four other men, in the presence of two more. Both before and after these events, she was asked about the whereabouts of her husband. Other witnesses reported that Hazim Delić would boast about this incident and about having raped at least 18 women, claiming that "it was his intention to rape more in the future" (Delić sentencing judgment, 16 November 1998, para. 928, p. 325). Mrs. Ćećez testified that Hazim Delić had told her, while she was being raped, that she was in the camp because of her husband (who was thought to be hiding in the vicinity of Konjic) and that she would not have been there if he had been around (Delić sentencing judgment, 16 November 1998, para. 929, p. 325). The other victim, Ms. Antić, was raped on three occasions by Hazim Delić. Another witness, Witness P, stated that Hazim Delić had said that he was keeping Ms. Antić for himself and that she was a virgin (Delić sentencing judgment, 16 November 1998, para. 948, p. 331). The story of Ms. Antić is also mapped out in the judgment, where it is made clear that she was not married, was 44 years old at the time of the crimes, and was living with her mother when she was arrested in her village and taken to the Čelebići camp, where the following events took place:

> Upon her arrival at the Čelebići prison-camp, she was immediately interrogated together with another woman, by Hazim Delić, Zdravko Mucić and another person. In answer to a question by Mr. Mucić, she stated that she was not married, at which point Mr. Mucić said to Mr. Delić, "[t]his is just the right type for you."
> (Delić sentencing judgment, 16 November 1998, para. 955, p. 333)

The judgment then proceeds to detailed descriptions of rapes that were violent, intimidating and physically damaging for the victims. In its summary of how it viewed Hazim Delić's behaviour, the court wrote:

> The rapes were committed inside the Čelebići prison-camp and on each occasion Hazim Delić was in uniform, armed and viciously threatening towards Ms. Antić. The purpose of these rapes was to intimidate, coerce and punish Ms. Antić. Further, at least with respect to the first rape, Delić's purpose was to obtain information from Ms. Antić, as it was committed in the context of interrogation. In addition, the violence suffered by Ms. Antić in the form of rape, was inflicted upon her by Delić because she is a woman. As discussed

Perpetrators of sexual violence 161

above, this represents a form of discrimination which constitutes a prohibited purpose for the offence of torture. Finally, there can be no question that these rapes caused severe mental and physical pain and suffering to Ms. Antić. The effects of the rapes that she suffered at the hands of Hazim Delić, including the extreme pain of anal penetration and subsequent bleeding, the severe psychological distress evidenced by the victim while being raped under circumstances where Mr. Delić was armed and threatening her life, and the general depression of the victim, evidenced by her constant crying, the feeling that she was going crazy and the fact that she was treated with tranquilizers, demonstrate most emphatically the severe pain and suffering that she endured.

> (Delić sentencing judgment, 16 November 1998,
> paras 963–4, p. 335)

Hazim Delić was found guilty of torture for the multiple rapes of Ms. Antić. In the court's discussion of factors relevant for sentencing, a number of issues pertaining to Hazim Delić's personality were raised and the following formulation was used: "Hazim Delić [is] guilty of committing a series of violent crimes upon detainees who were at his mercy in the Čelebići prison camp" (Delić sentencing judgment, 16 November 1998, para. 1253, p. 429). In other words, the prisoners were not only extremely vulnerable owing to the fact of their incarceration, but had also been subject to Delić's whims and impulses, as the prosecution pointed out. In its closing statements, the prosecution stated that "he participated in monstrous crimes [. . .] he brutally raped a number of the women in the prison camp and then boasted about it [. . .] he took sadistic pleasure in the infliction of pain [. . .] he would laugh in response to pleas for mercy from the victim" (Delić sentencing judgment, 16 November 1998, para. 1254, p. 429). Further, the prosecution submitted that the Trial Chamber should regard, as an aggravating factor, that the suffering of the victims took place within the context of the conditions of their imprisonment (Delić sentencing judgment, 16 November 1998, para. 1256, p. 429). The defence, on the other hand, argued that Delić had had no prior trouble with the law, had been charged with no criminal offences before this time, and had no training prior to his assignment to the prison camp (Delić sentencing judgment, 16 November 1998, para. 1257, p. 429). The court, however, found few mitigating circumstances for Hazim Delić. Rather, and in relation to the rapes in particular, the Trial Chamber pointed out that:

> Hazim Delić is guilty of torture by way of the deplorable rapes of two women detainees in the Čelebići prison-camp. He subjected Grozdana Ćećez not only to the inherent suffering involved in rape, but exacerbated her humiliation and degradation by raping her in the presence of his colleagues. The effects of this crime are readily apparent from the testimony of the victim when she said ". . . he trampled on my pride and I will never be able to be the woman that I was." Before the first rape of Milojka Antić, Hazim Delić threatened her and told her that, if she did not do whatever he asked, she would be sent to another prison-camp or shot. He then forced her to take her clothes off at gunpoint, ignored her pleas for mercy and cursed and threatened her while raping her.

162　*Inger Skjelsbæk*

The following day he compounded her fear and suffering by stating ". . . [w]hy are you crying? This will not be your last time." This rape was followed by two others, one of which involved painful and physically damaging anal penetration. These were committed by Hazim Delić when he was armed, in total disregard of his victim's pleas for mercy. Ms. Antić testified as to the effect these crimes had on her, including feelings of misery, constant crying and the feeling that she had gone crazy. In a victim impact statement submitted by the Prosecution for the purposes of sentencing, she stated, "[t]he wounds that I carry from the rapes in Čelebići will never go away."

(Delić sentencing judgment, 16 November 1998,

paras 1262–3, p. 431)

The Trial Chamber further commented on the way in which Hazim Delić was said to have behaved in the prison facility, and concluded that both the crimes (and their underlying motivations) were some of the most serious offences a perpetrator can commit. Further, the Trial Chamber commented that the "manner in which these crimes were committed are indicative of a sadistic individual who, at times, displayed total disregard for the sanctity of human life and dignity (Delić sentencing judgment, 16 November 1998, para. 1268, p. 433). The next paragraph stated:

As well as having a general sadistic motivation, Hazim Delić was driven by feelings of revenge against the people of Serb ethnicity. Before raping Ms. Antić, he stated that "the Chetniks were guilty for everything that was going on. He [Delić] started to curse my Chetnic mother."

(Delić sentencing judgment, 16 November 1998,

para. 1269, p. 433)

The frequent use of words like pathetic pleasure, revenge, sadistic motivation, whims and impulses, etc., in the sentencing judgments suggest that the court views the perpetrators as having low self-control and that the possibility to commit acts of sexual violence was something they sought out, because the opportunity was there. In addition, it is underscored that these perpetrators were particularly violent and thus the shifts when they were on guard stood out. The fact that these men stand out in the setting they were in is further underscored by their respective defense lawyers, who attempt to build a case narrative in which it is the perpetrators' deviant personalities which are in focus, and where attempts were made to view their deviant personalities as mitigating circumstances.

A final narrative format which emerged in the sentencing judgments was when *remorse was expressed* and a guilty plea was submitted. Miroslav Bralo admitted guilt on all counts against him, including the rape and imprisonment of Witness A, whom he violated over a period of approximately two months. In his guilty plea, he expressed deep discomfort with the person he was at the time of the war and the actions and behaviors he admitted having carried out:

These were acts which I always knew to be wrong, which anyone would know to be wrong, and for which there really can be no excuse at all. I know

Perpetrators of sexual violence   163

I acted badly, and compounded this later by my words. Our wrongs were so terrible – I include others here – that we clung to them, and tried to justify them. I tried to be proud of my actions and to think they were the actions of a successful soldier. Today I am ashamed of my conduct and ashamed how I behaved. No, these were not the actions of the soldier I once wanted to be. I was present when women and children were gunned down in front of me, and at that moment the good soldier in me was gone, silent.

(Bralo, guilty plea, 19 July 2005)

Dragan Zelenović, on the other hand, was found guilty of committing, aiding and abetting and co-perpetrating multiple rapes at various times and at different locations in Foča over an extended period of time in 1992. On 17 January 2007, he pleaded guilty to seven counts of rape and torture. In his plea statement, he focused on the religious dimensions of his regrets:

Guided by Biblical teachings that the truth is not to be feared because that is the only thing that will help all, I have confessed as to my guilt, and I am prepared to bear all the consequences of that. I know that not a single form of punishment can erase the sufferings sustained by my victims. However, faith teaches us that admission of having committed injustice to someone is the best way of helping them. [. . .] I feel sorry for all the victims who were victimized by anything that I did, and that is why I express from this forum my deepest remorse and regret. I am a human being with virtues and vices, and I didn't know how to deal with these vices when I should have. [. . .] I will courageously take any sentence meted out, and I hope that God will give me strength to go through all of this and that I go back to my family.

(Zelenović, guilty plea, 17 January 2007)

In these judgments, the expression of guilt itself is at the core and the perpetrator himself agrees, by and large, to the factual basis and gives an assessment of his own behavior. In other words, in these judgments the voices of the perpetrators are the most pronounced. In all three of these cases, the fact that the accused entered a plea of guilty was given considerable weight by the court, and the sentences the accused men received for grave offences were substantially lighter than those in the other cases examined. The central element in the evaluation of the court was not just the fact that a plea of guilty had been entered, but also its timing, its wording and whether it was seen as being sincere and a true expression of remorse. The way in which this admission of guilt was formulated in the guilty pleas varied, but the central tenet was that the perpetrators distanced themselves from the persons they were at the time when the admitted crimes took place. The individual saw himself as a damaged soldier; as a person tormented by guilt (i.e. that he committed acts he knew to be wrong); as a failed human being who did not deal appropriately with his own virtues and vices, for which he was prepared to pay the appropriate cost both in a legal and in a religious sense. All three cases contain descriptions of altered identities: the soldier, the person of conscience

164   *Inger Skjelsbæk*

and the humane person. These insights and admissions were given considerable punitive leverage by the court, even though the crimes the accused men admitted committing were arguably among the gravest instances of humanitarian violation in the war.

When summarizing these narratives, two extremes emerge. On the one hand, the narrative of the sexual violence perpetrator attempting to be cast as a chivalrous militarized individual. We are presented with the claim that the perpetrator(s) commit(s) acts of sexual violence out of lust and not hatred, that they could have been more violent (but refrained to be), that they are seduced by (very young girls) and that there is a love relationship between perpetrator and victim. All of these events are further set within the framework of a protectionist aim, and the sexual violence behavior is construed as part of normalized military behavior, albeit strongly contested by the judges and the prosecutors. At the other end of the extreme lies the narrative of opportunistic military perpetrators who commit acts of sexual violence because they have authority and access to defenseless women and because they display sadistic pleasure in inflicting humiliating pain. In these cases, acts of sexual violence serve to set the perpetrators apart from other military individuals; they are seen as deviant and abnormal individuals. These narratives are mutually reinforced by the judges, defense lawyers and prosecutors, albeit with different legal concerns in mind. In addition to these opposite extremes, there are the remorseful perpetrators who plead guilty and express regret, shame and guilt. At the core of their guilty plea statements are what they portray as failed soldiers. The acts for which they plead guilty are in contrast to how a good soldier should behave. Sexual violence, then, does not simply set these individuals apart from other soldiers, but becomes a different expression of a failed military identity altogether. What sets the remorseful narratives apart from the two others is that they refer to an aberrant, or temporarily abnormal, behavior that the perpetrator recognizes in hindsight. The judges' assessment of the perpetrator focuses on the validity of this temporality: is the perpetrator really sincere in his expression of remorse and thereby distancing himself from who he was during the war?

How then do these narratives add to the understanding of perpetrators of mass atrocities in armed conflicts? What do these narratives represent? The notions of the chivalrous, opportunistic and remorseful perpetrators overlap to a large extent with the categorizations by Smeulers (2008) and others. In different ways, these narratives suggest criminal masterminds, fanatics, criminal sadists, profiteers and devoted warriors, which Smeulers discusses in her overview. Yet sexual violence crimes involve the notion of sexual pleasure in addition to the infliction of pain; a way of thinking which enables a conceptualization whereby the crimes can be narrated in a way that is different to torture and mass atrocities. One could there-fore question if these crimes come across as more normal to the perpetrators than other kinds of crimes: the victims are not seen as dehumanized in the context of the armed conflict, but as gendered objects of masculine lust, which is what the chivalrous narratives would suggest is in a way normal behavior. At the other extreme, sexual violence crimes set perpetrators apart from other perpetrators in the same setting, as the opportunistic narrative would suggest, identifying the perpetrators as abnormal individuals. Finally, the narrative of remorse is perhaps most in compliance with the more established conceptualization of perpetrators of mass atrocities: a new identity (the soldier) takes precedence over other identities and primes the individual for behavior and reasoning that seem aberrant for the civilian in the aftermath.

Conclusion

The analysis shows that by committing sexual violence crimes military individuals in the context of war are situated as perpetrators in different ways. Having presented here the three conceptualizations, one could argue that acts of sexual violence place the perpetrators on a continuum where it is the notion of the militarized individual that is cast in a different light, depending on how the discussions in the court unfold. These findings do not suggest a linear instrumental use of sexual violence on a group level, as was the approach of Cohen et al. (2012), but takes the acts themselves as the starting point and asks how they reflect back on the perpetrator and how the perpetrator is situated as a militarized individual through these acts. What we find by doing this is that sexual violence in war has at least two opposing consequences for the perpetrators: it can enhance a militarized masculinity, but it can also do the opposite. Kimberly Hutchings asks whether war provides an arena for hegemonic masculinities to be played out or whether it could be that the so-called new wars force us to focus on the "formal, relational properties of masculinity as a concept" (Hutchings 2008: 390). Perhaps the discussions of the three perpetrators in this category constitute a good illustration of Mary Kaldor's (1999) discussions of the so-called new wars, as Hutchings sees them. She argues that Kaldor diagnoses the "masculinity of the new warrior as pathological, something that takes a recognizable form of human behavior to new and extreme limits and that needs to be countered by responsible and autonomous action on the part of the cosmopolitan law enforcer" (Hutchings 2008: 399). The nature of wars has changed and the perceptions of hegemonic (and militarised) masculinity has changed accordingly. The response is not a privileged status but potential international criminal prosecution. These insights suggest that the ICTY represents a strong conceptual shift from the laissez-faire attitude expressed in the memoirs of General Patton that "unquestionably there shall be some raping" (quoted in Brownmiller 1975: 31) to harsh moral condemnation of this allegedly normal state of affairs.

Notes

1 This chapter is a reworked version of Inger Skjelsbæk, "The Military Perpetrator: A Narrative Analysis of Sexual Violence Offenders at the International Criminal Tribunal for the Former Yugoslavia (ICTY)." *Journal of Social and Political Psychology* 3, no. 1 (2015): 46–70.
2 The Russian ambassador to the UK at the time called Beevor's descriptions "acts of blasphemy," regarding them as an affront to the troops that saved Europe from Nazism (Summers 2002).

166 *Inger Skjelsbæk*

3 However, both de Brouwer (2005) and Henry (2011) argue that there was evidence but that it was ignored and overlooked.

4 In addition, a set of United Nations Council Resolutions (one adopted in June 2008 (UNSCR 1820), one in September 2009 (UNSCR 1888), one in December 2010 (UNSCR 1960), and one in June 2013 (UNSCR 2106)) have formulated how sexual violence in war is perceived by the international community at large. They all focus on the protection of women and vulnerable groups against sexual violence – based on the central argument that lack of protection perpetuates vulnerability, which in turn may be detrimental to international peace and security. This is the essence of the conceptual shift that has taken place regarding crimes of sexual violence.

5 Particularly UNSCR 1820; 1888; 1960; 2106; and 2242.

6 Despite their differences, there are certain narrative elements that characterize all of the sentencing judgments in the ICTY Trial Chamber: a list of the charges against the accused, the evidence presented to the court, a discussion of the applicable law, the findings of the Trial Chamber and, finally, a discussion of the factors considered relevant for sentencing. In cases where a guilty plea has been entered by the accused, this plea is given considerable weight in the sentencing judgment.

7 *See* Commentary to Article 46 'Sentencing,' Draft Statute for an International Criminal Court, *Report of the International Law Commission on the work of its forty-sixth session*, UN Doc A/51/10 (1994), p. 123 (Article 46, Commentary, para. 1).

8 Miller (2004), Zimbardo (2008) and Baum (2008) argue for a distinction between evil actions and evil inactions. This distinction proved very useful, because it permitted me to distinguish between those who had perpetrated acts of sexual violence with their own bodies or with tools/weapons they held and used directly on other persons and those who had not. The 'inactive' perpetrators were by no means passive, but they were not as directly involved in the crimes of sexual violence for which they were held responsible as those who actually committed such acts. It turned out, however, that the 'inaction category' needed to be further subdivided, as the cases classified under this heading comprised a wide variety of inactions. There was a subgroup to which the label "evil inaction" did not seem to belong, because the individuals concerned had given direct orders to others to commit acts of sexual abuse, rather than committing such acts themselves. These individuals seemed to fall somewhere between being personally active and being inactive. It therefore seemed useful to distinguish this group further into those who had instigated sexual violence by ordering or being physically present and those who had known about such events but had not intervened to prevent them. In sum, the case material revealed 15 people who had been found guilty of crimes of sexual violence on the basis of their inactions, and four who were held responsible because they had issued direct orders, but who had not themselves directly committed acts of sexual violence. All of the sentencing judgments for these cases were read through as background material, but do not form part of the material analysed in this chapter.

9 This list is taken from the details of the *Kunarac, Kovačand Vuković* trial provided in de Brouwer (2005: 363–4).

References

Arendt, Hannah. *Eichmann in Jerusalem: A Report on the Banality of Evil*. New York: Penguin Classics, 2006 [1963].

Baaz, Maria Eriksson, and Maria Stern. "Why Do Soldiers Rape? Masculinity, Violence, and Sexuality in the Armed Forces in the Congo (DRC)." *International Studies Quarterly* 53, no. 2 (2009): 495–518.

Baaz, Maria Eriksson, and Maria Stern. *Sexual Violence as a Weapon of War? Perceptions, Prescriptions, Problems in the Congo and Beyond*. London: Zed Books, 2013.

Perpetrators of sexual violence   167

Baum, Steven K. *The Psychology of Genocide: Perpetrators, Bystanders, and Rescuers*. New York: Cambridge University Press, 2008.

Beevor, Anthony. *Berlin: The Downfall 1945*. London: Penguin Books, 2002.

Brownmiller, Susan. *Against Our Will: Men, Women and Rape*. New York: Simon and Schuster, 1975.

Cohen, Dara Kay, Amelia Hoover Green, and Elisabeth Jean Wood. *Wartime Sexual Violence: Misconceptions, Implications, and Ways Forward*. Special Report 323. Washington, DC: United States Institute of Peace (USIP), 2013. www.usip.org/publications/wartime-sexual-violence-misconceptions-implications-and-ways-forward. Accessed 27 November 2017.

Cohen, Dara Kay, and Ragnhild Nordås. *Sexual Violence in African Conflicts, 1989–2009: What the Data Show*. CSCW Policy Brief. Oslo: Centre for the Study of Civil War (CSCW), 2012. http://file.prio.no/publication_files/cscw/Nordas-Cohen-Sexual-Violence-in-African-Conflicts-1989-2009-CSCW-Policy-Brief-02–2012.pdf. Accessed 27 November 2017.

Crelinsten, Ronald D. "In Their Own Words: The World of the Torturer." In *The Politics of Pain: Torturers and Their Masters*, edited by Ronald D. Crelinsten and Alex P. Schmid, 35–65. Boulder, CO: Westview Press, 1995.

de Brouwer, Anne-Marie L. M. *Supranational Criminal Prosecution of Sexual Violence: The ICC and the Practice of the ICTY and the ICTR*. Antwerpen: Intersentia, 2005.

de Brouwer, Anne-Marie L. M., Charlotte Ku, Renée G. Römkens R., and Larissa J. Herik (eds.). *Sexual Violence as an International Crime: Interdisciplinary Approaches*. Antwerpen: Intersentia, 2013.

Elshtain, Jean Bethke. *Women and War*. New York: Basic Books, 1987.

Enloe, Cynthia. *Bananas, Beaches & Bases: Making Feminist Sense of International Politics*. Berkeley: University of California Press, 1989.

Fineman, Martha Elbertson, and Estelle Zinsstag (eds.). *Feminist Perspectives on Transitional Justice: From International and Criminal to Alternative Forms of Justice*. Antwerpen: Intersentia, 2013.

Henry, Nicola. *War and Rape: Law, Memory and Justice*. London: Routledge, 2011.

Houge, Anette Bringedal. *Wartime Rape and Sexual Violence*. Master Thesis, University of Oslo, Department of Political Science, Oslo, 2008.

Hutchings, Kimberly. "Making Sense of Masculinity and War." *Men and Masculinities* 10, no. 4 (2008): 389–404.

Kaldor, Mary. *New and Old Wars: Organized Violence in a Global Era*. Stanford, CA: Stanford University Press, 1999.

Leiby, Michele L. "Wartime Sexual Violence in Guatemala and Peru." *International Studies Quarterly* 53, no. 3 (2009): 445–68.

Lily, Robert J. *Taken by Force: Rape and American GI's in Europe During World War II*. New York: Palgrave Macmillan, 2007.

Miller, Arthur G. (ed.). *The Social Psychology of Good and Evil*. New York: The Guilford Press, 2004.

Neitzel, Sönke, and Harald Welzer. *Soldater: Beretninger om Krig, Drap og Død [Soldiers: Stories of War, Killings and Keath]*. Oslo: Forlaget Press, 2011 [1st German ed. 2011].

Nordås, Ragnhild. *Preventing Conflict-Related Sexual Violence*. PRIO Policy Brief. Oslo: Peace Research Institute Oslo (PRIO), 2013. http://file.prio.no/publication_files/prio/Nordas-Preventing-Conflict-related-Sexual-Violence-PRIO-Policy-Brief-02-2013.pdf. Accessed 27 November 2017.

Payne, Leigh A. *Unsettling Accounts: Neither Truth nor Reconciliation in Confessions of State Violence*. London: Duke University Press, 2008.

168 *Inger Skjelsbæk*

Sarbin, Theodore (ed.). *Narrative Psychology: The Storied Nature of Human Conduct.* New York: Praeger, 1986.

Skilbrei, May-Len. "Taking Trafficking to Court." *Women and Criminal Justice* 20, no. 1 (2010): 40–56.

Skjelsbæk, Inger. "Sexual Violence and War: Mapping Out a Complex Relationship." *European Journal of International Relations* 7, no. 2 (2001): 211–37.

Skjelsbæk, Inger. *The Political Psychology of War Rape: Studies from Bosnia and Herzegovina.* London: Routledge, 2012a.

Skjelsbæk, Inger. "Responsibility to Protect or Prevent? Victims and Perpetrators of Sexual Violence Crimes in Armed Conflicts." *Global Responsibility to Protect* 4, no. 2 (2012b): 154–71.

Skjelsbæk, Inger. "The Military Perpetrator: A Narrative Analysis of Sentencing Judgments on Sexual Violence Offenders at the International Criminal Tribunal for the Former Yugoslavia (ICTY)." *Journal of Social and Political Psychology* 3, no. 1 (2015): 46–70.

Smeulers, Alette. "Perpetrators of International Crimes: Towards a Typology." In *Supranational Criminology: Towards a Criminology of International Crimes*, edited by Alette Smeulers and Roelof Haverman, 233–63. Antwerpen: Intersentia, 2008.

Summers, Chris. "Red Army Rapists Exposed." *BBC News Online* (2002). http://news.bbc.co.uk/2/hi/europe/1939174.stm. Accessed 27 November 2017.

Waller, James E. *Becoming Evil: How Ordinary People Commit Genocide and Mass Killing.* Oxford: Oxford University Press, 2007.

Wood, Elisabeth Jean. "Variation in Sexual Violence During War." *Politics and Society* 34, no. 3 (2006): 307–41.

Young, Iris Marion. *Global Challenges, War, Self-Determination and Responsibility for Justice.* Cambridge: Polity Press, 2007.

Zimbardo, Philip. *The Lucifer Effect: Understanding How Good People Turn Evil.* New York: Random House Trade Paperbacks, 2008.

9 Cross-border perpetrator recruitment in the Ivorian civil war

The motivations and experiences of young Burkinabe men in the *Forces Nouvelles* rebel movement

Jesper Bjarnesen

Introduction

The armed conflict in Côte d'Ivoire in the first decade of the new millennium resonated throughout a region already marked by the civil wars in Sierra Leone and Liberia and an unstable political environment in Guinea-Conakry.[1] Despite this regional instability, and the gradual build-up of hostilities in Côte d'Ivoire, there was a sense of disbelief in the early reports from both national and international observers (e.g. Daddieh 2001; Human Rights Watch 2002; Le Pape and Vidal 2002; Maddox Toungara 2001), not only by way of the disturbing images of its most obvious victims: the dead bodies in mass graves on the outskirts of Abidjan in October 2000, or the Burkinabe laborers killed in the town of Tabou in 1999, but also as a further fall from grace of the former regional economic superpower. The deterioration of financial and political stability, as well as the receding possibilities for labor migrants, affected livelihoods across the Ivorian borders and changed political outlooks of actors across the continent.

In addition to these structural and symbolic regional impacts, the perpetrators of armed aggression on both sides of the conflict were a corollary of nationalities and ideological affiliations. The three rebel groups constituting the *Forces Nouvelles* movement, which originated in Côte d'Ivoire's northern regions and waged a war against what they perceived as their deliberate marginalization and persecution by successive regimes since the early 1990s, employed Sierra Leonean and Liberian mercenaries as well as *dozo* hunters from the north and from Burkina Faso. President Laurent Gbagbo's loyalist forces, consisting of the Ivorian armed forces as well as the irregular urban youth militias known as the *Jeunes Patriotes* (young patriots), in addition to Liberian fighters and *dozo* hunters of their own, employed South African, Angolan, and European mercenaries. Finally, the French army's *Licorne* forces in collaboration with peacekeeping forces from the Economic Community of West African States (ECOWAS) and the United Nations Operation in Côte d'Ivoire (ONUCI) were deployed to keep the two sides apart (Banégas and Marshall-Fratani 2003: 8). In this sense, the regional entanglements of the Ivorian crisis covered a vast array of actors and social spheres, assisted by the gradual

170   *Jesper Bjarnesen*

loosening of national border controls in order to accommodate refugees and, allegedly, arms trafficking, to and from Burkina Faso, Ghana, Guinea, and Liberia.

This chapter explores the involvement of young Burkinabe fighters in the Ivorian crisis, through their recruitment into the *Forces Nouvelles* rebel movement by recruiters stationed in the regional capital of Bobo-Dioulasso during the period 2000–2004. Rebel recruitment and the perpetration of violence is analyzed on the premise of the motivations and practices of mobility as akin to other forms of mobility. The analysis employs an anthropological approach to the study of perpetrators of violence in armed conflict, emphasizing the structural violence that conditions the participation in war as well as the socio-cultural idioms that shape and legitimize perpetration in specific social contexts. The chapter thereby advocates an approach that resists a normative or moral judgment of acts of violence, or rather that explores the normative orders that provide the context for the perpetration of violence in armed conflict empirically. This stance implies an understanding of the concept of perpetration that distances itself from the common connotations of the term, which, as Merriam-Webster's dictionary bluntly summarizes, implies "to do (something that is illegal or wrong)"! Advocating a less normative conceptualization of perpetration does not concern the question of whether the analyst condones the acts of violence studied but posits that acts of violence, as other exchanges between subjects, carry intentions and outlooks that should be explored empirically rather than preconceived (see Jackson 2002).

In the case of Burkinabe recruits in the *Forces Nouvelles* rebel movement, generations of labor migrants across the Ivorio-Burkinabe border provided the dominant moral template for assessing perpetration of violence in the Ivorian armed conflict, on the part of the perpetrators themselves as well as their neighbors, families, friends, and of local authorities upon their return to Burkina Faso. The empirical material that informs this chapter was collected through ethnographic fieldwork in southern Burkina Faso between January and December 2010. This chapter is based on extended participant observation and open-ended questioning through semi-structured interviews with eight former rebel combatants as well as a larger number of other residents in the same urban area. The chapter begins by contextualizing *Forces Nouvelles* cross-border recruitment and proceeds by considering the experiences and narratives of three former combatants upon their return to Burkina Faso. These three cases serve as a reflection on the conditions of combatant recruitment and return, and explore the circumstances as well as the social and existential effects of perpetrating violence in the Ivorian armed conflict. The overall argument suggests that the perpetration of violence must be understood not only in relation to the socio-cultural significance of these acts in and of themselves but, more importantly, in the broader socio-economic context of regional labor migration as well as the political context of transnational identity politics.

Perpetration in armed conflict

The study of perpetration in mass violence in the social sciences has so far focused primarily on genocidal violence, and particularly on the emblematic cases of the

Perpetrator recruitment in the Ivorian war   171

Holocaust and the Rwandan genocide. Furthermore, much attention has been given to the motivations and outlooks of the figure heads of genocidal movements such as Adolf Hitler or Pol Pot, neglecting the study of "foot-soldiers at the local level" (Williams 2014: 73). This chapter provides an anthropological approach to perpetration that emphasizes the motivations and outlooks of young men without previous experience of mass violence who were recruited into the *Forces Nouvelles* rebel movement in Côte d'Ivoire. The analysis thereby broadens the scope of the study of perpetrators to consider cases of armed conflict that may not be considered genocidal.

This chapter thus inscribes itself in a well-established anthropological paradigm of searching for structural explanations behind the actions and outlooks of individuals. In relation to armed conflict, several studies have pointed to the dynamics between personal or idiosyncratic motivations or predilections and the societal conditions that enable and impede the individual combatant's outlooks and room for maneuver (e.g. Hoffman 2011a; Vigh 2006a; Utas 2003; Nordstrom 2004; Richards 2004). From this perspective, the most significant motivating factor that lead young Burkinabe men into battle was undeniably the lack of employment opportunities at home, which implied the lack of possibilities for realizing a process of social becoming (cf. Christiansen et al. 2006). Similarly, Ghassan Hage argues that, "[t]he impossibility of making a life is one of the most important factors to consider when trying to understand the emergence of the [Palestinian suicide bombers]" (Hage 2003: 78). Hage refers to the lack of such possibilities as a state of 'social death,' whereby the potential perpetrator loses all social significance and sense of purpose – an existential void that the prospects of becoming a martyr promises to fill posthumously. The ideology of martyrdom, in Hage's case, becomes the sociocultural idiom that provides the potential suicide bombers with a morally sanctioned path out of their social moratorium (cf. Vigh 2006b).

It should be noted that outside such ethnographically anchored analyses, the search for the structural conditions that enable the perpetration of (mass) violence goes against the normative inclination to reserve structural explanations for social contexts that are far removed from the sociocultural sphere of the analyst or commentator. Instead of applying structural analyses in cases closer to home, the notion of 'a few bad apples,' which locates the incentives in the (deviant) behavior of the individual perpetrator(s) is generally evoked to explain violent acts that are not morally sanctioned in the US or in Europe; the school shootings across the US and the mass killings in Norway by Anders Behring Breivik being prime examples. Conversely, the same analytical gaze consistently blames the 'barrel' in violence labeled as 'terrorist' – a label that in itself has become increasingly reserved to the cultural Other. As David Keen argues in relation to the US-lead 'war on terror,' there has been

> a persistent tendency to exaggerate the decentralization of violence in relation to one's 'friends.' Alongside this has been an enduring habit of underplaying the decentralization of violence among one's 'enemies.'
>
> (Keen 2006: 87)

172 *Jesper Bjarnesen*

By "decentralization," Keen intends the ascription of agency, or blame in an explicitly moralizing perspective, to actors outside the centers of ideological and political authority, such as lower ranking or civilian perpetrators of mass violence. In the analysis of cases closer to home, then, the uncomfortable questions regarding the structural explanations for mass killings are replaced by an insistence of the singularity of the perpetrator(s), while a phenomenon classed as belonging to a different (and almost by default, a lesser) cultural sphere is understood almost purely in terms of its structural causes, such as Islamist ideology or chronic poverty. The challenge of a less normative analytical approach to the perpetration of violence, therefore, consists in the consideration of both structural and idiosyncratic conditions for such acts (Williams 2014).

In the present case, the tendency to emphasize the structural conditions of unemployment, ethnic allegiance, and lack of political leadership risks a neglect of the full cultural repertoires that provide moral justification and rationale for engaging in the perpetration of violence, as well as the political consciousness and capabilities of individual combatants. Danny Hoffman's (2011a) work on combatants in the Mano River wars, for example, provides an elegant and insightful contextualization of perpetration through the conceptualization of non-state violence as driven by dissident 'war machines.' Hoffman argues explicitly that the notion of war machines, derived from Gilles Deleuze and Felix Guattari's influential treatise *Capitalism and Schizophrenia* (2004a, 2004b), should not be confused with a popular imagining, which might evoke "mindless, amoral violence – a machine perhaps operated by human beings but ultimately grinding away under its own steam for the sole purpose of destruction" (Hoffman 2011a: 3). But although Hoffman proceeds to elaborate a nuanced conceptualization of 'war machines,' one is still left with a view of the combatants he studies as drawn into violence almost entirely by circumstances that mute their own intentionalities, condemning marginal young men to a life of day-to-day maneuverings to stay alive and make a living (see also Utas 2003; Vigh 2006a). Despite its praiseworthy illumination of the social contextualization of recruitment into armed conflict, this view of combatant incentives has relegated political imagination and ideological motivations to analytical obscurity, bordering a portrayal that echoes Deleuze and Guattari's analogy between the war machine and the game Go:

> Go pieces, in contrast [to Chess pieces] are pellets, disks, simple arithmetic units, and have only anonymous, collective, or third-person function. . . . Go pieces are elements of a nonsubjectified machine assemblage with no intrinsic properties, only situational ones.
>
> (Deleuze and Guattari 2004a: 389, quoted
> in Hoffman 2011a: 9)

Despite Hoffman's conceptual caveats, I would argue, the Deleuzian imagery of the war machine as a structural complex that conditions and enables large-scale recruitment of combatants retains the connotations of a machinery wherein its constitutive parts are replaceable, anonymous cogs rather than full-fledged social beings. This analytical priority has had its legitimacy not only as a counterbalance to the decentralized ascription of agency considered earlier, but also as a significant contribution to the analysis of that complex, *from the vantage point of the war machine*. As an account of the incentives of the combatants themselves, on the other hand, the overemphasis on the structural conditioning of potential 'cogs in the machinery' require a complementary consideration of the political imaginaries and socio-cultural repertoires of the combatants as full-fledged social beings.

This chapter, therefore, offers an analysis that builds on the well-established structural analyses of participation in mass violence in West Africa, as exemplified by Hoffman's Deleuzian framework, and adds an emphasis on the spectrum of ideological reasonings that legitimate violence in the eyes of the perpetrators themselves. In order to grasp the ideological spectrum evoked by Burkinabe ex-combatants, it is necessary to consider the political and cultural history of transnational connectedness between Burkina Faso and Côte d'Ivoire. The following section offers a brief summary to that extent.[2]

Cross-border recruitment in the Ivorian crisis

The territory of present-day Côte d'Ivoire was a cornerstone of French colonial rule in West Africa. Contrary to the Sahelian region to the north, the fertile lands along the Atlantic coast favored agricultural production and during the first half of the twentieth century, Côte d'Ivoire's southern half was developed into a productive plantation economy, with cocoa and coffee as the primary export crops. Labor was initially recruited by force from the interior, characterized by less fertile lands and a high population density – particularly in the territory of present-day Burkina Faso. This regional division of labor has retained its basic structure, despite the considerable political and economic transformations of both countries since independence (Amin 1995; Cordell et al. 1996). The Ivorian plantation economy continues to be manned primarily by labor from Burkina Faso, as well as other regional neighbors such as Mali and Guinea, who lack an equivalent agricultural sector (Beauchemin 2004; Beauchemin and Bocquier 2003).

This uneven division of labor is central for understanding the recruitment of young Burkinabe men in the Ivorian civil war. Labor migration to Côte d'Ivoire has been an important livelihood option for generations and the lack of employment opportunities at home still motivates many young men and women to pursue a migrant career. Such migrant aspirations generally reflect a fundamental desire to establish a family, to contribute to the subsistence of the extended family, and to become an economically capable person with resources necessary for marriage. To fulfill these expectations would entail a transition from a status of youth to one of social adulthood. Maturity, in this view, is not primarily concerned with biological age but rather with social status and relative economic independence (Barrett 2004; Bucholtz 2002; Christiansen et al. 2006; Cole and Durham 2007; De Waal and Argenti 2002; Durham 2008; Vigh 2006a). The *Forces Nouvelles* rebel movement in Côte d'Ivoire seem to have been well aware of the demand for migrant opportunities in Burkina Faso. Prior to the Ivorian civil war, which began

174   *Jesper Bjarnesen*

with the attempted military coup by the *Forces Nouvelles* on 19 September 2002, rebel commanders were recruiting youths into a well-organized rebel army. The *Forces Nouvelles* were anchored in the Ivorian army in the northern parts of Côte d'Ivoire, which enabled the use of the military infrastructure in the training of new recruits (Fofana 2008; Konate 2003).

The Ivorian crisis thereby added a new movement to the migratory flows across the Ivorio-Burkinabe border, namely that of young Burkinabe men joining the rebel forces against the regime of Laurent Gbagbo in Côte d'Ivoire. This cross-border recruitment was not only hazardous for the recruits who generally had no prior experience or military training: it was also a potentially dangerous political issue on both sides of the border, both in terms of the illicit border transgressions, and in terms of the identity politics in Côte d'Ivoire and the diplomatic crisis between the two neighbors. Since the early 1990s, the political elite around the Ivorian presidency had gradually articulated a rhetoric that constructed northern-ers as foreigners and, eventually, the *Forces Nouvelles* movement as a foreign invasion rather than party in a civil war (Dembélé 2002). This made the presence of Burkinabe recruits within the rebel ranks potentially problematic for the legiti-macy of the *Forces Nouvelles*. President Gbagbo's allegations against Burkina Faso's president, Blaise Compaoré of supporting the rebels, similarly, made any Burkinabe affiliation with the *Forces Nouvelles* a diplomatic liability for the Burkinabe authorities (Hagberg and Bjarnesen 2011). Despite the precarious political situation, rebel recruitment meetings were said by local residents to have been a public secret in Bobo-Dioulasso in the time around the failed military coup on 19 September 2002, in which the *Forces Nouvelles* coordinated simultaneous attacks on the Ivorian urban centers of Korhogo, Bouaké, and Abidjan – which marked the escalation of Côte d'Ivoire's political crisis into a nationalized armed conflict. Some former fighters claimed to have been recruited as early as 1999 or 2000 while others only crossed the border in 2004.

Given this historical contextualization, and as the following case studies will show, to ex-combatants in Bobo-Dioulasso, military recruitment presented at once a rupture with societal norms, in the sense of being a self-fulfilling search for adventure and engaging in activities that would generally be labelled as immoral, and a continuation of the mobility practices of earlier generations of young men, in the sense of a labor migration trajectory intended to provide an income in the context of overwhelming youth unemployment. The following three sections present the narratives of three former rebels, who all took part in the perpetra-tion of violence against the Ivorian army and its mercenaries during the period 2002–06. The sections are ordered to reflect the chronology of a combatant career, with Didier's narrative emphasizing recruitment; Gérard's emphasizing camp life and combat; and Bouba's emphasizing demobilization. All three cases outline all these phases, and are intended to evoke subjective experience of perpetration as socially embedded acts of violence. The forms of these informants' narratives in and of themselves emphasize the overall argument of this chapter; that the act of perpetrating violence was inscribed into ideological narratives of labor mobility and political resistance.

The public secrets of a Burkinabe rebel

Didier was the first ex-combatant I met in Bobo-Dioulasso. He said that his '*chef,*' who had recruited him here in Bobo-Dioulasso was still around. I asked an elaborative question which he understood as being about the superior officer's identity and the jovial atmosphere between us vaporized in a blink. I clarified that I was not asking for his commander's name and that seemed to reassure him. Didier embarked on a narrative that we often returned to during the ten months that followed, and particular events and dates are still unclear to me, as I believe they were to Didier himself. I include some of these confusions to illustrate the form the narrative took, but also to prioritize Didier's sentiments and retrospective evaluations.

Didier explained that he had been invited to a secret meeting by a friend of his in which they had been told about the possibility of going to Côte d'Ivoire as soldiers in a rebellion against the Gbagbo regime. Most people I spoke to, including a local journalist, said that they had known of the public secret of recruitment meetings and that they were being held all around Bobo-Dioulasso during the year preceding the 2002 attacks on Korhogo, Bouaké, and Abidjan. The journalist had decided not to write about these meetings out of an awareness of the diplomatic sensitivity of the issue. Didier said that he had been motivated to partake in the fight against Gbagbo in defense of Burkinabe citizens living in Côte d'Ivoire but that the considerable sums of money they had been promised obviously had played a large part in making him consider taking up arms in the first place. Didier's parents were against his recruitment into the rebel forces from the beginning. They had pleaded with him not to leave, and his father had fallen ill with worry while he was away, Didier said.

When Didier and his friend had decided to join, they went to the recruiter who asked them to hand over all their identity papers and any other possessions that might reveal them to be Burkinabe. Even cigarettes of the brands sold in Burkina Faso were confiscated. They were given 25,000 fCFA[3] each, which my assistant found to be outrageously little, but Didier explained that they were promised 100,000 *per day* (a decent month's salary in his current situation) for their service in Côte d'Ivoire – which, they were told, would only last for three days or one week at the most. With a pensive smile, Didier added that in the end he had spent more than five years 'over there.' Didier and the other recruits were taken at night along the back roads to the Ivorian border in carriers belonging to the Burkinabe army and left at the banks of the Léraba River, which straddles the border due north of the city of Kong for about forty kilometers, before joining the larger Comoé River, which flows southwards across Côte d'Ivoire into the Atlantic Ocean. At Comoé they waited from 3 until 9 a.m., when canoes arrived from the Ivorian side and transported them across. On the other side, trucks awaited them to bring the new recruits to the main training barracks in the North, in Korhogo, via a brief stop in the nearest rebel base, in Ferkéssédougou. Didier claimed that Commander Fofié[4] received them in person at the banks of the Léraba River.

After the first few days in Korhogo, the recruits were told that their initial 'mission' was over and that they now had to decide for themselves whether they would

176 *Jesper Bjarnesen*

stay on. The proposition was, of course, rhetorical: no one who had come this far would turn back before being sent into battle and the rebels were unlikely to dish out the initial allowances and then let people simply return home. So Didier, as his fellow recruits, stayed. The 100,000 fCFA a day allowances would obviously no longer apply but they were promised 500,000 fCFA at the end of their service and 1 million fCFA in compensation to their families, should they be killed in battle.

The *Forces Nouvelles* movement consisted of three groupings, the MJP, the MPIGO, and the MPCI, who eventually joined forces under the leadership of Guillaume Soro around the Linas-Marcoussis peace talks in January 2003. To Didier, however, these groupings were present but fairly irrelevant to his combatant career. He held membership cards for all three groups, which he still kept and showed me, and moved from the alleged territory of one to the other without knowing, or without having to relate to any shift in authority other than on the level of individual commanders and unit leaders. In this way, Didier moved from the territory of the MPCI in the north, through the MJP heartland in and around Man, into the home of the MPIGO movement around Danane in the west. Didier was at this point part of the rebel frontline fighters, facing the Ivorian army and moving the frontline further south and west with each invaded town. After a successful attack on a town, Didier's unit would call for reinforcements and proceed once another unit arrived to secure the town.

Didier described the development of the plight and organization of the fighting units as being one of gradual degradation. As the frontline's progression was halted south of Man and Danane in the west, Didier was stationed at roadblocks along some of the main roads into rebel territory: initially to secure the occupied territory but eventually to search for 'infiltrators' or spies who were feared to have integrated into the rebel movement to provide the Gbagbo regime with intelligence about rebel positions and capacities. Didier said that there were so many roadblocks that you couldn't take a walk without bumping into one and as lower-ranking rebels took charge, the main purpose of the roadblocks became to extrapolate money and other valuables from travelers. Passengers travelling with Burkinabe papers were particularly ill-treated and this had pained Didier and made him doubt the sincerity of whole movement. Towards the end of Didier's career as a rebel soldier, the roadblocks were manned by nine soldiers in shifts of three days.

During that time, Didier relied on what he could earn from the travelers passing through to pay for his subsistence. Extolling pennies from fellow Burkinabes was not his idea of an armed rebellion against the Gbagbo regime: "At the roadblocks . . . and . . . me, I'm Burkinabe. You often collect identity papers like that, you'll see parents, brothers, all that." Seeing the family names of Burkinabe travelers that were associated with his own ethnic group made Didier doubt the task he had been given. He had joined the rebels, in part, to take part in the struggle against the Gbagbo regime's repression of Burkinabe immigrants in Côte d'Ivoire, and now the rebels themselves were mistreating his social kinsmen. Manning a roadblock was worse than risking one's life and having to take the lives of others on the frontline. The combination of boredom and this less than honorable assignment

Perpetrator recruitment in the Ivorian war 177

made him consider desertion. He thought of his parents back home, who were expecting him to come home – as any successful migrant – with money and presents at the end of his stay. He had to come to terms with the fact that a successful return seemed less likely by the day. His decision was made easier by his past experience as a carpenter and mason. Didier was confident that he would, in fact, be able to make a better living in Bobo-Dioulasso than he did manning one of the innumerable roadblocks in the stagnated political landscape of the Ivorian crisis.

War changes a man

Gérard was born in Côte d'Ivoire, in Bouaké in the center of the country, to a Burkinabe father and an Ivorian mother. His father worked in the transportation business in Bouaké until his retirement in 2005. His employer was a white guy, Gérard impressed upon me. Gérard was twenty-eight years old at the time of my fieldwork and had attended school in Bouaké until the ninth grade, by which time his studies were interrupted by what he referred to as "the crisis." I asked Gérard to recall the first time he became aware of 'the crisis' and he described the imposition of a curfew following shootings in town in September 2002. They had thought that it was a strike by the police or military.

The curfew lasted for about a week, and then things calmed down. However, a week later, gunshots rang through the streets of Bouaké once more. Gérard had thought that it would be the same scenario as the week before, but this time it was a confrontation between rebel soldiers and the Ivorian army. It was a Sunday, and everyone was running through the streets, looking for cover. The fighting took place on the outskirts of town and ended with a victory for the rebels, who managed to take control. One of Gérard's friends was killed on his way home during the fighting. He was stopped by Gbagbo's mercenaries who had identified him as a Burkinabe from his ID papers. They had ordered him to undress and led him into the bush. A woman who had witnessed the incident informed Gérard and his friends, who immediately went out looking for him. It took a couple of days to find his body, which had already started to decompose. They had no way of finding a car to transport the body, so they borrowed a push cart and brought it home, to clean the corpse up before taking it to the morgue. A few days after his friend's burial, Gérard's father went to Burkina Faso to visit his family. The border was closed at that time, and he had passed through Ghana to enter the country. It was during his father's absence that Gérard had decided to join the rebel forces. He said that he was worried that Gbagbo's men would avenge their defeat and return to kill all the Burkinabes, including his own family.

Gérard and Didier had been in the same camp, and had come to realize that they both had their origins in Burkina Faso. Gérard said that there was a large group of Burkinabe recruits among the rebels. I asked him if he was asked to discard of his identity papers indicating his Burkinabe origins through his last name and his father's village of origin but he said that he had been too young to hold proper identity papers when he joined the rebels, and only had his student card. He told me that it was easy to enlist. In fact, the rebels were forcefully conscribing young men

178 *Jesper Bjarnesen*

in and around Bouaké, so joining voluntarily was quickly done. They had trained for about a week before they were given guns and uniforms and sent out to different bases around the rebel-held territory. Gérard's father returned to Bouaké a few days later and had summoned his son to demand an explanation for his enlistment. Gérard had argued that he was acting to defend their family but his father would have none of it. Gérard had returned to the base without settling the argument with his father. A few days later he was sent out on his first mission – to seize the town of Touba, near the Guinean border in the west, which was held by Angolan mercenaries. He had seen his mother before he left and she had given him her blessings. Unlike his father, she understood his motivation for taking up arms.

They descended from the truck outside of Touba. The senior officers gave them unspecified narcotics; 'things' that made them brave. In this case, it was a potion that was mixed in a large pot in the barracks. It was so pungent that you had to hold your breath while you drank it. They were told to apply the potion to their skin as well and that this would make them impenetrable to bullets. They had taken Touba. Gérard stayed in camp in Touba for two months. The rebels were bored and unruly, and during one quarrel two rebels injured each other with gunshots. At one point Gérard was also shot in the foot by one of his comrades. He had thought that if they remained in camp much longer, they would begin killing each other. A few weeks later they were sent to Man further south, one of the most unstable places in the Ivorian crisis, to push back "the Angolans," Gérard's generic shorthand for the forces they faced in battle, once more. Once again the rebels descended from their trucks outside of town and prepared to attack. But this time the enemy had been warned and was positioned on the hills surrounding the town. They had allowed Gérard and his group to advance and then closed an ambush behind them. Fighting had lasted more than twenty-four hours. Eventually, the rebels began sneaking out through enemy lines. Many had left their weapons behind. They had been forced to march the whole way back to Touba, a walk of about ninety kilometers.

Back in Touba, the rebel commanders had called for the aid of Liberian mercenaries, who knew the area much better and were better trained and equipped. They had led the next attack on Man, with Gérard's unit as backup. It was around that time that Gérard's mother received news that Gérard had been killed in battle during the ambush in Man. Gérard was unaware of the rumor when he returned to Bouaké on leave, following the successful second attack on Man. His family had been relieved to learn that he was all right but they were unable to convince Gérard to abandon his combatant career. After his leave of absence, Gérard re-joined his group at Man, and proceeded from there to Danane. He was appointed 'chef de poste' under ComZone Traoré, with the responsibility of collecting levies at a roadblock outside town. Initially, the roadblocks were installed to control vehicles, not to collect money. The rebels on guard were paid 10,000 FCFA per day and were in no hurry to menace passengers for petty change. Once the salaries dried out, they began collecting money from travelers as compensation.

In 2005 Gérard took leave to accompany his father to Bobo-Dioulasso to visit their relatives. Once in Burkina Faso, his parents told him that they intended to

Perpetrator recruitment in the Ivorian war   179

remain here and they soon moved into a rented house. Gérard had thought that he would return after a month but he appreciated the calm pace of life in the neighborhood and his father, intent on persuading him to leave the rebels, had provided him the opportunity of working as a driver for Sofitex, one of Burkina Faso's leading cotton-processing companies. He accepted the job without having made up his mind about the future and began earning a little money. He gradually realized that it would make no sense to go back to war and risk his life. He found an even better job with another company, through one of his former rebel commanders who now lived in hiding in Bobo-Dioulasso, and made a steady income as a driver of his own truck. He had never really articulated the decision to desert – and claimed that his friends still called him from Bouaké, asking him to return to camp. To avoid their questions, he just made up stories about familial duties or other reasons for staying on in Burkina Faso. He imagined that his name was still called out at roll call in 'Camp Wattao' in Bouaké every morning.

"War changes a man," Gérard said. "Seeing so many dead bodies. Seeing yourself search a corpse for money and valuables." Angolans would often carry 50,000 or more in cash. Gérard seemed to be haunted by the memories of war, much more so than the other rebels I met in Bobo-Dioulasso. His personal trauma led him to drink abusively, which in turn affected his relationship with his parents and his reputation in the neighborhood.

From wartime empowerment to peacetime displacement

Bouba explained that he had been recruited in Bobo-Dioulasso, following his failed attempt to enlist in the Burkinabe army. He had done well at the try-outs but had failed to provide the 25,000 fCFA fee required for inscription. Two months after the try-outs, he had been contacted by men claiming to be army personnel who were looking for recruits for a mission in Côte d'Ivoire. They had said that the reward for a completed mission would be a permanent employment in the Burkinabe army and that he would be serving his country by taking the mission. Unlike the other ex-combatants I met in Sarfalao, Bouba was adamant that he had enlisted in the rebel movement on these terms and that the promise of a considerable financial gain and the adventurous life of a soldier had nothing to do with it.

Like the other ex-combatants I met, Bouba felt that his commanders had lost sight of the movement's cause and were now simply 'harassing people' at the ubiquitous roadblocks, as well as in the increasing armed robberies and carjackings in Northern Côte d'Ivoire since the signing of the 2007 peace agreements. This sentiment contributed to his perception of rebel life as immoral and self-indulgent. Although he might have argued that enlisting had been a 'clever' choice in order to provide for himself, Bouba now perceived the 'easy life' of being a soldier as being without prospects, as being indulgent and only serving the present. He saw himself as better than that, with more capabilities to take care of himself, as opposed to those remaining 'over there' as soldiers who he believed remained out of a lack of other options. Being aware of the Burkinabe authorities' wariness towards the presence of a considerable number of ex-combatants, Bouba

180 *Jesper Bjarnesen*

was articulating a prospect for himself as a good citizen who would provide for himself through an honest trade – he said that he was trained as both a welder and a mason – rather than relying on his connections or skills as a rebel soldier. As it turned out, Bouba was hired by the largest security company in Bobo-Dioulasso, but he insisted that he had said nothing of his past as a high-ranking security officer in Côte d'Ivoire:

> Me myself I don't want the label rebel . . . "rebel" . . . to be stuck to my . . . documents. No no no . . . Because I don't want . . . their label. Yeah. For it to be in my records. The word "rebel" . . . it's a bad omen. It's a bad omen.

Despite his reference to his own agency in turning his back on his rebel past, a sense of exclusion underlies this quote. While many of Bouba's reflections posited himself as strong and independent enough to resist the 'easy life' of the rebellion and return to the honest hard work in Burkina Faso, he spoke of the word 'rebel' being imposed upon him, it being 'their label.' In this quote 'their' refers to potential employers, judging him to be undeserving of a job, but also to the authorities, and in a broader sense to the Burkinabe public in general. In his everyday life, his sense of exclusion was primarily felt in relation to his neighbors and former 'pals' in Bobo-Dioulasso.

Bouba's sense of marginalization upon his return to Bobo-Dioulasso was both related to his reception in the neighborhood as well as the broken promises of his recruiters, who had told him that his services in Côte d'Ivoire would be rewarded with a post in the Burkinabe army: "Had I known, that it was a lie, ah, that I would become an enemy of my . . . country, of the community, I wouldn't have gone over there [to Côte d'Ivoire]. Because . . . I don't want to be an enemy of the community." He told me that it was not only the Burkinabe authorities who were now hostile towards the former combatants, who were feared to have been turned into violent vigilantes that would pose a threat to their home communities. Back in his house in Bobo-Dioulasso, he had noticed his neighbors' hostility as well. If he approached a group of ten youths talking, nine of them would get up and leave, he exemplified. People blamed the rebels for the war in Côte d'Ivoire, he said, and most of all for the suffering and impoverishment it had caused on this side of the border. Things here in Burkina Faso were much worse than before the war, he admitted.

The disorientation of having to reassess a social terrain that was once so familiar made all three ex-combatants suspicious of their surroundings and motivated them to guard themselves in the company of others. Although the psychological trauma of armed combat may be part of the reason for their feeling of unease, both Didier and Bouba faced the tangible hostility of their neighbors, which made the achievement of their essential life projects harder to realise. In contrast to other former combatants, who exploited their experience in war to further new careers as security guards, mercenaries, or drug traffickers, Bouba and Didier only discussed their violent past with outsiders and preferred to look for more conventional occupations in the neighborhood. Bouba did in fact work as a watchman

Perpetrator recruitment in the Ivorian war 181

but insisted that he had not disclosed his combatant past to his employers, nor relied on his commanders' social networks for the connection. In response to my repeated questioning, he did admit that his employers may have been able to recognize his military training in his behavior and vocabulary but I believe that he did see his affiliation with the *Forces Nouvelles* as a disadvantage, despite the nature of his work tasks as a watchman.

The perpetration of violence and the quest for social worth

The three men's narratives about their time in the ranks of the *Forces Nouvelles* are conspicuously free of descriptions of actual acts of violence. Although we came to know each other well, and could share conversations about other sensitive or potentially shameful issues, they never told me about the people they had killed. Their efforts to put those experiences behind them and take up their old lives in Bobo-Dioulasso probably discouraged them to think too much of what they had witnessed and done as soldiers. Rather than dwelling on the experience of engaging in violent acts in and of themselves, the narratives are charged with a sense of duty and professionalism; of taking pride in describing their tasks and the movements and larger efforts that they were part of. This sense of duty suggests a different repertoire of meaning than one concerned with visions of the enemy or other moral justifications for inflicting harm on others. This sense of duty also challenges the stigma that combatants faced upon their return to Bobo-Dioulasso, by which their recruitment was primarily seen as having indulged in killing for cash; of being hired guns at the hands of an unsuccessful rebel movement. Rather than perceiving the quest for enrichment as an immoral act, outside the normal social order, then, the three narratives invite us "to think of violence as literal work, to think of the labor of war as labor" (Hoffman 2011b: 34), as Hoffman has suggested in relation to young combatants in Sierra Leone.

Approaching mass violence as a form of labor does not imply, in this context, a disaffected, robotic, perpetration of violence, akin to the image of the war machine in his work, discussed above. Gérard's trauma in particular testifies to the emotional scars that the combatants carried with them. Rather, war as labor should be understood here as a form of culturally valued and meaningful practice: "[w]ork, in short, is a positive aspect of human activity, and is expressed in the making of self and others in the course of everyday life" (Comaroff and Comaroff 1987: 197). By evoking their professionalism as soldiers, the recruits were attempting to inscribe their activities into a socio-moral framework of meaningful labor, evoking the history of labor migration between Burkina Faso and Côte d'Ivoire which has been a socially and economically significant livelihood option for young Burkinabe since the colonial period (Bjarnesen 2013; Hagberg and Ouattara 2010: 111).

In these ways, the three narratives of recruitment into the *Forces Nouvelles* reflect a familiar predicament in the West African context, of un- or underemployed young men being available to military recruiters in the quest for a livelihood and a sense of social worth. The unprecedented wealth promised to the

182 *Jesper Bjarnesen*

recruits was certainly a decisive factor in motivating their enlistment but chronic poverty in and of itself cannot be seen as the singular causal factor that turned poor carpenters, meat vendors, and mechanics in the town of Bobo-Dioulasso into skilled rebel fighters. Approaching war as labor also implies an attention to the perpetration of violence as inscribed into the logics of a work ethics rather than a political or moralizing view of the object of this violence. Fighters were given responsibility and recognition they had never imagined and took pride in their severity and uncompromising aggression as leaders of units, responsible for ammunitions, or other tasks within the group. At the same time, success on the battlefield – whether personal or collective – was often remembered with nostalgia and a sense of history in the making. In this sense, they remembered themselves as a part of a historically important movement, against the injustices committed by the Gbagbo regime in Côte d'Ivoire towards Burkinabe migrants in particular. Another important motivating factor for all three men in this chapter, therefore, was the persecution of Burkinabe labor migrants in Côte d'Ivoire by the regime that they were given the opportunity to fight against. This aspect does not mean that recruits saw themselves as selfless heroes but simply that the injustice committed against their countrymen across the border was a motivating factor in its own right. Analyses emphasizing the structural explanations for combatant perpetration of violence (Hoffman 2011b; Hage 2003) tend to neglect the possibility of such ideological callings being anything but rhetorical or post-facto rationalizations.

Upon their return to Burkina Faso, none of the former rebels I met had been able to accumulate anything but a few memorabilia, such as military boots or photos of themselves in uniform, sporting machine guns or other weapons. Materially, they were no better off than before their recruitment. As with other migrant aspirations, of course, the eventual failure to accumulate the envisioned capital from participating in the rebellion takes nothing away from the fact that rebel recruitment was approached by young Burkinabe as a livelihood option as much as it was an ideological calling. In this way, military recruitment was perceived simultaneously as an ideological choice to join the ranks of the rebels under the banner of a common cause, and as a different form of labor migration that had arisen due to changing socio-political circumstances. The perception of a combatant career as fundamentally different from that of a plantation worker or a migrant working in Abidjan's informal sector may relate more to normative preconceptions about morally appropriate forms of labor than to the motivations for engaging in war, and the material and social effects of this engagement (see also Elwert 1999). As Bouba's narrative illustrates, the moralizing judgments of neighbors upon their return weighed heavily on the former combatants, as they saw their noble cause recast as the self-interested search for enrichment through immoral killing in Côte d'Ivoire.

Conclusion

As other studies of wartime mobilization have shown (e.g. Hoffman 2011a; Honwana 2005; 2006; Richards 1996; Utas 2003; Vigh 2006a, 2006b), joining a

Perpetrator recruitment in the Ivorian war 183

rebel movement and becoming a soldier is often experienced as an empowering adventure that changes one's outlook on life and the opportunities for enrichment (see also Förster 2010: 712–13). But more than the quest for adventure, the former combatants in Bobo-Dioulasso in this chapter evoked the lack of other possibilities and their wish to contribute to the struggle against the oppression of their compatriots in Côte d'Ivoire. While the lack of viable alternative livelihood strategies has been well-documented to provide incentives for participation in armed conflict, a more nuanced consideration of the cultural and ideological repertoires that informed the decisions of Didier, Gérard, and Bouba has been shown to include the historical precedent of transnational mobility, as well as the political condemnation of the identity politics informing the xenophobic violence of the Gbagbo regime in Côte d'Ivoire.

While perpetration tends to be framed in more or less explicitly normative terms, as the morally dubious acts of one's enemies rather than the justifiable acts of one's friends, this chapter has instead evoked the socio-moral repertoires of the perpetrators themselves. In this regard, anthropological analysis of ethnographic data offers a particularly suitable approach to studying subjective experiences and rationalizations of the perpetration of violence in armed conflict. Furthermore, the empirical cases add an important dimension to our understanding of the Ivorian civil war, in which Burkinabe migrants often figure as the voiceless victims of xenophobic violence but so far have remained unconsidered as active participants in the armed conflict. Finally, this case selection also contributes to an emerging literature on perpetration in armed conflicts other than the emblematic cases of genocidal violence. This ongoing expansion of the perpetrator literature has the potential to add an important counterweight to the normative view of perpetration evoked in these emblematic cases, as well as a more nuanced anthropological analysis of the incentives for participating in armed conflict.

Notes

1 The regional overlaps and interlinkages of these conflicts have been well-documented to concern the mobility of combatants as well as the movement of arms, and shifting political alliances across these borders (e.g. Banégas and Fratani 2003; Michel Galy 2003; 2004; Magnus Jörgel and Utas 2007; Richards 2004, 2005; Utas 2012).
2 For a fuller discussion of this historical contextualization, see Bjarnesen (2013).
3 25,000 fCFA is equivalent to approximately 45USD.
4 According to Till Förster, Kouakou Martin Fofié was chief security officer of Korhogo between 2002 and 2005. He held more power in the city than the official commanders of the area Messamba Koné and Youssouf Diarrasouba and eventually succeeded them, in part because of his popularity among the city's youth (Förster 2012:13).

References

Amin, Samir. "Migrations in Contemporary Africa: A Retrospective View." In *The Migration Experience in Africa*, edited by Jonathan Baker and Tade Akin Aina, 29–40. Uppsala: The Nordic Africa Institute, 1995.

184 *Jesper Bjarnesen*

Banégas, Richard, and Ruth Marshall-Fratani. "Côte d'Ivoire, un conflit régional?" *Politique Africaine* 89 (2003): 5–11.

Barrett, Michael. *Paths to Adulthood: Freedom, Belonging and Temporalities in Mbunda Biographies from Western Zambia.* PhD Thesis, Uppsala University, 2004.

Beauchemin, Cris. "Pour une relecture des tendances migratoires internes entre villes et campagnes: une étude comparée Burkina Faso-Côte-d'Ivoire." *Cahiers québécois de démographie* 33, no. 2 (2004): 167–99.

Beauchemin, Cris, and Philippe Bocquier. "Migration and Urbanization in Francophone West Africa. A Review of the Recent Empirical Evidence." *Document de travail DIAL.* Paris: DIAL/Unité de Recherche CIPRÉ, 2003.

Bjarnesen, Jesper. *Diaspora at Home? Wartime Mobilities in the Burkina Faso-Côte d'Ivoire Transnational Space.* PhD Thesis, Uppsala Studies in Cultural Anthropology, no. 53. Acta Universitatis Upsaliensis, Uppsala, 2013.

Bucholtz, Mary. "Youth and Cultural Practice." *Annual Review of Anthropology* 31, no. 1 (2002): 525–52.

Christiansen, Christine, Mats Utas, and Henrik E. Vigh. *Navigating Youth – Generating Adulthood: Social Becoming in an African Context.* Uppsala: Nordic Africa Insitute; New York and Oxford: Berghahn Books, 2006.

Cole, Jennifer, and Deborah Durham. *Generations and Globalization: Youth, Age, and Family in the New World Economy.* Bloomington: Indiana University Press, 2007.

Comaroff, Jean, and John Comaroff. "The Madman and the Migrant: Work and Labor in the Historical Consciousness of a South African People." *American Ethnologist* 14, no. 2 (1987): 191–209.

Cordell, Dennis D., Joel W. Gregory, and Victor Piché. *Hoe and Wage: A Social History of a Circular Migration System in West Africa.* Boulder, CO: Westview Press, 1996.

Daddieh, Cyril K. "Elections and Ethnic Violence in Côte d'Ivoire: The Unfinished Business of Succession and Democratic Transition." *African Issues* 29, no. 1/2 (2001): 14–19.

Deleuze, Gilles, and Felix Guattari. *A Thousand Plateaus: Capitalism and Schizophrenia.* London: Continuum, 2004a.

Deleuze, Gilles, and Félix Guattari. *Anti-Oedipus: Capitalism and Schizophrenia.* London: Continuum, 2004b.

Dembélé, Ousmane. "La Construction économique et politique de la catégorie 'étranger' en Côte d'Ivoire." In *Côte d'Ivoire. L'année terrible 1999–2000*, edited by Marc Le Pape and Claudine Vidal, 123–71. Paris: Karthala, 2002.

De Waal, Alexander, and Nicolas Argenti. *Young Africa: Realising the Rights of Children and Youth.* Trenton: Africa World Press, 2002.

Durham, Deborah. "Apathy and Agency: The Romance of Agency and Youth in Botswana." In *Figuring the Future: Globalization and the Temporalities of Children and Youth*, edited by Deborah Durham and Jennifer Cole, 151–78. Santa Fe: SAR Press, 2008.

Elwert, Georg. "Markets of Violence." In *Dynamics of Violence: Processes of Escalation and De-Escalation in Violent Group Conflicts*, edited by Georg Elwert, Stephan Feuchtwang and Dieter Neubert, 85–102. Berlin: Duncker & Humblot, 1999.

Fofana, Moussa. "Les déterminants de l'enrôlement des jeunes combattants de la rébellion du Nord de la Côte d'Ivoire." *CRISE Working Paper.* Oxford: Centre for Research on Inequality, Human Security and Ethnicity, 2008.

Förster, Till. "Maintenant, on sait qui est qui. Political Re-Configuration of an African Society After Conflict." *Development and Change* 41, no. 4 (2010): 699–722.

Förster, Till. "Statehood in a Stateless Society: Political Order and Social Memory in Northern Côte d'Ivoire." *Basel Papers on Political Transformations.* Vol. 4. Basel: Institute of Social Anthropology, University of Basel, 2012.

Galy, Michel. "Les espaces de la guerre en Afrique de l'Ouest." *Hérodote* 111, no. 4 (2003): 41–56.

Galy, Michel. "De la guerre nomade: Sept approches du conflit autour de la Côte d'Ivoire." *Cultures & Conflicts* 55, no. 3 (2004): 163–96.

Hagberg, Sten, and Jesper Bjarnesen. "'Good Guys' and 'Bad Guys': The Burkinabe Public Debate on the Ivorian Crisis." In *Une anthropologie entre pouvoirs et histoire. Conversations autour de l'oeuvre de Jean-Pierre Chauveau*, edited by Eyolf Jul-Larsen, Pierre-Joseph Laurent, Pierre-Yves Le Meur and Éric Léonard, 509–34. Paris: Karthala, 2011.

Hagberg, Sten, and Syna Ouattara. "Vigilantes in War: Boundary Crossing of Hunters in Burkina Faso and Côte d'Ivoire." In *Violent Demeanors: Vigilantism, State, and Struggles for Encompassment in Africa*, edited by Tilo Grätz and Thomas G. Kirsch, 98–117. Oxford: James Currey, 2010.

Hage, Ghassan. "'Comes a Time We Are All Enthusiasm': Understanding Palestinian Suicide Bombers in Times of Exighophobia." *Public Culture* 15, no. 1 (2003): 65–89.

Hoffman, Danny. *The War Machines: Young Men and Violence in Sierra Leone and Liberia*. Durham: Duke University Press, 2011a.

Hoffman, Danny. "Violence, Just in Time: War and Work in Contemporary West Africa." *Cultural Anthropology* 26, no. 1 (2011b): 34–57.

Honwana, Alcinda. "Innocent and Guilty: Child-Soldiers as Interstitial and Tactical Agents." In *Makers & Breakers: Children & Youth in Postcolonial Africa*, edited by Alcinda Honwana and Filip De Boeck, 31–52. Oxford: James Currey, 2005.

Honwana, Alcinda. *Child Soldiers in Africa*. Philadelphia: University of Pennsylvania Press.

Human Rights Watch. "Côte d'Ivoire: Government Abuses in Response to Army Revolt." *Human Rights Watch Report* 14, no. 9 (A) (November 2002): 1–19.

Jackson, Michael. *The Politics of Storytelling: Violence, Transgression and Intersubjectivity*. Copenhagen: Museum Tusculanum Press, 2002.

Jörgel, Magnus, and Mats Utas. *The Mano River Basin Area: Formal and Informal Security Providers in Liberia, Guinea and Sierra Leone*. Stockholm: FOI, Swedish Defence Research Agency, 2007.

Keen, David. "War Without End? Magic, Propaganda and the Hidden Functions of Counter-Terror." *Journal of International Development* 18, no. 1 (2006): 87–104.

Konate, Yacouba. "Les enfants de la balle. De la Fesci aux movements de patroites." *Politique Africaine* 89, no. 1 (2003): 49–70.

Le Pape, Marc, and Claudine Vidal (eds.). *Côte d'Ivoire. L'année Terrible 1999–2000*. Paris: Karthala, 2002.

Nordstrom, Carolyn. *Shadows of War: Violence, Power, and International Profiteering in the Twenty-First Century*. Berkeley, Los Angeles and London: University of California Press, 2004.

Richards, Paul. *Fighting for the Rain Forest: War, Youth, and Resources in Sierra Leone*. Portsmouth NH: Heinemann, 1996.

Richards, Paul. "Controversy Over Recent West African Wars: An Agrarian Question?" *Occasional Paper*. Copenhagen: Centre of African Studies, January 2004.

Richards, Paul. "La terre ou le fusil? La jeunesse rurale et les racines agraires des conflits de la région du fleuve Mano." *Afrique Contemporaine* 214, no. 2 (2005): 37–58.

Toungara, Jeanne Maddox. "Ethnicity and Political Crisis in Côte d'Ivoire." *Journal of Democracy* 12, no. 3 (2001): 63–72.

Utas, Mats. *Sweet Battlefields: Youth and the Liberian Civil War*. PhD Thesis, Uppsala University, Uppsala, 2003.

Utas, Mats (ed.). *African Conflicts and Informal Power: Big Men and Networks*. London: Zed Books, 2012.

186 *Jesper Bjarnesen*

Vigh, Henrik E. *Navigating Terrains of War: Youth and Soldiering in Guinea-Bissau*. London and New York: Berghahn Books, 2006a.

Vigh, Henrik E. "Social Death and Violent Life Chances." In *Navigating Youth – Generating Adulthood: Social Becoming in an African Context*, edited by Catrine Christiansen, Mats Utas and Henrik E. Vigh, 31–60. Uppsala: Nordic Africa Institute, 2006b.

Williams, Timothy. "The Complexity of Evil: A Multi-Faceted Approach to Genocide Perpetrators." *Zeitschrift für Friedens- und Konfliktforschung* 3, no. 1 (2014): 71–98.

10 *Judenjagd*

Reassessing the role of ordinary Poles as perpetrators in the Holocaust

Tomasz Frydel

Introduction[1]

The framework of categories introduced by Raul Hilberg – perpetrators, victims, and bystanders – once conventionally employed in understanding the destruction of European Jewry (Hilberg 1992), has started to fall out of fashion among historians of the Holocaust. In the case of East Central Europe, particularly Poland, the people situated at the edges of the volcanic eruption of genocide have invariably begun their slide from "bystanders" to "perpetrators" in the recent turn in scholarship since the publication of Jan T. Gross's *Neighbors* (Gross 2001). Apart from the national debate unleashed in Poland in 2001, the major contribution of the book to the historiography was to banish a view of ethnic Poles solely as victims of Nazi Germany and to substantiate a long-standing claim found in Jewish survivor testimonies that Poles sometimes acted as perpetrators of the Judeocide (Polonsky and Michlic 2004: 30–43). The Jedwabne pogrom of 11 July 1941 has become the cornerstone of discussions about collaboration and perpetrators at the grassroots level in East Central Europe.

The seeds of a second, though much slower, paradigm shift can be found in the work of Polish historians focused on what they call the 'third phase' of the Holocaust, namely the attempt by the Germans to destroy the remaining Jews who survived Operation Reinhard – the code name given to the secret Nazi plan to murder all Polish Jews in the gas chambers of Bełżec, Sobibór, and Treblinka. These fugitives from Nazi German law fled ghettos and jumped off trains headed for death camps as they sought shelter among peasants in rural areas. The working assumption among these historians is that approximately 250,000 Jews – roughly 10 per cent of the 2.5 million Jews still alive in the summer of 1942 – made the escape to the so-called Aryan side. Of these, it is estimated that fewer than 50,000 survived (Grabowski 2013: 172–3). Unlike in the previous stages of ghettoization and deportation to death camps, where Polish society could do little to divert the Nazi steamroller of genocide, here, in the space of the 'hunt for Jews' (*Judenjagd*), allegedly out of reach of German authority, ethnic Poles had a larger say in the fate of the 200,000 fugitive Jews who did not survive. The issue of Polish behavior on this measurable "periphery of the Holocaust" thus represents the load-bearing question of Polish responsibility (Gross and Grudzińska-Gross

188 *Tomasz Frydel*

2012). Arguing against an older framework born under Poland's Communist regime (1944–89) that regards Polish participation in anti-Jewish acts as carried out by the criminal dregs found on the 'margins' of every society, these historians are careful to emphasize that the perpetrators often represented 'ordinary' Poles, not uncommonly well-respected members of local communities. The recent wave of scholarship – which makes reference to the murder of Tutsi in Rwanda and Bosnian Muslims in Srebrenica (Gross and Grudzińska-Gross 2012: 84, 86) – is poised to interpret these events as part of a tradition of ethnic cleansing on the historiographical map. The vision of violence here is a kind of mobile Jedwabne in the Polish 'killing fields.'

In this chapter, I argue that something like the opposite of grassroots ethnic cleansing can be demonstrated. Peasant society participated in the capture and killing of Jews, but mostly within locally situated dynamics of communal fear and survival – not necessarily ethnic hatred or extreme nationalism – and this after the structures of village authority were reconfigured for the purpose by the occupation authorities. I offer a reappraisal of this phase of genocide using a different methodology to interrogate the meaning of 'perpetrators' and 'collaboration' within this framework. First, I contextualize the shelter and the hunt for fugitive Jews with parallel processes aimed at other fugitive groups, such as Soviet prisoners of war (POWs), Roma, deserters from the German army, and others. Second, I situate the actions of the perpetrators within a broad system of surveillance operations that conditioned local societies in obedience to German law. Third, I suggest the German occupation gave rise to two different trajectories of experience between Poles and Jews, which frequently culminated in an existential competition. This competition, in turn, helps us to understand the specific dynamics of grassroots violence. Fourth, I focus on the unique case of perpetrators who participated in both harming Jews and helping them.

Studying perpetrators in a different light

My approach is informed by a simple observation. While the Second Polish Republic witnessed official support for discriminatory anti-Jewish measures and growing outbursts of anti-Jewish violence, particularly in the period of accelerated democratic erosion following the death of Józef Piłsudski from 1936–39 (Zimmerman 2015: 14–20), the vast majority of Poles – as the majority of Germans at this time – had no experience with murder as a category of thought or action. Yet within a few years of the Second World War, in specific moments of the occupation, the denunciation and murder of Jews would be met with a significant level of social approval. It is in the 'hunt for Jews' that the German occupation authorities co-opted segments of Polish society into active complicity in genocide. How can a segment of society be shaped into an accessory of murder? This chapter is concerned with the social mechanisms that helped to transform ordinary people into perpetrators. A close study such as this is particularly suited to observing the gradual shift in attitudes and behavior that this transformation required. My overarching goal is to examine the actions of 'perpetrators' from a

Judenjagd 189

variety of angles. In the broadest sense, perpetrators are defined here as those who participated in impeding the survival of members of a targeted group.

For both historical and moral clarity, the approach taken here aims to disaggregate the notion of the Holocaust into 'smaller' genocidal episodes or phases. Unlike other genocides, the Holocaust was unprecedented in that it compressed various forms of destruction within a short time period: mass executions, pogroms, ghettoization, death camps, hunts for Jews, and so-called death marches. Each of these stages introduced its own structure and dynamics of violence. The 'Final Solution of the Jewish Question' was a continent-wide undertaking applied in widely varying contexts. In the territories of the former Second Polish Republic under German occupation, now within the larger *Lebensraum*, it was superimposed on distinct policies targeted at other groups within the indigenous population. These policies rearranged the relations of its various victim groups. The focus here is on the *Judenjagd* from 1942–45, but unlike the approach taken by the recent wave of scholarship discussed earlier, the source base is significantly widened to observe peasant behavior within the broader dilemmas faced by rural societies. This is not to suggest that the *Judenjagd* was a mere byproduct of the occupation, but that it was part of a wider social space and cannot be understood solely by recourse to cases that involved Jews.

A related innovation here is to apply a model of 'integrated history' on the scale of a microhistory in keeping with an approach advocated by historian Saul Friedländer (Friedländer 2010: 21–9). It is not that the findings in the previously discussed works are false, but that it is precisely their isolation from the broader context that helps sustain a range of sharp theses. The approach taken here will help avoid the 'bracketing' of the Jewish experience in order to foreground a causal interplay between victim groups that had an impact on the course of the *Judenjagd* and gave rise to sub-categories of perpetrators on the local level. This methodological aim is akin to Clifford Geertz's anthropological "thick description" (Geertz 1973: 3–30) employed by Gross in *Golden Harvest* (Gross and Grudzińska-Gross 2012: 19, 58–9), though it differs fundamentally in its application and conclusions. At the same time, the figure of the Righteous among Nations, so prevalent in the scholarship on Polish rescue, will be kept out of the historical reconstruction, as it is a moral and commemorative – not a historical – category that emerged in the postwar period (Dreifuss 2012: 77–81). Neither the figure of the Righteous Rescuer, nor a sacralized notion of martyrology and victimhood, belong on the historical landscape of an *Alltagsgeschichte*. This close study of genocide is committed to a notion of history as a "discipline of context and of process" (Bloxham 2009: 323–33).

The geographical focus is a region that corresponded to the eastern part of District Krakow of the General Government, or historic Western Galicia.[2] The primary archival sources used here are postwar investigation and trial records of individuals tried for collaboration on the basis of the so-called Decree of 31 August 1944 issued by the pro-Soviet puppet government, which today are housed at the archives of the regional branches of the Institute of National Remembrance (AIPN). These were generally off-limits to researchers during the time of the

190   *Tomasz Frydel*

Polish People's Republic (1944–89), but historians of the Holocaust have begun to draw on them in the last two decades. It is primarily this trial material that makes a reconstruction of the *Judenjagd* possible. Other sources include Jewish survivor testimonies deposited with the archives of the Jewish Historical Institute (AŻIH) in the immediate postwar period, as well as real-time underground reports by the major partisan formations of occupied Poland.

Who, after all, speaks today of the annihilation of the Soviet POWs?

A crucial change undergone by rural society during the war resulted from the restructuring of village authority and accountability. A new set of responsibilities was imposed on village society that profoundly altered its choice architecture and social relations. The occupation authorities were primarily interested in the Polish province as a source of food quotas to feed the German army and 'human quotas,' or forced laborers, for the Third Reich. The village head (*sołtys*) bore the brunt of the responsibility for meeting these quotas. In order to help the village head carry out his duties, the Germans instituted a system of village guards (*Ortschutzwache* or *Ortschutz*), whose members were often drawn from the local fire brigades. The *Ortschutz* was de facto a kind of local militia headed by a commander. A secondary system of 'hostages' (*zakładnicy*) made these men personally responsible for maintaining 'security' over their areas of jurisdiction. If the village guards were not sufficient, a village head could always turn to the Polish "Blue" Police (*Polnische Polizei*/PP). The Blue Police – named informally after the color of their uniforms – was itself drawn from the prewar state Police, which was subordinated to the German Order Police (*Ordnungspolizei*; in rural areas, the gendarmerie).

After the invasion of the Soviet Union and the commencement of Operation Reinhard, the screws of this system were tightened and its scope broadened. It was the responsibility of each village head not only to apprehend Polish laborers, but to report and deliver any Jews, Soviet prisoners of war, partisans ('bandits'), strangers, or outsiders to the nearest gendarmerie or PP station. Thus, the same system that was already turned against ethnic Polish society in the forceful extraction of various quotas was expanded into a system of surveillance against all categories of people targeted by Nazi Germany. On 10 November 1941, Hans Frank, Governor of the GG, instituted the death penalty for people who offered any help to Jews outside of ghettos, a measure which could be – and often was – exercised in the form of collective punishment. But in the context of the village system, this punishment was extended to 'failure' to report and apprehend fugitives. In essence, villages were now weaponized against outsiders and the whole system was held in place by draconian threats at each level of authority. It is no accident that the overwhelming majority of individuals tried for collaboration after the war – the village heads, members of the village guard, messengers, foresters, and gamekeepers, who figure in these cases – were indeed 'ordinary' Poles. But in most cases, they did not represent a random sample of peasants, but those tried for collaboration precisely on the basis of their position in the 'security' gridlock that

Judenjagd 191

they found themselves in, not a shared ideological profile. It was the institutional role that largely determined the range of behavior.

Thus, at its root, the village surveillance system was aimed at a variety of fugitives, and Soviet POWs represented the largest parallel group next to Jews. Although history has provided researchers with a control group, it is a wonder that no historian has taken advantage of this fact in the enormous scholarship on the rescue of Jews in Poland. What is striking here is that the hunt for Jews bears a remarkable similarity to the hunt for Soviet POWs. To take a few examples: in 1943, the village of Brzezówka (Rzeszów county) witnessed two cases of captured prisoners of war. In the first case, Rozalia Żurek took in a young man who was asking for food and shelter. She later learned that he was an escaped Soviet POW and let him stay, as he helped her with the fall harvest and entertained her children by writing in Cyrillic. However, word got out and members of the village guard appeared at her home to take the POW away. He turned to the guard commandant "with a plea to spare his life, as he's a young man, he wants to live and return to his parents, he's a prisoner of war, who explained clearly to the accused that he's from Leningrad, that he took part in fighting the Germans and was wounded."[3] He then tried to escape, but one of the guards struck him down with an axe. The prisoner was taken to a Polish Police station, where he was likely shot.

In the second case, Franciszek Sowa, the village head, notified the Polish Police in Błażowa that Aniela Mitał was sheltering a Soviet POW of Russian background who had jumped off a transport. The denunciation was passed up the chain of command, and the following day the German gendarmerie and Polish Police were dispatched to Mitał's home. When they failed to find the escaped prisoner, they shot Aniela Mitał, her nine-year-old daughter, and 10-year-old son. Her home was set on fire and the village guard was ordered to throw their bodies into the burning building.[4] Likewise, in the village of Przyszów (Stalowa Wola county), Marcin Kotwica, the gamekeeper (*gajowy*) was accused of apprehending and handing over to the German police three escaped French POWs, one of whom attempted to trade his coat in exchange for a piece of bread.[5] In yet another case, Jan Kostak, the village head of Turza (Kolbuszowa county), along with hostage Ludwik Matuła and village messenger (*goniec*) Tomasz Mika, apprehended three young Soviet POWs, who were looking for shelter for the night.[6] They delivered the young men to the German police, where they were shot.

Still, manhunts went beyond Jews and Soviet POWs – peasants were also drawn into hunts against fellow villagers evading forced labor in Germany. For example, in the village of Przykop (Mielec county) in July 1942, Józef Racławski, the commandant of the *Ortschutz*, received an order to apprehend Poles to be sent to Germany. One of the people he was forced to capture was his own sister.[7] In a number of cases, the village guard and local peasants were mobilized in the hunt for partisans or 'bandits,' in the nomenclature of the occupation authorities. In the village of Las (Żywiec county), Emil Michałek was ordered by the commandant of a German police station to report for such a hunt. When Michałek failed to make it to the police station on time, as he had no shoes, the commandant

192   *Tomasz Frydel*

threatened him, saying he should have "wrapped his feet in rags and reported for the hunt."[8] Sometimes the very presence of a stranger was cause for alarm. When an unknown woman with a child appeared in the village of Wola Wielka (Dębica county) in January of 1943, the entire community was thrown into an existential dilemma as villagers debated how best to proceed. Some claimed she was a Jew, others that she was a Roma, she herself claimed that she was a wandering beggar. In the end, the locals decided not to take a risk and applied pressure on the village head to deliver mother and child to the police.[9]

It is here that Geertz's "thick description" is most relevant in capturing the broader social world that conditioned the actions of would-be perpetrators. Hunts for Jews were entangled with hunts for other fugitives. People who sheltered Jews sometimes sheltered prisoners of war. A hunt for Polish laborers could bring into its orbit a hunt for Jews and vice versa. Village heads were forced to act against Jews as well as members of the ethnic Polish collective, though certainly not in the same genocidal capacity. Perpetrators on the local level could thus be viewed along several axes. Taken on their own and harnessed to a narrative, such incidents could be seen as the smoking gun of unique peasant hatred against a particular victim group; when combined, they force the historian to reconsider the motivation within the broader framework that informed such actions.

Informers: weeding out the Good Samaritans

Obedience to this system was reinforced by informers working for the German police. For our purpose, informers are significant for two reasons. First, knowledge of their presence and operations conditioned the behavior of locals to propel peasants along a path leading to inaction or perpetration. A particularly sinister role was played by agent provocateurs under various covers. These informers, or *V-Personen*,[10] compiled lists of those who gave them shelter, inquired about who possessed weapons or maintained contact with partisans. The use of informers posing as escaped Soviet POWs appears to have been the most widespread practice. The village of Styków (Rzeszów county) was 'tested' three times by such informers.[11] In the village of Żurowa and Racławice (Tarnów county), "an incident took place where members of the Gestapo dressed up as Russians . . . [and] caused the burning down of two homes and the shooting of two families."[12] The two men dressed in Soviet uniforms returned the following day in the uniforms of the SS and in the company of other policemen to execute those who had opened their doors to them.

The plot thickens when the Polish province emerges as a zone teeming with every variety of informer, Gestapo agent, and false-flag operation, fueling an atmosphere of distrust. In the town of Łańcut and vicinity, Maria Steinberg was seen by locals walking around "dressed as a chimney sweep," only to be later seen (along with another informer) in the uniform of the German gendarmerie, assisting in the 'pacification' of the village of Żołynia, where 14 people were killed.[13] Monthly underground reports carefully observed intricate false-flag operations. Still, locals unwittingly often stepped into these traps. In the spring of 1943, the

Judenjagd   193

Kripo and gendarmerie of Dębica had set up base in the village of Łączki Kucharskie (Ropczyce county), dressed up as armed partisans, and walked through neighboring villages. They passed through the village of Glinik on 10 April 1943 and returned there the following day now as German policemen to execute locals for failing to inform them about the presence of partisans in the region. They executed a few villagers, stopping only when some locals identified the German policemen as the very same group of 'partisans' that had passed through the village the previous day.[14]

Second, some categories of informers, recruited as they were from among victim groups, tell us something important about the dramatic transformation of victims into perpetrators that took place during the war. Within the above set of practices, the use of informers posing as fugitive Jews was hardly off limits. Various partisan formations of the underground movement were acutely aware of this. For example, a unit of the Peasant Battalions in the Krosno region "sold a machine gun for 3,000 zł to a member of the Jasło Gestapo, Becker [Oskar Bäcker], posing as a Jew," and once contact was established, the entire unit was eventually penetrated and destroyed by the German police.[15] Similarly, a Home Army report from the fall of 1942 warned: "Over 15 spies have been dispatched into each county, who are to roam the region as peddlers, Jews, nuns, and soldiers escaping from camps."[16]

But perhaps the most counterintuitive is the participation of Jews themselves with the Gestapo in the surveillance of the local population and the *Judenjagd*. After the war, Christoph Führer, who was part of the German civilian administration, reported the following scenario: "[In 1942] I met two Jews on a country road, who had previously lived in Dębica, equipped with identity cards issued by the Gestapo. They had an assignment to ferret out hidden Jews."[17] The Mielec Gestapo used several Jewish *V-Leute* in the region. One of these was a 20-year-old woman with the pseudonym of Sophie, who was transferred to the Mielec post in the spring of 1943 and was dispatched into the region to penetrate the underground movement (Krempa 2013: 20–2). A labor camp established by a German firm, Bäumer und Lösch, in the Czekaj forest near Mielec included a special barracks for Jewish informers and their families, who were drawn from the Jewish Councils (*Judenräte*) of the Mielec and Dębica ghettos and Pustków labor camp, as well as the Jewish ghetto police (*Ordnungsdienst*) of Dębica (Krempa 2013: 146–53). Izak Kapłan from Mielec, Herman Immerglück from Dębica, and Max Bitkower from Tarnów were its three main agents. They were exempt from work in the camp, were permitted to bring their families (Bitkower brought his wife and child from Tarnów), and were issued special papers by the Gestapo to allow them to walk around freely. "In the morning, they left on bicycles and returned at night. We knew that the Gestapo came to visit them – they drank, ate and had fun together. Later it turned out that they rode to the woods where Jews were hiding and denounced them," stated Jakub Grynblum, who worked in the camp.[18] When they succeeded in persuading fugitive Jews to come to the camp, they were usually taken out and shot by members of the Mielec Gestapo in the nearby forest of Berdechów. On 23 April 1943, members of the *Ortschutz* of nearby Chrząstów

194 *Tomasz Frydel*

apprehended one of these informers – perhaps Kapłan himself – and handed him over to the Polish Police in Mielec.[19] The man was subsequently released and was seen walking around in the company of the German police. These informers operated in the region from the end of 1942 to the summer of 1943, when they were executed by the Gestapo.

Surprising as it may be, the participation of Jewish informers in the *Judenjagd* was in line with the Nazi policy of divide et impera of its colonial subjects. But the fact alone that victims of genocide could be so dramatically transformed into collaborators and perpetrators ought to take the wind out of sharp claims about the *Judenjagd* as an exclusively grassroots, peasant-driven 'social movement' to rid society of its Jews. The effect of these widespread surveillance practices was undoubtedly to condition an automatic response among villagers to immediately report and apprehend any strangers that made their appearance. It seems impossible to understand the irrational fears shared by rural society without taking these factors into account.

Beyond ethnic categories: the teleology of survival

In her study of peasant violence toward Jews, historian and psychologist Barbara Engelking quotes Roza Majerfeld, who experienced the paralyzing taste of death during a German patrol: "My heart and legs became numb, it's as if my speech was taken away from me. It was a feeling of death – a faint, sweet taste for a fraction of a second" (Engelking 2011: 195–6). Such feelings undoubtedly accompanied many Jews in their desperate search for shelter, which deepened as the *Judenjagd* swept across the countryside and farmers increasingly refused to open their doors to strangers. Majerfeld herself tasted it many times over, but lived to see liberation. But was the fear experienced by those sheltering Jews any less profound? The German occupation introduced a unique dynamic in which the Poles who undertook the shelter of Jews arguably partook in a shared taste of death. But the taste could evoke different responses.

This tension is captured in the story of Perel Faust and her husband Chaim, who escaped the Dębica ghetto to hide with a Polish family for a period of 22 months in return for payment. When a member of the Gestapo moved into the room next door, the Polish woman asked their Jewish charges to leave, but a granddaughter exclaimed: "Grandmother, if they leave, they will shoot us, for they will certainly reveal that they were with us!" (Faust 2016: 289). Here began the toxic relationship between the rescuers and the rescued. The Gentile family believed that releasing the Faust couple would lead to their eventual capture – and the betrayal and death of those who gave them help. At the same time, with the German policeman and the Jewish family separated by a thin wall, they could not endure the daily experience of fear. Eventually the Polish couple began making threats that they would have to kill their Jewish charges. "They did not want to keep us anymore, but they could not let us go, for then they would be in danger. Indeed, they were in great danger," wrote Faust. During those 22 long months, a series of murder attempts on the Jewish couple using poison, suffocation, and starvation followed.

The preceding case is a microcosm of the larger dynamic that emerged between Poles and Jews during the *Judenjagd*. On an existential level, one family's will to survive was pitted against another's. It was the fundamental 'Faustian' bargain that ordinary people found themselves in during the course of shelter, and it gave rise to a new teleology of murder. In the preceding case, a denunciation by formerly sheltered Jews only appears as a possibility, but a close study of the Subcarpathian region reveals a number of reported incidents. In the same area combed by Kapłan's group of informers, an older Jewish woman from the village of Grochowe (Mielec county) was captured in the spring of 1943 by the German police. She was marched through the neighboring village of Malinie and beaten into revealing which families had offered her food or shelter. One of the several homes that she indicated was the Witek household. When the German police arrived, they beat the 65-year-old woman living there and, as punishment, ordered her to dig a grave for the Jewish woman underneath her door entrance.[20]

In other cases, it appears that German policemen were able to exploit the vulnerabilities of young people who were captured. For example, Małka Schönfeld, an 18-year-old Jew from the village of Pantalowice (Przeworsk county), was hiding with her family in a forest bunker. On 4 December 1942, she was captured by German gendarmes and denounced the Poles who had provided the family with food. The German policemen took Schönfeld on a horse-drawn cart, as she indicated who in the village had given them help. As a result, the gendarmes executed three young Polish brothers in Pantalowice and six Poles in the village of Hadle Szklarskie.[21] In another case, Nathan Haske was wounded during a hunt for Jews and turned himself over in the village of Wólka Ogryzkowa (Przeworsk county). The German policemen "gave him water to drink and promised him that if he tells them everything that they ask, they will send him to a hospital and then to Germany, where he would live."[22] According to the village head, Haske supplied the policemen with the names of members of the Peasant Battalions in nearby Gniewczyna Tryniecka and Jagiełła. When the information was exhausted, "Gestapoman Zajder told him [Haske] to get up so that he could be taken to a hospital" and shot the young man in the forehead.

Such incidents in the Subcarpathian region could be multiplied (Rączy 2008: 113–15). They came to inform 'Polish' anxieties about the dangers of sheltering or even maintaining contact with fugitives and left a strong mark on real-time documents produced during the war. They can be found in the diary of Franciszek Kotula, who kept a chronicle of the "voice of the street" in the city of Rzeszów. The motif of Jews denouncing Poles who gave them shelter appears several times throughout the chronicle. Among others, his entry on 16 December 1942 reads:

> Rumors are coming in from all sides that the Germans are murdering entire Polish families if any hidden Jews are found. Whoever is still hiding someone, that person is pushed out and, when captured by the Germans, he most often reveals where he stayed and who gave him food – even though he knows that he will face death anyway.
>
> (Kotula 1999: 147)

196 *Tomasz Frydel*

His entry on 11 January 1943 captures the case of Małka Schönfeld, among others:

> In the region around Hyżne, twenty Jews were killed and 10 Poles, who had given them food and shelter. Three sons of the forester in Hadle Szklarskie were killed for sheltering Jews and five peasants in Grzegorzówka. The Jews can't hold out during torture. Even though they know they will die, they betray their hosts.
>
> (Kotula 1999: 151)

Every major partisan formation in the region registered this danger. On 12 March 1943, the following order was issued by the Home Army in the Rzeszów region:

> There has not been a single incident in which a captured Jew did not denounce everyone who offered them help. In many cases, they maliciously give surnames [of individuals] who are completely uninvolved. All are shot on the spot. We have borne many losses because of this. Therefore, I forbid any contact with and help to fleeing Jews.[23]

A report by the Communist People's Guard (GL), which was the most sympathetic to Jews, stated the following: "Recently two partisans were killed, who were given away by a Jewish woman hiding among our people."[24] The Peasant Battalions reported: "Certainly more of them [Jews] could have remained in hiding if it wasn't for their poor tactics during interrogation when captured by the gendarmerie. In such situations, they reveal everything they know – whom they hid with, who gave them food. The accused face unfortunate consequences, including the loss of life, and so fall victim sooner."[25] Yet it is important to bear in mind that the accusation was not aimed solely at Jews, but was inherent to the danger of hiding any fugitives. For example, an underground newspaper complained of Soviet POWs denouncing their former shelterers:

> Facing imminent danger, the unavoidable bullet, he [the POW] gives away the names of those who had previously given him food and protected him. [. . .] There are only a few exceptions among Russian prisoners of war, who responded to the Germans with silence and contempt during interrogation and the barrage of questions, without betraying those who helped them in difficult times. The rest, although they knew without a doubt that their fate was sealed, extended their life by a few days.[26]

On one level, Polish-Jewish tensions could be viewed through the prism of ethnicity. Yet the preceding cases suggest that they were also profoundly informed by a competing teleology of survival. The 'faint, sweet taste' of death was undoubtedly experienced by everyone caught in the dynamics of sheltering, even if money was involved. While each case was specific, the fundamental tension was located on a spectrum of existential competition. It is hard to understand the strained conflict between Poles and Jews in this context without appreciating the ever-present fear of death, which, as we have seen, was based on real incidents, but also likely magnified by fear and the power of rumors in a time of war. The struggle for survival had the potential of becoming a zero-sum game, which sometimes left a trail of bodies in its wake.

The rise of a unique cohort of perpetrators: the people of two faces

At the institutional level, the occupational authorities had tilted the entire legal, economic, and social landscape toward facilitating genocide, causing a gradual landslide into a moral abyss and social breakdown, especially when Polish government structures above the village level were hijacked and political elites decapitated. At the local level, the lifting of all forms of state protection from Polish society encouraged a kind of 'tribalization' of social relations in rural areas, with lines of mutual distrust and hatred deepening along ethnic lines. Within the vacuum of legitimate state authority, underground structures aside, it was the Polish Police that often played a role of 'stabilizing' the volatile situation, especially in preempting the unpredictability of German terror. These conditions produced a unique type of 'perpetrator' – individuals who participated in ways of both harming and helping Jews. Take the case of Karol Stachak, who was both commandant of the PP in Czudec (Strzyżów county) and the commander of the local underground Home Army unit (AK Czudec). Among other accusations, he was tried after the war for killing a Jewish man who was brought to the PP station of Lubenia in the spring of 1942 while Stachak was its commandant. During questioning, the man allegedly "gave the names of eight families who sheltered him. The accused and his colleagues were afraid that if they handed him over to Czudec [gendarmerie], the Jew would also denounce these eight families, who would be shot."[27] Stachak and two other policemen thus shot the man behind the police station.

However, in the course of the investigation, it was also revealed that Stachak had sheltered a Jewish boy in his home – who survived the war – as everyone in the village was afraid to take him in. Stachak also knew that a Jewish girl was being hidden in a mill by a farmer in Hyżne, yet, according to one witness, "he protected her and did not turn her over to the German authorities."[28] Further, as a member of the Home Army, he procured "Aryan papers" for Jews and had a good reputation in the Jewish community.[29] The court did not know what to make of this man. On the one hand, as a "member of the AK, he sympathized with people of communist convictions, Jews, did a lot of good for people, helped them in various situations, often at the risk of his own life [. . .] helped people avoid being sent to Germany, helped to hide Jews – moreover, he hid a Jewish child in his own home." On the other hand, he was a member of the PP "under the control of German authority," whom the Germans could always trust. He was "a man of a vacillating character, of indecisive and unsettled political convictions – a man of two faces," concluded the court, as it sentenced him to death.[30] The case of the Polish Police is all the more relevant, because in the Second Polish Republic their

198 Tomasz Frydel

duties included preventing the outbreak of violence against its Jewish minority, but during the *Judenjagd* they appear on the horizon as key perpetrators.

In many ways, the story of Karol Stachak is emblematic of the wider dilemmas of Polish society under occupation, which eluded the established legal and political categories of collaboration (Connelly 2005: 771–81). The "people of two faces" had to straddle two universes – satisfying state-level German regulations from above and communal survival pressures from below. The case of the Polish policemen foregrounds these 'contradictions' most dramatically, as they had to navigate this fraught relationship. This 'triangular' relationship faced by local police forces differed fundamentally from the situation of the 'ordinary men' of Police Battalion 101 in Christopher Browning's classic study (Browning 1992). After the liquidation of ghettos throughout the GG in the summer of 1942, members of the PP were to apprehend Jews, take down their testimony, and deliver them to the German police, resorting to shooting only in the case of escape. From February 1943, however, they were under German orders to shoot Jews on the spot, though this could differ from region to region. But oftentimes, as in the case of policeman Stachak, they acted as a kind of killing squad or 'willing executioners' of Jews in the name of protecting the local population from the onslaught of German state terror and collective punishment.

It is in the context of acts of repression that the role of the Blue Policemen emerges most visibly in the capacity of 'willing executioners.' Manhunts initiated by ordinary peasants without ties to the village security system, or the "active involvement of large masses of peasants in the *Judenjagd*" in each village (Grabowski 2013: 75–8), were the exception rather than the rule and took place in specific circumstances. A close study of the Subcarpathian region suggests that it was rather in the immediate aftermath of a major act of repression for the shelter of Jews – precisely the moments that represented the greatest existential threat to the community – that we see a popular upsurge of expelling, capturing, or killing of Jews. The 'pacification' action of the village of Podborze (Mielec county) is a case in point: it resulted in the capture and death of over 30 Jews across three communes in a matter of two weeks (Frydel 2016: 147–66). When local policemen arrived on the scene, they encountered peasants pleading with them not to hand over the Jews for fear that they might denounce their shelterers, but to shoot them on the spot.

These perpetrators, the 'people of two faces,' recur regularly throughout the archival record. What do they tell us? It was precisely the people who were part of the institutional framework tied to genocide, whether the Polish Police or the village security apparatus, who faced this dilemma most sharply. The village head of Nagoszyn (Dębica county), Stanisław Biduś, was tried for handing over Jews and Soviet POWs to the police. He was indeed found guilty, but what angered locals during the house searches was his alleged hypocrisy. A witness echoed a refrain heard during the searches: "He's sheltering Jews himself, but goes to others' homes looking for them."[31] In all these cases, the perpetrators had to conform to an outward facade. The messenger of the village of Zwiernik (Dębica county), Mieczysław Fiołek, was ordered to report to the home of the village head at dawn, where the PP was organizing a hunt for Jews in a nearby forest. Some 80 villagers were called out from their homes and were divided into search parties. Although Ryba himself sheltered a Jewish woman, Sala Teifelbaum, who survived the war, he had to participate in the search.[32]

A discernible dividing line in these cases lies at the level of kinship, which was a determining factor in who to help and who to hand over or kill, if it came to that. Marian Lenartowicz, a Polish policeman from Żyrardów in central Poland with ties to the Home Army, who was transferred to Jasło during the war, participated in delivering Jews to the Gestapo. At the same time, the goods that he confiscated from peasants for illegal slaughter or black marketeering were sent to help Jews in the Warsaw ghetto. He "sent packages for Jews in the Warsaw ghetto, who came from Żyrardów. These packages were repackaged by me and my father and sent by post with the help of Stachecki," testified his sister.[33] Another policeman, Michał Strzępka, mentioned above, killed over a dozen Jews during his time at the Radomyśl Wielki PP station. Surprisingly, one of the people who came to his defense in the trial was Wiktoria Wolińska (née Berl), whose family (Wiktoria, Salomon, and Adela Berl) had received help from the entire Strzępka family since 1940. Strzępka, his wife, and daughter helped coordinate the relocation of the Berl family from village to village, provided them with food, information, and false papers, without receiving any payment in exchange. Remarkably, the duality of the policeman was unknown to Berl: "During my stay in the Radomyśl Wielki region and nearby villages, I never heard or saw Strzępka persecuting Jews. [. . .] I never heard that Strzępka ever participated in the capture or shooting of Jews."[34]

These cases might normally be treated as odd 'exceptions' within the conventional legal and political understanding of perpetrators and collaboration, but there are grounds to treat them as a cohort, which shows that the participation in persecution and killing was not specific to any social group or ideology. These good acts represented neither brief sparks of humanity nor an insurance policy taken out in the event of a change in political winds, but were structural to the situation of society under occupation. Further, there is reason to believe that such paradoxical behaviors were more salient in the General Government due to the lack of political collaboration with Nazi Germany, compared to other Eastern European states, such as Lithuania, Ukraine, or Slovakia, where the social energy of collaboration was harnessed to an organizing political principle. The brutalized occupational conditions of the General Government had given rise to an arithmetic of survival, in which the killing of fugitive Jews was at times re-imagined as a way of protecting the larger community. If the Holocaust was a "legitimate resident in the house of modernity," in the words of Zygmunt Bauman (1989: 17), the paradox of perpetrator-helpers was one way that local societies learned to coexist with it under occupation.

Conclusion

This analysis has harnessed the data to an explanatory framework that makes acts of perpetrators of violence toward Jews comprehensible primarily within an institutional framework in which a system of draconian control was imposed on village life. The violence thus flowed from the top in what could be called 'genocide

200 Tomasz Frydel

from above' – as well as from 'abroad,' as it was largely imported by an occupying power and imposed on a defeated and dismantled state. This chapter argues that the majority of peasant acts of violence against Jews constituted a form of genocide from above. However, at the same time, the specific conditions of the German occupation in the General Government gave rise to 'killing from below,' rooted in the restructured social reality that set its fragmented victim populations on a collision course. Genocidal policies issued by the occupation authorities from the top ricocheted in surprising ways on the local level. In this analysis, Nazi German racial reasons for the killing of Jews from 'above' can begin to be distinguished from the causes of Polish killing of Jews from 'below.'

What does this tell us about perpetrators and motivation? The complex reality examined here cannot be poured into the mold of antisemitism alone. This is not to suggest that antisemitism, like greed, did not co-exist with this system or to say that Gentiles were otherwise waiting to jump forward to save the Jews. But it can be overworked as an explanatory concept when confronted with the complex reality of local violence, particularly in the paradoxical case of the perpetrator-rescuer. The system of pressures examined here formed the baseline of causes that informed the actions of the perpetrators. No doubt the system benefitted from antisemitism, but it was a sufficient, not a necessary, condition for participation. It only gets us so far in explaining why killing on the local level proceeded the way that it did. A genocide that took the form of the *Judenjagd*, it seems, was an enterprise that harnessed multi-ethnic participation, driven by German policy from the top. In the broad hunts examined here, there was little ideological consistency to peasant behavior or to the profiles of the policemen.

At stake in a study of perpetrators is the question of why people kill – here, quite ordinary people. A microhistory, with its proximity to the intimacy of violence, can perhaps bring us closer to an answer. The primary forces that held the system in place and propelled the *Judenjagd* along its tracks were fear and the will to survive. In the shadow of mass killing, social relations were rearranged along an axis of kinship networks. A related observation is that times of catastrophe and communal crisis appear to give rise to utilitarian thinking, constraining altruism to family and acquaintances. Further, short-lived episodes of violence that eventually petered out, such as the Jedwabne massacre and the pogroms in the summer of 1941 more broadly, are not the best lens for examining a long-term process that was drawn out for a period of three years. The German occupation was a period of radical social transformation and the "perpetrator" was a fluid category in this landscape. Without a broader contextualization, a study of perpetrators can become unmoored, which is evident in ongoing treatments of the subject. If we ignore the parallel hunts against other groups, the dilemmas that compromised village society, and remove the teleology that often informed decisions to denounce or kill, then indeed the *Judenjagd* emerges as killing done for its own sake, which fits in more readily with a model of ethnic cleansing. Yet, as this chapter shows, killing took place within a different set of coordinates.

In setting out his approach to writing the history of the English working class from below, the historian E.P. Thompson (1980: 12) famously wrote that he sought to

Judenjagd   201

rescue the 'backwardness' of his subjects from "the enormous condescension of posterity." It seems that a similar intervention is needed from another "condescension of posterity" when writing about peasant society and the Shoah.

Notes

1 I am grateful to Irene Eber, David Engel, Jeffrey Kopstein, Antony Polonsky, and Piotr Wróbel for their comments on drafts of this chapter. Responsibility for content rests with the author.
2 The General Government (GG) was a part of occupied Poland not annexed to the Third Reich, but was not a collaborating puppet state. It was subdivided into five districts governed by German civil and police administrations: Warsaw, Lublin, Radom, Krakow, and Galicia (added in August 1941). District Krakow was subdivided into 12 counties (*Kreise*). The counties that fall under the purview of this chapter are Tarnów, Dębica, Rzeszów, Jarosław, Jasło, Krosno, Przemyśl, and Sanok.
3 AIPN Rz, 358/38, trial of village guard commandant Piotr Zembroń and others, indictment of the accused, p. 140. On 8 May 1951, the Voivodship Court of Rzeszów sentenced Zembroń to five years and six months in prison.
4 AIPN Rz, 357/10, trial of village head Franciszek Sowa, testimony of gendarme Wiktor Waszek, pp. 4–6. Sowa was found not guilty by the District Court of Rzeszów on 14 May 1947.
5 AIPN Rz, 357/31, trial of gamekeeper Marcin Kotwica, testimony of Józef Wojtak, pp. 39–41. According to Wojtak, a crowd of about 30 people had witnessed the incident and Kotwica therefore believed he had no choice but to hand the fugitives over. Kotwica was found not guilty by the District Court of Rzeszów on 31 October 1947.
6 AIPN Rz, 358/32, trial of village head Jan Kostak, Ludwik Matuła, and Tomasz Mika, court sentence by the Voivodship Court of Rzeszów on 18 April 1951, pp. 313–8. Kostak and Matuła were sentenced to six years in prison.
7 AIPN Rz, 363/4, trial of village guard commandant Józef Racławski, statement by the defense drawing on the testimony of Józef Leszkowicz, pp. 64–6. Racławski was found not guilty by the District Court of Tarnów on 16 April 1951.
8 ANK, SAKr, 1002, K 54/50, trial of Emil Michałek, deposition of the accused, pp. 32–3.
9 AIPN Rz, 358/119, trial of village guards Władysław Chorąży, Stanisław Dural, and others, court sentence by the Voivodship Court of Rzeszów on 25 June 1953, pp. 369–71. All of the accused were found innocent.
10 *V-Personen* or *V-Männer*, from *Vertrauensperson* in German for "trusted person."
11 AIPN Rz, 352/153, trial of village head Franciszek Pruchnik, sentence by the Special Penal Court of Rzeszów, 9 August 1946, pp. 198–200. The village head was found innocent.
12 AIPN Rz, 354/52, trial of deputy village head Andrzej Kawa and village guard commandant Franciszek Mika, court sentence by the District Court of Jasło, 10 December 1947, p. 99.
13 AIPN Rz, 352/149, trial of Maria Steinberg (Pelc), pp. 92, 154–5. Steinberg was sentenced to death by the Special Penal Court of Rzeszów on 4 November 1946.
14 AIPN Rz, OKŚZpNP, S 20/09/Zn, Vol. II, testimony of Jan Dziedzic, 1946, pp. 366–7.
15 CAW, II.33.44, Peasant Battalions, Rzeszów District IV-Bez, "Oracz" to "Zawojny," 28 October 1943, pp. 1–11.
16 AAN, 1673/XI/50, "Pług" to "Rzemiosło" (Rzeszów), "Political Intelligence" report, 4 November 1942, "German intelligence" section, pp. 35–7.
17 BAL, B 162/7460, testimony of Christoph Führer, deputy *Kreishauptmann* of Dębica county, pp. 65–74.
18 AŻIH, 301/3503, testimony of Jakub Grynblum, 1947, pp. 1–2.
19 AIPN Rz, 353/61, pp. 258–61, trial of Jan Miłoś and other night guards, testimony of Bogdan Protter, a Jewish fugitive who came into contact with one of these informers.

202 *Tomasz Frydel*

20 AIPN Rz, 358/48, trial of Jan Malczyński, testimony of Władysław Witek, pp. 20–1.
21 AIPN Rz, OKŚZpNP, S 133/12/Zn, testimony of Julia Bura, pp. 11–13; testimony of Aleksandra Dec, pp. 16–18.
22 AIPN Rz, 359/21, trial of village head Jan Janas, deposition of the accused, pp. 16–17.
23 AIPN Rz, 105/7, Order No. 3, Point 21 of instructions issued by the commander of district AK Rzeszów-South, Col. Józef Maciołek, alias "Żuraw," p. 120. The order itself was issued earlier by the central command in Krakow.
24 AAN, 191/XXIV/2, People's Guard, Krakow District IV, Report No. 2, "Krakow," 1 December 1942, p. 3.
25 AZHRL, VI/32, Subregion (Podokręg) Rzeszów – District Przeworsk, "To the Inspectorate of the People's Security Guard (LSB)," Section IV, 1 July 1944, p. 3.
26 *Wieści*, no. 6, 6 February 1944, "Ivans and Vasyls," 3–4.
27 AIPN Rz, 046/991, trial of PP Karol Stachak, sentence by the District Court of Rzeszów on 12 March 1949, p. 4.
28 AIPN Rz, 353/18, trial of PP Karol Stachak, testimony of Edward Brydek, pp. 116–17.
29 Ibid., testimony of witness Chaskel Wiesenfeld, pp. 240–1. Wiesenfeld's Jewish friends instructed him to seek the help of Stachak, who was generally regarded by them as a 'good man.'
30 AIPN Rz, 046/991, court sentence, p. 1–12. The sentence was commuted to 10 years in prison by the Appellate Court of Rzeszów on 24 October 1949.
31 AIPN Rz, 353/81, Vol. II, trial of village head Stanisław Biduś and others, testimony of Karolina Cieśla, pp. 75–7.
32 AIPN Rz, 353/285, trial of Mieczysław Fiołek and Władysław Ryba, court sentence, p. 149; Teifelbaum's letter, pp. 43–43v.
33 AIPN Rz, 107/1783, Vol. IV, Part I, trial of PP Władysław Malawski and others, testimony of Aniela Iżycka, sister of Lenartowicz, pp. 378–9; testimony of Marian Leczysłowski, a mailman in Brzostek, 379–80. Both witnesses testified that Lenartowicz sent food packages to prisoners in Auschwitz and Łódź, as well as Żyrardów Jews resettled to the Warsaw ghetto.
34 AIPN Rz, 34/61, Vol. I, trial of PP Michał Strzępka, testimony of Wiktoria Wolińska, 25 May 1965, pp. 183–8.

References

Archival sources

Archive of the Institute for the Study of the Popular Movement [Archiwum Zakładu Historii Ruchu Ludowego (AZHRL)] VI/32, Subdistrict Rzeszów [Podokręg Rzeszów].
Archive of the Jewish Historical Institute [Archiwum Żydowskiego Instytutu Historycznego (AŻIH)] 301/3503, testimony of Jakub Grynblum.
Archive of Modern Records [Archiwum Akt Narodowych w Warszawie (AAN)] 191/XXIV/2, People's Guard [Gwardia Ludowa], Krakow District IV.
Archive of the Rzeszów Branch of the Institute of National Remembrance [Archiwum Instytutu Pamięci Narodowej w Rzeszowie (AIPN Rz)] 358/38, 357/10, 357/31358/32, 358/119, 363/4, 352/153, 354/52, 352/149, 353/61, 358/48, 359/21, 105/7, 046/991, 353/18, 046/991, 107/1783, 34/61, 353/81, 353/28.
Central Military Archives in Warsaw [Centralne Archiwum Wojskowe w Warszawie (CAW)] II.33.44, Peasant Battalions [Bataliony Chłopskie].
Federal Archive of Ludwigsburg [Bundesarchiv Ludwigsburg (BAL)] B 162/7460.
IPN – The Rzeszów Branch of the Main Commission for the Prosecution of Crimes against the Polish Nation [Główna Komisja Ścigania Zbrodni przeciwko Narodowi Polskiemu w Rzeszowie (IPN Rz, OKŚZpNP)] S 20/09/Zn, S 133/12/Zn.

Judenjagd 203

National Archives of Krakow [Archiwum Narodowe w Krakowie (ANK)] Krakow Appellate Court [Sąd Apelacyjny w Krakowie (SAKr)] 1002, K 54/50; 1042, IV K, 252/50.
Periodical *Wieści* [News].

Secondary literature

Bauman, Zygmunt. *Modernity and the Holocaust*. Cambridge: Polity Press, 1989.

Bloxham, Donald. *The Final Solution: A Genocide*. Oxford: Oxford University Press, 2009.

Browning, Christopher R. *Ordinary Men: Reserve Police Battalion 101 and the Final Solution in Poland*. New York: HarperCollins, 1992.

Connelly, John. "Why the Poles Collaborated So Little: And Why That Is No Reason for Nationalist Hubris." *Slavic Review* 64, no. 4 (2005): 771–81.

Dreifuss, Havi. *Changing Perspectives on Polish-Jewish Relations During the Holocaust*. Jerusalem: Yad Vashem, 2012.

Engelking, Barbara. *Jest taki piękny słoneczny dzień . . . Losy Żydów szukających ratunku na wsi polskiej 1942–1945*. Warszawa: Stowarzyszenie Centrum Badań nad Zagładą Żydów, 2011.

Faust, Perel. "Twenty-Two Months of Hiding with the Gentiles." In *The Book of Dembitz (Dębica, Poland)*, edited by Daniel Leibl, translated by Sefer Dembitz, 287–92. New York: JewishGen, 2016.

Friedländer, Saul. "An Integrated History of the Holocaust: Possibilities and Challenges." In *Years of Persecution, Years of Extermination: Saul Friedländer and the Future of Holocaust Studies*, edited by Christian Wiese and Paul Betts, 21–9. London: Continuum, 2010.

Frydel, Tomasz. "The Pazifizierungsaktion as a Catalyst of Anti-Jewish Violence: A Study in the Social Dynamics of Fear." In *The Holocaust and European Societies: Social Processes and Dynamics*, edited by Frank Bajohr and Andrea Löw, 147–66. London: Palgrave Macmillan, 2016.

Geertz, Clifford. "Thick Description: Toward an Interpretive Theory of Culture." In *The Interpretation of Cultures: Selected Essays*, 3–30. New York: Basic Books, 1973.

Grabowski, Jan. *Hunt for the Jews: Betrayal and Murder in German-Occupied Poland*. Bloomington: Indiana University Press, 2013.

Gross, Jan T. *Neighbors: The Destruction of the Jewish Community in Jedwabne, Poland*. Princeton, NJ: Princeton University Press, 2001.

Gross, Jan T., and Irena Grudzińska-Gross. *Golden Harvest: Events at the Periphery of the Holocaust*. New York: Oxford University Press, 2012.

Hilberg, Raul. *Perpetrators, Victims, Bystanders: The Jewish Catastrophe, 1933–45*. New York: Aaron Asher Books, 1992.

Kotula, Franciszek. *Losy Żydów rzeszowskich 1939–1945. Kronika tamtych dni*. Rzeszów: Społeczny Komitet Wydania Dzieł Franciszka Kotuli, 1999.

Krempa, Andrzej. *Zagłada Żydów mieleckich*. Mielec: Muzeum Regionalne w Mielcu, 2013.

Polonsky, Antony, and Joanna B. Michlic. *The Neighbors Respond: The Controversy Over the Jedwabne Massacre in Poland*. Princeton, NJ: Princeton University Press, 2004.

Rączy, Elżbieta. *Pomoc Polaków dla ludności żydowskiej na Rzeszowszczyźnie, 1939–1945*. Rzeszów: Instytut Pamięci Narodowej, 2008.

Thompson, Edward Palmer. *The Making of the English Working Class*. London: V. Gollancz, 1980.

Zimmerman, Joshua D. *The Polish Underground and the Jews, 1939–1945*. Cambridge: Cambridge University Press, 2015.

11 Is a comparative theory of perpetrators possible?

Scott Straus

Introduction

The chapters in this volume represent a compelling approach to the study of violence. In various ways, they seek to address fundamental questions in the social scientific study of violence: Who commits violence? Why do they commit violence? How do they commit violence? What is the balance of psychological, social, political, and situational factors that shape the decision to commit violence? By bringing together scholars from various disciplines, sometimes in the same chapter, and in examining examples from multiple continents, the chapters underscore how rich, interesting, and unchartered this area of research remains. While the study of violence has taken a "micro-turn" in recent years, and while the study of micro-level dynamics and perpetrators in certain cases, such as the Holocaust, have advanced tremendously, there remains a lack of systematic comparative research on perpetrators. To the extent that general theories on perpetrators can develop, systematic comparison that builds findings across cases is an essential part of that intellectual project. The volume is a welcome step in that direction.

The chapters demonstrate the complexity of the subject. They show that there is no single motivation that explains the participation in the harm of others. Some chapters emphasize ideological factors, such as that by Leader Maynard. Others emphasize gender and social norms, including the desire to appear decent, as Gertz, Brehm, and Brown show. Still others show how the desire for survival prompted some to participate in violence, even if they were actively protecting potential victims, as Frydel shows. The diversity of social, political, and situational factors represented across these chapters is refreshing. The authors are not confined to staid debates between social situational factors, on the hand, versus deep-seated animosity, on the other. Indeed, the authors seek to move well beyond such debates, opening up new ways to conceptualize the problem. Similarly, the authors in this volume lean towards viewing perpetrators as "ordinary" people, in the sense of reflecting their societies and of having no particular pre-crisis proclivity for violence. But again the authors move well beyond that argument. While the authors recognize that perpetrators are reflective of the societies from which they emerge, there remains a great deal left to explore about perpetrators.

One of the key questions that the book implicitly raises is: Is a comparative theory of perpetrators possible? Can scholars determine, based on comparative analysis, some essential commonalities in who perpetrates violence, how they do, and the reasons why they do. In examining perpetrators across different historical periods and across multiple different kinds of contexts, that question lurks behind this volume. At the very least, that question will be of interest to some readers of the volume, in particular those who engage directly and indirectly in comparative research.

In this closing chapter, I wish to address that question and in particular to raise some problems with a comparative theory of perpetrators that this volume exposes. I do not rehearse the arguments in the interior pages, as they are available to readers, but rather to draw attention to some questions and problems that the chapters collectively bring to the fore. I address these in the spirit of the volume – an effort to advance the systematic, comparative study of perpetrators.

Conceptualization and theorization

A comparative approach requires a baseline concept to bring a research field together. That baseline concept for this volume is perpetrator. But what is a perpetrator? What does a perpetrator perpetrate? Is the concept a useful social scientific one? What distinguishes a perpetrator from a non-perpetrator? Is it a concept to describe a category of people or is it a concept to describe a category of action? In different ways, several chapters address these questions. All the same, the question is fundamental for any field of "perpetrators studies" to have coherence.

The standard definition of perpetrators, which Raul Hilberg espoused, conceptualizes perpetrators as that class of people who directly or indirectly participated in the destruction of civilian lives. As some chapters point out, that concept has an implicit normative element. Individuals commit acts of violence against non-combatants; their violence is illegal, not right, because they kill civilians. In the extreme, such violence is genocide or another form of mass atrocity in which there is sustained destruction of a category of people. Several chapters in the book focus on direct perpetrators, those that took part in the destruction of lives or those who ordered or condoned such violence. Others focus on the indirect perpetration, in which individuals may have participated in a system that led to the overall destruction of lives but not (as being part of a bureaucracy that itself was part of a state committed to genocide or as stealing property from those who were targeted, as in the Rwanda case).

To the extent that a field of "perpetrator studies" exists, I would argue that the field depends on the analytical and implicitly normative distinction between violence and warfare. Violence is the non-sanctioned (in a normative, legal sense) deliberate physical harm against civilians and non-combatants. Perpetrators commit violence. War (or combat) is sanctioned violence between combatants. Soldiers engage in warfare. Perhaps that is too strong a contrast but for those who would object to such a stark difference, I would push them to define what a perpetrator is. How is a perpetrator different from a soldier? When does a soldier become a perpetrator, as the Harrisville chapter on the Wehrmacht implicitly asks? When does a policeman or policewoman become a perpetrator? Not all violence is illegal. Implicit to the concept of perpetrator, it seems to me, is the idea that the commission of violence is unacceptable from a normative point of view.

There is, however, another approach as reflected in this volume which undermines the distinction I am drawing. Some chapters consider perpetrators those actors who participated directly in warfare and who were not necessarily directly involved in direct violence against civilians, for instance Bultmann's chapter on low-level soldiers in Cambodia or Bjarnsen's chapter on recruitment into the Ivoirian civil war. The tension between soldier and perpetrator is perhaps most central to Harrisville, who studies how soldiers rationalize what he calls "criminal violence" in their letters home. He calls them "Wehrmacht perpetrators." These soldiers cite a variety of motivations, but in the end their rationales are consistent with their service as soldiers: they are defending Germany, they are surviving as military units on the Eastern Front, and they are preempting Russian attacks, or responding to them. They become "perpetrators" only in as much as the "combat" is directed at a perceived threat from civilians or non-combatants, such as prisoners of war. This is fascinating because, judging from the letters they write home, they see continuity between their actions as soldiers and their actions as perpetrators. Even though one can point to these arguments as rationalizations, the actor perspective, so well brought out in the chapter, raises the question as to what the distinction in analytical and explanatory terms is between a perpetrator and a soldier. Similarly, O'Byrne's analysis of civil servants in Germany also breaks down the distinction, implicitly, between government workers and perpetrators. In his words, they "serv[ed] the system."

If this is the case – that is, if perpetration is synonymous with state or military-backed orders and if perpetration is thus, to the actors, consistent with their normal roles – the following question arises: What is to be explained in perpetrator studies? What is the analytical puzzle in perpetrator studies? Is the issue how and why they come to see their roles as consistent with committing violence against civilians? Is it how individuals come to see "abnormal" behavior as "normal"? That is, implicitly in these chapters, perpetrators are undoing the normative distinction that lies at the heart of the field; they are showing how they came to see violence as consistent with their social, political, and military roles.

Similarly, in each of the chapters, the actors whose behavior is being explained did not initiate violence against civilians, as far as we can tell. Rather, they adapted to their institutional environment, as in the Nazi case. Perhaps saying that they "followed orders" is a cliché; they had agency; they made decisions. But they did not design the policy of targeting civilians; they did not create a policy of genocide. Again, that raises the question as to what utility there is in studying their behavior. The question seems to me less, "why did genocide happen" or "why did violence happen" and more "how and why do individuals come to commit such violence"? The distinction is perhaps subtle for some but seems fundamental to me.

Is a comparative theory possible? 207

The tensions here are explicit and carefully analyzed in the Poland chapter, where Harrisville describes the actions of villagers as a response to directives from above. The actors seem to me "compliers," rather than or as much as they are "perpetrators." Or, in some chapters, perpetrators are simply army recruits. Is the question then a negative one: why did individuals not resist the shift from soldiering to violence? Why did they not adapt in a different way? In a military hierarchy, their job was to follow orders. To me, these questions lead away from conceptualizing the problem as one of explaining "perpetrator" behavior and more to questions about disobedience and moral courage.

Moving away from a focus on "perpetrators" is most explicit in Williams' conceptualization, and to an extent in Leader Maynard. In both of these cases, the focus is not on individuals per se but on action. That which is to be explained is the act of violence, not a category of people who commit it. These frameworks are intuitively appealing because they move away from the unstable dichotomy of perpetrator/non-perpetrator. They allow a much more fluid understanding of how a Polish civilian or policeman could be a perpetrator and a rescuer in exactly the same moment or how a Wehrmacht soldier could easily slip between being a soldier and a perpetrator, and back again. The focus here is not what motivates actors, but rather what are the conditions in which such actions are taken? If perpetrators are simply soldiers and ordinary people who adapt to their environmental and institutional circumstances, the behavior seems less of a puzzle as opposed to the circumstances demanded such action.

I am not arguing against "perpetrators" as a useful analytical category; the concept of a perpetrator describes individuals who participate in atrocity or criminal violence against civilians and non-combatants. Such a term is an efficient and evocative way to label such action. But this volume calls into question whether we could ever have a theory of perpetrators. Perhaps there could be a theory of violence perpetration. The pertinent questions are: Why did the policy become one that targeted civilians? Why did the policy succeed, including why did individuals not resist the move to criminal violence? We are not dealing with a class of people – of perpetrators – but rather with situations, circumstances, and institutions that lead individuals to commit violence. The puzzle is not the individual behavior but rather the conditions that facilitated such behavior.

Contexts and situations

A second problem with developing a theory of perpetrators is that the chapters all emphasize context. This is the case for the chapters on Côte d'Ivoire, Rwanda, Poland, Cambodia, and the German chapters in particular. The authors of these contributions take their context seriously and look to embed the action of violence in the context in which it was taken. This focus emerges from a nuanced understanding of how ordinarily nonviolent people or trained soldiers come to participate in murderous acts. Indeed, this emphasis on context is precisely that which drives my theoretical concerns in my first set of comments.

208　*Scott Straus*

But how can scholars generalize from these context-focused explanations? Are there any cumulative findings across different contexts? In other words, is there any way in which one can see commonalities across these very different contexts? How is Rwanda 1994 comparable to Poland 1941–42? How is rural civilian behavior in Poland comparable to elite Nazi behavior in Germany? The strongest commonality is that these chapters primarily describe contexts of warfare in which authorities label the enemy in a particular way. In each case, the context is one of crisis and armed conflict. But even that is not satisfactory – the Cambodian chapter is not really about violence against civilians; the same is true for the Ivoirian situation.

That leads to the observation that to generate careful generalizations, or indeed to insist on comparability, one must limit the range of violence being explained. If both the type of perpetration and the context vary the ability to generate anything close to common, cumulative findings will be extremely difficult. So, while I laud the idea of a broad range of types of perpetration, such variation plus the significant variation in context represented in this volume create steep challenges for inference. For future endeavors, it could be a useful analytical exercise to develop more fine-grained questions – ones that hold perpetration or context constant. For example, why do soldiers shift from fighting other soldiers to targeting civilians? That seems to be a question that is askable across multiple contexts. Or, why did civilian or military authorities command those below them to target civilians? Were the contexts and circumstances in location 1 the same as location 2? By contrast, one could place the emphasis in variation on the type of perpetration. For example, were the reasons why Polish rural actors committed violence in 1941 similar or different from the reasons why German rural actors did the same or were the Polish rural actors similar in their rationales to Polish elite urban actors? In sum, to build a field of comparative research on perpetrators, constructing tighter comparisons would seem to be a valuable next step.

Methodology

The authors in this volume are fairly silent about methodology, but the question of evidence must be central to any study of perpetrators. The field is layered with problems of inference. As the Wehrmacht chapter makes clear, individuals who commit violence have a strong social desirability bias. Given that we know perpetrators want to present themselves in a particular way, how do we interpret what they say and write? Are there particular methodologies that are less susceptible to these kinds of biases than others? What is the role of triangulation? Do we need to compare perpetrator statements to other types of evidence, such as court rulings or victims' statements?

How can researchers build a representative sample of perpetrators? Researchers often look to court documents, prisons, memoirs, or in this case letters. But is there anything in who survives or who ends up in court to suggest that there is something particular about that class of perpetrators that would lead to a certain set of results? Is there systematic bias in which perpetrators can access? Perhaps not

Is a comparative theory possible? 209

every piece of research wants to insist on "representativeness," but the question of inherent biases in the evidence with which researchers work must be addressed.

Lastly, should we be comparing perpetrators to perpetrators or perpetrators to non-perpetrators (or both)? In recent work, I have emphasized the importance of studying the negative case – why did situations that have the ingredients of genocide not result in genocide? But the question seems quite pertinent to perpetrator studies. Why did some individuals not join armed groups? Why did some soldiers refuse to commit violence? Why did some political elites seek to steer policy away from violence, assuming that did happen? For a theory of violence perpetration to develop, researchers need to know not only what is common among perpetrators but also what distinguishes them and their situations from non-perpetrators.

This volume is a wonderful, rich contribution to a research on perpetrators and the perpetration of violence. My comments here are an effort to take stock of the cumulative findings with an eye towards extending the research agenda into the future. Research on violence is much enriched with a direct focus on those who commit it, their mobilization, and the conditions under which they commit such violence. For those reasons, a research agenda on perpetrators and violence perpetration are essential.

Index

actions: continuous spatial classification of 26–8; definition of 38–9; figuration of 41–3; frames of 40–1, 45–7; of heroes 31; individual impact and proximity as defining indicators of 23–6; intent of 24; mentality of 40; morals of killing 110–11; motivations of perpetrators and 22–3, 63–4; practices and 48–51; psychology of 45; social change and 39–40; theories of 44–7; types of 25–6; typology of 28–32; violence as 36–52
active encouraging actions 29–30
active facilitating actions 30
active inhibiting actions 30
adherents 66, 71, 73, 75
adjustment 47–8
agency 142–3
agitating actions 28–9, 32
analytical sociology 24
antagonists 68–9
apathetics 67–8
appropriation 47–8
Arendt, Hannah 20, 125, 155
armed groups: drug use 109, 178; morals of killing 110–11; perpetration in armed conflict 170–3; recruitment into 102–3, 173–83; refusal of orders 111–12; routinisation of 108–9; self-discipline of 107–12; social order of 100–4, 112–13; spiritual discipline 109–10; symbolic violence and 104–7, 112–13
Armée Nationale Sihanoukiste (ANS) 100
Armenian genocide 18–20, 23, 27
assisting actions 29, 31, 32

behaviour 45
being disengaged actions 30, 32
Bralo, Miroslav 156–8, 162
Browning, Christopher 37, 58, 84, 117, 134
bystanders 21, 23, 30, 37–8

Cambodian genocide 17–21
Coalition Government of Democratic Kampuchea (CGDK) 100, 104–5, 110
commanding actions 29, 32
Côte d'Ivoire: perpetration of violence and quest for social worth 181–2; perpetrator recruitment in armed conflict of 169–70, 173–4; personal trauma of rebel 177–9; public secrets of a Burkinabe rebel 175–7; wartime empowerment to peacetime displacement 179–81

decency 125–8
defection 111–12
Delic, Hazim 156–7, 160–2
devotees 65–6, 71, 75
discouraging actions 30, 31, 32
drug use 109, 178

Eckener, Hans-Peter 119–20, 123–4, 127
Efendi, Mehmet Alî 20, 22, 23, 27, 29, 31
Eichmann, Adolf 20, 23, 25, 27, 155
Elias, Norbert 41–2
encouraging actions 29–30, 31, 32
enforcing actions 29, 31, 32

facilitating actions 24–5, 31, 32, 197
figuration 41–3, 51
Forces Nouvelles rebel movement 170, 173–4
frame 40–1
Friedländer, Saul 83, 189

German soldiers: cultivating sense of decency 125–8; ideological diversity of 61–3, 73; justifying criminal war 122–5; killing of 51–2; legacy of Wehrmacht 42, 117–29; legitimating atrocities 119–22; war crimes 40; *see also* Nazi perpetrators
Goffman, Erving 40

212 *Index*

Goldhagen, Daniel 117
Göring, Hermann 89
Gröning, Oskar 84–5

habitus 45, 48, 49, 51
Habyarimana, Juvénal 137
heroes 31
Heydrich, Reinhard 88
high-level individuals 21
Hilberg, Raul 21–2, 37, 83
Himmler, Heinrich 110
Hitler, Adolf 20, 27, 28, 61, 70, 90, 91, 92, 118, 125, 126
Holocaust: behavioural manifestations of actions by individuals in 19–20, 24–5; ideological compositions of potential perpetrators in 61–3, 72–3; literature on types of perpetrators 37–8; role of ordinary Poles as perpetrators in 187–201; role of political civil servants in Third Reich in 83–96; women perpetrators 134; *see also* Jews
Hutu 20, 23, 67

ideological diversity: amongst intermediaries 73–4; conceptualizing 63–4; hypothetical post-radicalization distribution 71–2; pre-radicalization ideological distribution 70–2; role of 60–3; theorizing 58–75; typology of ideological internalization 64–72; violence and 72–5
ideology 64
implementing actions 24
individual impact 25–6, 28
information processing 45–6
informers 192–4
inhibiting actions 30, 31, 32
intentionality 24, 36
International Criminal Tribunal for the Former Yugoslavia (ICTY) 152, 155–7

Jews: behavioural manifestations of actions by individuals toward 20, 22, 24–5; ideological compositions of potential perpetrators and 60–1, 69, 72–3; legacy of Wehrmacht and 42, 117–29; perpetrators of actions against 37, 41–3, 187–201; role of political civil servants in Third Reich and 83–96; *see also* Holocaust
justifications 122–5

Kaplan, Izak 193–4, 195
Keo Rithy 21, 22, 25

Khmer People's National Armed Forces (KPNLAF) 100, 104
Khmer Rouge 17–18, 20, 21, 73, 74, 111
Kritzinger, Friedrich-Wilhelm 86–93
Krohn, Johannes 86, 89–95
Kunarac, Dragoljub 156–8

Landžo, Esad 156–7
leakage 62, 74
lone-wolf perpetrators 100, 113
low-level individuals 21, 24

masculinity 157–65
mentality 40, 123
middle-level individuals 21
Milgram, Stanley 60, 106
militarism 157–65
Moldenhauser, Wilhelm 123, 124
moral disengagement 118
morals of killing 110–11
motivations 22–3, 24, 63–4, 107–8, 200

National Army of Democratic Kampuchea (NADK/Khmer Rouge) 100; *see also* Khmer Rouge
Nazi perpetrators 22, 66, 69–70, 83–96, 110; *see also* German soldiers

obedience 60, 99, 104, 106, 108, 112, 126, 137, 146, 188, 192
Operation Barbarossa 62
Operation Reinhard 190
opportunism 22
Ottoman Empire 20

passive encouraging actions 29–30
passive facilitating actions 30
passive inhibiting actions 30
perpetration: in armed conflict 170–3; aspects of symbolic violence in participation and 104–7; definitions of 17, 100; legacy of Wehrmacht 117–29; by political civil servants in Third Reich 83–96
perpetrators: categorising actors 18, 21–3; civil servants not being 92–5; comparative theory of 204–9; complicity of 23; conceptualization and theorization of 205–7; contexts and situations of 207–8; definition of 17–18, 38–9, 205; ideological diversity of 60–75; individual impact as factor on outcome 25–6, 28; methodology of study on 18–19, 208–9; motivations of

22–3, 24, 63–4, 107–8, 200; as 'people of two faces' 197–9; political civil servants in Third Reich 83–96; portrayals of 58–60; positions of 21–2; potential 61–2; proximity as factor on outcome 25–6, 28; roles of 23, 187–201; self-discipline of 107–13; of sexual violence in armed conflict 151–65; types of 18, 19–21, 37–8, 63–4, 197–9; typology of ideological internalization in 64–72; women 47–8, 133–46

Poland: German order to slaughter civilians in 61; murder of Jews by German soldiers in 117; role of ordinary Poles as perpetrators in Holocaust 187–201

Polish "Blue" Police (*Polnische Polizei/ PP*) 190, 198

Pol Pot 20, 27, 28

Popitz, Heinrich 43–4, 48

power 72

practices 48–51

prejudice 42

prisoners of war (POWs) 190–1, 196

proximity 25–6, 28

Radic, Milorad 159

rationality 45

rescuing actions 30–1, 32

routines 46–7, 50–1, 108–9

Russian soldiers 73, 117–29, 151, 190–1, 196

Rwandan genocide 18, 20, 23, 73, 133

Schindler, Oskar 20, 22, 24, 27

Schlegelberger, Franz 86–93

Schreibtischtäter (desk perpetrators) 20

self-discipline 107–12

sexual violence: court trials 152; narratives along a normal–abnormal continuum

157–65; narratives on perpetration at ICTY 155–7; perpetrators of 151–65; rape committed by Russian soldiers 151; researching perpetrators of 153–5

shared ideologies 64

Smeulers, Alette 63, 134, 154–5, 164

social change 39–40

social norms 43–4

social theory 39–40

Stachak, Karol 197–9

structural individualism 18, 24

Stuckart, Wilhelm 86, 90–5

subversive leading actions 31, 32

supporting actions 31, 32

survival 194–7

symbolic violence 104–7, 112

sympathizers 66–7, 73, 75

Trapp, Wilhelm 20, 26, 28–9, 30

Trocmé, André 60–1

Tutsi 20, 23

victims 37–8

von Galen, Clemens August Graf 68–9

Welzer, Harald 37, 152

witnessing actions 30, 32

women perpetrators: agency of 142–3; guards in German concentration camps 47–8, 135; involvement in mass violence 134–5; in Rwandan genocide 133, 137–40, 143–6; situating actions 140–2; structural constraints and opportunity 143–5

Yugoslavia 67, 152, 155–65

Zelenovic, Dragan 156–8, 163

Zimbardo, Philip 60